EXPLORING DIGITAL HUMANITIES IN INDIA

This book explores the emergence of digital humanities in the Indian context. It looks at how online and digital resources have transformed classroom and research practices. It examines some fundamental questions: What is digital humanities? Who is a digital humanist? What is its place in the Indian context?

The chapters in the volume:

- study the varied practices and pedagogies involved in incorporating the 'digital' into traditional classrooms;
- showcase how researchers across disciplinary lines are expanding their scope of research, by adding a 'digital' component to update their curriculum to contemporary times;
- highlight how this has also created opportunities for researchers to push the boundaries of their pedagogy and encouraged students to create 'live projects' with the aid of digital platforms; and
- track changes in the language of research, documentation, archiving and reproduction as new conversations are opening up across Indian languages.

A major intervention in the social sciences and humanities, this book will be of great interest to scholars and researchers of media studies, especially new and digital media, education, South Asian studies and cultural studies.

Maya Dodd received her PhD from Stanford University in Modern Thought and Literature. Subsequently, she received postdoctoral fellowships at Princeton University, USA, and Jawaharlal Nehru University, India. She also taught in the Department of Anthropology at Princeton University and in English departments at Stanford and the University of Florida. Currently, she is Assistant Dean of Teaching, Learning and Engagement and is a part of the Department of Humanities and Languages, and she teaches Literary and Cultural Studies at FLAME University, India. Her research interests include Indian law and cultural studies, and her teaching is focused on the digital classroom and archiving practices in South Asian cultural studies.

Nidhi Kalra is a doctoral candidate working on affect and conflict at the Department of Humanities and Social Sciences at IIT Bombay and is also Assistant Professor in the Department of Humanities at FLAME University, Pune, India. She has taught at the English Department in Savitribai Phule Pune University and Gargi College in the University of Delhi, India. Nidhi received her MPhil in English Literature from the University of Delhi, for which she worked on problematising Holocaust memoirs. Her research interests include memory studies, trauma studies, oral history, digital humanities and children's/young adult literature.

EXPLORING DIGITAL HUMANITIES IN INDIA

Pedagogies, Practices, and Institutional Possibilities

Edited by Maya Dodd and Nidhi Kalra

Routledge
Taylor & Francis Group

LONDON AND NEW YORK

First published 2021
by Routledge
2 Park Square, Milton Park, Abingdon, Oxon OX14 4RN

and by Routledge
52 Vanderbilt Avenue, New York, NY 10017

Routledge is an imprint of the Taylor & Francis Group, an informa business

British Library Cataloguing-in-Publication Data
A catalogue record for this book is available from the British Library

Library of Congress Cataloging-in-Publication Data
A catalog record for this book has been requested

ISBN: 978-1-138-50319-9 (hbk)
ISBN: 978-0-367-34793-2 (pbk)
ISBN: 978-1-003-05230-2 (ebk)

Typeset in Bembo
by Apex CoVantage, LLC

CONTENTS

FIGURES

CONTRIBUTORS

Rahul Chopra is currently the coordinator of a climate education project (TROP-ICSU) of the International Council of Science, based at the Indian Institute of Science Education and Research (IISER), Pune, India. He is the former Chair of the Centre for Earth and Environment at FLAME University, Pune, and was Associate Professor of Environmental Studies there. His interests are multidisciplinary and include curriculum development in earth and environmental studies, the use of satellite-derived remotely sensed and in situ data to evaluate our changing environment, field-based geological and environmental studies, and the use of high-resolution chemical analysis instruments and data to study various earth and environmental processes. He received his PhD in Geophysical Sciences from the University of Chicago, USA.

Maya Dodd received her PhD from Stanford University in Modern Thought and Literature. Subsequently, she received postdoctoral fellowships at Princeton University, USA and Jawaharlal Nehru University, India. She also taught in the Department of Anthropology at Princeton University and in English departments at Stanford and the University of Florida. Currently, she is Assistant Dean of Teaching, Learning and Engagement and is a part of the Department of Humanities and Languages, and she teaches Literary and Cultural Studies at FLAME University, India. Her research interests include Indian law and cultural studies, and her teaching is focused on the digital classroom and archiving practices in South Asian cultural studies.

Dhrubo Jyoti is a journalist working with the *Hindustan Times* in New Delhi, India. They write on national affairs at the intersection of caste, gender and sexuality and divide their time (unequally) between being queer and being Bengali. They received a master's degree in physics before abandoning the sciences for journalism, and are interested in interrogating the role of caste and gender in digital humanities and journalism processes.

Nidhi Kalra is a doctoral candidate working on a ect and conflict at the Department of Humanities and Social Sciences at IIT Bombay and is also Assistant Professor in the Department of Humanities at FLAME University, Pune, India. She has taught at the English Department in Savitribai Phule Pune University and Gargi College in the University of Delhi, India. Nidhi received her MPhil in English Literature from the University of Delhi, for which she worked on problematising Holocaust memoirs. Her research interests include memory studies, trauma studies, oral history, digital humanities and children's/young adult literature.

Karan Kumar currently works at Intellecap, a development advisory firm in Mumbai, India. His expertise areas are innovation in the food system focused on smallholder farmers, historical GIS and the spatial humanities in India and post-harvest loss reduction. His work lies at the intersection of sustainability, technology and innovation for social good. His other expertise areas are geospatial mapping, the digital humanities, development anthropology and food studies. He wrote his thesis on the reconfigurations of rural-urban dynamics as a result of the emergence of urban farms in four metropolitan cities of India; convened one of India's first undergraduate student research conferences, titled 'Re-thinking Cultural Studies in India'; and supported the convening of a colloquium on digital studies in India with particular emphasis on pedagogy and the archive. He is a graduate in liberal arts from FLAME University, India, where he focused on literary and cultural studies and environmental studies.

C. S. Lakshmi, with the nom de plume **Ambai**, is a historian and a creative writer in Tamil who writes about love, relationships, quests and journeys in the Tamil region of India and elsewhere. Her stories have been translated by Lakshmi Holmstrom in two volumes entitled *A Purple Sea* and *In a Forest, a Deer*. Ambai was awarded the Lifetime Literary Achievement Award of Tamil Literary Garden, University of Toronto, Canada, for the year 2008. An independent researcher in Women's Studies for the last thirty-five years, Ambai is the author of several critical books and articles. She is currently the Director of SPARROW (Sound and Picture Archives for Research on Women).

Nirmala Menon leads the Digital Humanities and Publishing Research Group at the Indian Institute of Technology (IIT), Indore, India. She is Associate Professor of English in the School of Humanities and Social Sciences (HSS), IIT Indore. She is the author of *Migrant Identities of Creole Cosmopolitans: Transcultural Narratives of Contemporary Postcoloniality* (Peter Lang Publishing, 2014) and *Remapping the Post-colonial Canon: Remap, Reimagine, Retranslate* (Palgrave Macmillan, 2017). Menon is the project lead for KSHIP (Knowledge Sharing in Publishing), an IIT Indore digital humanities project in multilingual open access scholarly publishing in India. She is widely published in numerous international journals and speaks, writes and publishes about postcolonial studies, digital humanities and scholarly publishing.

Souvik Mukherjee has been researching video games as an emerging storytelling medium since 2002, examining their relationship to canonical ideas of narrative and also how these games inform and challenge current conceptions of technicity, identity and culture. He is the author of two monographs, *Videogames and Storytelling: Reading Games and Playing Books* (2015) and *Videogames and Postcolonialism: Empire Plays Back* (2017), and is currently co-editing a special issue on video games and postcolonialism. Besides a range of topics in game studies, Souvik researches and teaches early modern literature and digital humanities at Presidency University (formerly Presidency College) in Kolkata, India. He blogs regularly on 'Ludus ex Machina' (http://readinggamesandplayingbooks.blogspot.com/). He is also a founding member of DHAI (Digital Humanities Alliance of India) and has completed two digital archives of colonial cemeteries: the Dutch Cemetery in Chinsurah (http://dutchcemeterybengal.com/) and the Scottish Cemetery in Kolkata (http://scotscemeteryarchivekolkata.com/).

Padmini Ray Murray (PhD, Edinburgh) established India's first digital humanities master's programme at the Srishti Institute of Art, Design and Technology. Her research encompasses feminism and feminist protest, cultural specificity and how it shapes design practices, creativity and technology, as well as games, comics and publishing studies. Her work has been published in a number of peer-reviewed journals and volumes, and she has been the co-investigator on Two Centuries of Indian Print (funded by the Newton Fund, UK) and Gendering the Smart City (funded by the Arts and Humanities Council, UK). She is currently Head of Communications and Community at Obvious, a strategic design consultancy. In 2018 Padmini founded the Design Beku collective to help not-for-profit organisations explore their potential through research-led design and digital development.

Manasi Nene holds a bachelor's degree in Literary and Cultural Studies from FLAME University, Pune, India. Her research interests lie in new media, digital humanities and popular culture. She is also the founder of Pune Poetry Slam, one of the leading performance poetry groups in the country. She is interested in newer forms of art, such as beatboxing, and plans on pursuing digital ethnography and musicology.

Rochelle Pinto was a research fellow at the Nehru Memorial and Museum Library, New Delhi, India, from 2015 to 2017 and at the Centre for the Study of Culture and Society, Bangalore, from 2014 to 2015. She was Assistant Professor in the Department of English, Delhi University, from 2010 to 2014. Her PhD was from the School of Oriental and African Studies, London. Her book *Between Empires: Print and Politics in Goa* was published in 2007 by Oxford University Press.

Her current interests are legal and intellectual traditions framing land disputes in colonial Goa, the colonial novel and ethnography, and public access to archives.

Sneha Ragavan is Researcher at Asia Art Archive (AAA), New Delhi, India. Since 2012, she has conceptualised and overseen several research projects at AAA in India, including its language initiatives. She has a master's in Art History and Aesthetics from the Faculty of Fine Arts, M.S. University of Baroda (2008), with a specialisation in architectural history, and a PhD in Cultural Studies (2016) from the English and Foreign Languages University, Hyderabad, for her thesis 'Building the National Modern: The Discourse of Architecture in Twentieth Century India'.

Niruj Mohan Ramanujam has been interested in LGBT archiving for several years now. He believes that archiving is essential to combat forgetting and depoliticisation, as well as to sustain solidarities and help activism. In an era where historicity, contextualisation and nuance are increasingly trivialised, and in the LGBT context where the cultural generational span is much less than in the mainstream, archiving is a useful tool. Niruj is an astronomer by profession and is actively involved in astronomy outreach and science literacy. He is also interested in bringing science and technology tools to the LGBT archiving process. He has been associated with the Orinam Collective in their archiving work and is involved in the new QAMRA initiative. He was, until recently, employed at the National Centre for Radio Astrophysics in Pune, India.

Joyoti Roy is an arts and museum manager and heads her own partnership firm called Culture-Collective. She is also honorary Director of Achi Association India, a not-for-profit organisation engaged in the preservation of Himalayan Art. Until recently, she was heading the Outreach Department of National Museum and between 2011 and 2013. Thus far, she has successfully coordinated more than fifteen exhibitions, many of which have been international. She was trained as an art conservator from the National Museum Institute and worked at the Indian National Trust for Art and Cultural Heritage (Intach) from 2003 to 2010. She has been a Charles Wallace India Trust Awardee for the year 2008 for a fellowship programme in conservation of contemporary art at the Tate Gallery, London. She was the Clore Leadership Fellow in the UK in 2017–2018, working with a project for the upcoming museum and collection research facility in East London. Currently, she is the Head of Museum Marketing at Stategy at Chhatrapati Shivaji Maharaj Vastu Sangralay formerly known as the Prince of Charles Musuem in Mumbai.

Surajit Sarkar is currently Associate Professor and Coordinator of the Centre for Community Knowledge at Ambedkar University Delhi, India. He is the current President of the Oral History Association of India (OHAI), Executive Member of the International Association of Agricultural Museums (AIMA) and is on the Public Advisory Board of the Society for Cultural Anthropology (USA). He has been a photocopier salesman, a bank officer, a primary school teacher and developer of curriculum for primary schools. He has created weekly television programmes, as well as award-winning documentary and educational films. He has worked as a video artist for theatre and dance productions, and has created multi-media installations in museums and galleries in India and abroad.

Working in central India with small farmer organisations, Surajit became a member of the Catapult Arts Caravan. This travelling video+arts group believes that the stimulation of creative skills and cultural life in rural India must reflect an awareness of, and contain a response to, the major challenges facing rural India. And such engagement should involve the technologies that shape the twenty-first century horizon.

Puthiya Puriyal Sneha works with the Centre for Internet and Society (CIS), Bangalore, India. Her training is in English literature, and she has previously worked in the field of higher education. Her work at CIS primarily engages with shifts in modes and practices of knowledge production in the humanities and arts with the digital turn. Her areas of interest include methodological concerns in arts and humanities, digital media and cultures, higher education and pedagogy, and access to knowledge. She has published a report on mapping initiatives in the field of digital humanities in India, and co-edited a reader on digital activism efforts in Asia.

Vidya Subramanian is a postdoctoral fellow at the Centre for Policy Studies at IIT Bombay, India. Before this, she worked in the opinion section of the *Hindustan Times* in New Delhi. She got her PhD from the Centre for Studies in Science Policy at Jawaharlal Nehru University. Her work lies at the intersection of society and technology. She remains fascinated by communication and information technologies that enable the social milieu we currently inhabit, mediated as it is by screens, gadgets and 'connected' devices.

Shanmugapriya T. is a doctoral scholar at Indian Institute of Technology Indore, India. She completed her master's degree at Bharathiar University and worked on a postgraduate project titled *Virtual Spaces and Existential Territories of Aya Karpansika's Digital Poetry*. She is also part of the Digital Humanities and Publishing Research Group at IIT Indore. Currently, her research is focused on the impact of digital culture in twenty-first-century Indian literature, largely anchored with narration, publication and practice. Broadly, her interest focuses in digital culture, digital literary works and practising digital humanities methodology to explore literary and media works.

Mae Mariyam Thomas is a radio presenter, journalist, writer and voice-over artist, with more than a decade of experience in the radio industry. She began as a news editor for a community radio station in the UK. She eventually returned to India and worked at Chennai Live 104.8 FM, an English radio station in Chennai, as their Creative Manager. Thereafter, she moved to Bombay and joined erstwhile NH7.in as a music journalist/subeditor. She is most well-known for hosting the afternoon request show *Mumbai On Demand* on 94.3 Radio One. From broadcast radio, she explored the growing medium of podcasting and became the Creative Director of the biggest podcasting network in India, Indus Vox Media. She currently runs her own indie music podcast, *Maed in India*, and works as an audio industry consultant.

Dhanashree Thorat (PhD in English, University of Florida) is a postdoctoral researcher in digital humanities at the University of Kansas. Her research is situated at the intersection of Asian American Studies, postcolonial studies and digital humanities, and her current work focuses on the codification of hegemonic narratives about Muslims in digital archives and social media platforms. Dhanashree is a founding Executive Council member of the Center for Digital Humanities, Pune, in India. She serves as the lead organiser for a biennial winter school on digital humanities, and advises the Center on digital archival projects and DH curriculum development. She has written about her experiences with building DH networks in the Global South as a HASTAC Scholar (2015–2016), and is currently working as the issue editor for *Asian Quarterly*, a peer-reviewed scholarly journal, for a special issue on 'Digital Humanities in India' was published in 2018.

Xenia Zeiler is tenure track Professor of South Asian Studies at the University of Helsinki, Finland. Her research is situated at the intersection of digital media and culture in India and the worldwide Indian community. She is the author of numerous articles and book chapters on Indian video games, digital Hinduism, popular culture and religion in India, and of a monograph on current transformations of Tantric traditions. Her projects include the Digital Humanities Initiative (India-Finland,) Digital Educational Tools development (Duragapuja and Museums,) and her work is broadly focuses on Video Games and Cultural Heritage in Asia.

ACKNOWLEDGEMENTS

This book is a labour of love made possible by FLAME University, with the support of Dr Devi Singh, who strongly encouraged our forays into digital humanities (DH). We thank next our colleagues who have been part of our journey towards the making of this book: Ashutosh Potdar, Sonam Mansukhani and Renuka Kadapatti, who were co-organisers of *Learning Through Archives: A Colloquium on Digital Scholarship* held in October 2016. We acknowledge the help of Kunal Ray for introducing us to C. S. Lakshmi.

There are certain key individuals without whom this volume would have been a distant dream. We would like to start with Aakash Chakrabarty and Brinda Sen as well as the team of editors at Routledge India, and Chris Mathews for facilitating the production process for this book. Aakash, Brinda, and Chris have enabled the creation and improvement of this volume. P. P. Sneha and Sumandro Chattapadhyay have been invaluable for their work and scholarship at Centre for Internet and Society to the field of DH. Their intellectual rigour enables practitioners and researchers to follow emergent trends in the field, as well as survey the archive of issues and debates important to the history of DH in India.

We have benefitted immensely from interactions with scholars in the field, most of whom have graciously agreed to contribute towards this volume through hectic schedules, illnesses and all manner of difficulties, along with responding to hundreds of emails. We have to mention also one such interaction with Alex Gil, who was generous with his time through our work on this volume. Our students in Literary and Cultural Studies at FLAME University have been partners in crime in our academic endeavours and have willingly and perhaps unwittingly played along with our experiments in DH. We would like to thank especially Karan Kumar and Manasi Nene for many conversations and all the work we have shared in and outside of the classroom. We would also like to thank Manasi for her help while indexing. Thanks also go to Anoushka Zaveri for her help during C. S. Lakshmi's interview.

We end our note acknowledging the love and support of our family and friends, who have been pillars of strength through this book and much more than can be put in words. Thank you so much for being there. Maya Dodd would like to thank Lila for her patience and Rahul for his tech skills. Nidhi Kalra would like to thank her loved ones who have been there at the wings making this journey possible for her. Rani and Suresh Kalra have offered constant care and understanding. Meghna, Ayush, and Anil Kumar have nurtured and encouraged her through this process and beyond. She could not have done this work without the unwavering faith and strength offered by Usha Jawale and Shashank Jawale. Finally, she would like to thank Madhula Banerji for the moral support and help as this book journeyed through the publication process.

INTRODUCTION

Maya Dodd

Is it not possible that the entire society is seen as a vast university, every community in it an open treasurer of knowledge, as if they collectively a vast reference library, and the institution of learning a co-curator, a co-supervisor of that knowledge?

– G N Devy[1]

Digital humanities needs to be seen as an opportunity to question, contest, and remap the ways in which conditions of life, labor, and language are rapidly changing in the widely varied and uneven advent of digital modernity in the country. In its negotiation with the state infrastructure and its re-humanizing of the infrastructure centred debate, digital humanities can serve a dual function of building relevant and sensitive infrastructure of production and access to knowledge as well as build a critical voice that resists the dehumanizing principles of networked societies that reduce all human beings to actors and all human modes of engagement to actions and transactions

– Nishant Shah[2]

The title of this work has confused many. "What, Digital India? Who is a digital humanist? Humans have gone digital?" There were an abundance of queries on what exactly this work was about, and in gathering materials for this volume, we hope to have asked at least as many more questions as insights gained from exploring this subject. While there is no definitive view of digital humanities (henceforth, this will be referred to as DH) in India, there is no singular view of DH elsewhere either. Going by the names of publications in the field, (the series on *Debates in Digital Humanities* etc.) and many trails of arguments online (in HASTAC Scholars forums etc.) since its arrival, DH has almost been dominated more by arguments over its definition than suspicions over its utility.

And so, Puthiya Purayil Sneha's chapter kicks off this concern by raising the question asked by many with regard to the field: What is digital humanities in India, and why is it so difficult to pin down? Does the difficulty indicate a structural issue with the frameworks of knowledge and their dissemination, and therefore beyond that of the so-called humanities crisis? She suggests the contestations may themselves emanate from an ambiguity regarding the shifting episteme of both humanities and technology. This signals a move towards not only the interdisciplinary challenges of questions concerning society and academia, but also the whole process and praxis of knowledge making as such. In project formulation, selection of tools, and curation lies the chance to rethink traditional humanities scholarship and to render the maker as agentive in relating technology and authorship.

To instance how this is happening and for the purposes of identifying DH in India, let's look at works that represent the field: many of these are referenced in the volume such as the landmark project for textual studies, the digital variorum of Tagore's works in "Bichitra" done by the School of Texts and Cultural Records at Jadavpur University; the Dutch and Scottish cemeteries project at Presidency University; Two Centuries of Indian Print with the British Library and Jadavpur; KSHIP at IIT Indore; Indiancine.ma and Pad.ma.[3] This initial survey is a preliminary assortment of the wide range of practices, and Sneha reminds us that for makers and users of DH, "[i]n the Indian context, the question of digitality also becomes important from the perspective of technological obsolescence – where there is a great resistance to discontinuing or phasing out the use of certain kinds of technology; either for lack of access to better ones or simply because one finds other uses for it." This means that we must contend with challenges of the digital divide as a structural inequality as the circumscribes all questions of access. Questions raised on the opaqueness of maker culture are then further complicated in the Indian context, since they are linked to variance in economic, social, technological, and pedagogical access.

It is important to note that for these reasons – and also for the fact that much of Indian DH occurs in sites complementary to but outside of University spaces – the Indian definition of DH is far from derivative of a North American definition. Its meaning is still taking shape in India and hence this work is offered by way of an exploration of possibilities for what DH might be. In the end, what we are calling DH in India is decided by access to digital tools and resources that have been used across fields to impact humanities work in a new way but the field as such is still emergent and dispersed across several sites.

To start off, we scarcely have to emphasise the significance of the digital for our times. We are living in an era that may be retrospectively viewed as one when "Digital India" fundamentally shaped the country's discursive future. As the Digital India website proclaims, the programme is centred on three key vision areas: digital infrastructure as a core utility to every citizen, governance and services on demand, and digital empowerment of citizens. These goals will be achieved through the creation of a digital infrastructure and services. So, this entails building high speed Internet, digitising identity, finance, and creating public access to services through safe and secure cloud infrastructure. By making services user-centric, integrating services across departments, ensuring services are portable and online, leveraging Geographic Information System (GIS), and going cashless, governance would have entered a digital era. For empowerment, access is sought to be multiplied through universal digital literacy and making digital resources accessible via platforms such as e-Bhaasha to disseminate digital language content in many languages.[4]

Despite the lofty claims of Digital India, there is an undeniable re-making of our world (with or without our informed consent sometimes) and so our focus in this collection is on the impact of the digital on humanity and the humanities. The digital era is by no means unique or without precedent, and Dhanashree Thorat's piece on digital infrastructures reminds us of this by linking the history of communication technologies since imperial times to the present day. By making what at first may be seemingly improbable connections between the railways in the nineteenth century to Facebook basics and more in the twenty-first century, she demonstrates the uncanny ways in which history repeats itself. Whether it's in the realm of governance (digital India) or business, how colonial practices are recursively played out in the space of the digital is of interest to us all. Postcolonial DH is attentive to the longer histories of imperialism, and in her piece, Thorat says that to think differently entails imagining and articulating "new conceptions of postcolonial design, code, technology and infrastructure." DH is not just subsumed by issues of governance, as much as it amplifies concerns around issues of access. In this case, what DH scholar Roopika Risam says in the American context is equally true of India:

> The most significant contribution of digital humanities is to developing and sustaining the digital cultural record of humanity. We can debate about definitions and methods, but, fundamentally, the faculty, librarians, archivists, students, and those who work in galleries and museums who are equipped with digital humanities skills are uniquely poised to assemble this digital cultural record. They – we – do this by thinking critically about digital methods for humanities research and objects of knowledge and by building digital archives, maps, databases, and other digital objects that populate the digital cultural record.[5]

The reason DH is viewed foremost as an academic field in the West is that it has pedagogical goals. In India, too, DH retains that purpose but with a whole new valence for the fact that it is not some fully formed theology to be preached as much as it is the means to achieving a new faith for a new calling. As the HASTAC "Decolonizing the Digital" forum cites Roopika Risam's syllabus, "How might we begin to rethink the colonial topographies, architectures, and networks that so often structure emerging digital media/technologies? New conversations have emerged around essential questions: can the digital be 'decolonized?': what are the limits of decolonial, postcolonial, or anti-colonial approaches to digital cultures?; and how can these theoretical approaches be marshaled to build communities, tools, and justice?"[6]

This volume is an attempt to surveying the significant landmarks in how DH is decolonialising the humanities in India and adapting emerging digital cultures developing in India to wider uses. To those who accuse DH in the West of not having a politics or not being critical enough in the tradition of humanistic inquiry, we offer a different interpretation coming from the Indian context. In noting the differences between the careers of DH in the West and India, we reference the Indian story through the DH manifesto that defines it as a set of convergences of varied practices relating to access, equity, and participatory knowledge making.[7] Lately there has been an understanding that making is itself critique and the false oppositions between theory and practice cannot hold in digital times.

When surveying sites of digital practice, the potential that such a convergence holds is clearly visible. For instance, the IITs receive huge amounts of funding in India, linked to the state's developmental agenda, but this has turned into a surprising haven for humanities funding. Be it KSHIP at IIT Indore or Bichitra, the Tagore Varorium at Jadavpur, such institutional ventures demonstrate how some intense achievements have been birthed from public funding. In fact, one could view the digitalisation of scholarly and artistic practices in India as constituting a public sphere of a whole new kind – one that exists inside *and outside* of the confines of private universities, state institutions, official and unofficial collections, and spills out to personal blogs and tweets or podcasts to create communities. It is for this reason that this volume displays varied initiatives around digital efforts to expanding public access as constituting experiments in the Indian narrative of DH. The chapters discuss institutional experiences with digitisation, pedagogical experiments in the classroom, administrative challenges with innovation, subaltern DH and the possibilities of digital media for education and business. All these cases instantiate digital culture's trysts with what it means to be human in times of technological possibility.

The very making of these digital objects is part of a framework of varied uses and access across contexts and funding models, and at no point is it free of a politics of cultural critique. In this volume, DH is understood as a field that encompasses digital fields as form and the access desired by models of public humanities as content. Their intersection determines the always emergent nature of this field. In the Indian context, the stakes are also no doubt different. Uniquely Indian challenges also pertain to digitisation of content in Indian languages and public access. The cultural and linguistic diversity of the country alongside the fact that access was historically determined by archiving and curation as a selective colonial practice contends with the wide array of practices that conventional categories would discretely view as activism, identity politics, public history, oral history, cultural intervention, and more. By capturing all these under the umbrella term DH, we aim to capture the disruption of the digital alongside the attempts to bridge social divisions.

The quality of digital media to cross reference and multiply is manifested in an immediate expansion of activism, research and artistic publications. Through the digital, new registers are created that can cross question the official and enable many more to participate in the making of knowledge. To grant open access is already so much easier today with digital technologies. However, this does not mean that it doesn't meet with other challenges. In this regard, new technologies, whether it be the creation of digital surrogates or mp3s or infinite scans, all enable the passage from secret to manifest through endless reproducibility – at least in technical terms. Socially, though, the technology is often intercepted by other concerns, and as Rochelle Pinto reminds us in this volume, "Archives and libraries are constituted more by mandate than by content, and by both the past and the present."

Digital histories

P. P. Sneha greatly aided this work through her initial surveys on mapping DH in India. Given the different structures of academic spaces and careers of university systems, she notes, like many others in the volume, that the story of DH in India is divergent from its trajectory in North America. Consequently, Sneha raises an important question for the Indian context and particularly for this volume: If it is so different in India, why call it DH at all? She traces the history of humanities computing, textual studies, and archiving practices as leading up to the growth of digital humanities in the North American context. In India, DH is also born of interdisciplinary sharing and new institutional structures, but its growth is not primarily determined by university funding. Limitations on access to infrastructure, even as there is a push to democratising education through technology has produced new paradoxes in the Indian context.

In the same section on digital histories, Dhanashree Thorat's chapter also alludes to a history of continuity by tracing the public, corporate, and state discourse around digital infrastructure development in India as a sociotechnical construct. By focusing on infrastructural development propped by foreign investment, she examines in particular the case of Facebook's Free Basics initiative. In its two-year Indian campaign for Free Basics, to purportedly bring Internet access to a billion new users, Facebook touted the economic and social benefits of Internet access to underserved people, but Thorat notes how this rhetoric directly follows from colonial discourse, saying, "These technoutopian promises about the affordances of technology, particularly the claims about equality, opportunities, and rights, pre-date the digital era and are at least as old as the British colonization of India."

It is to undo these lineages that another imagination is necessary towards creating alternative infrastructure. One such path to realising what Arjun Appadurai calls "the right to research"[8] was the phenomenal pedagogical intervention through the Archive and Access project. Rochelle Pinto's chapter discusses the impetus for the project which began at the Centre for the Study of Culture and Society, Bangalore and was funded by the Sir Dorabji Tata Trust. The project was, at its most immediate level, a response to the perceived state of archiving in India. Much before Sahapedia and the National Digital Library of India, there existed a great deficit of access to archival resources in comparison with the experiences of scholarly access to libraries and archives in the USA and the UK. While some part of this disparity pertained to resources, it was equally evident that to a great extent it is also the political culture in India around questions of access, preservation, and citizenship anxieties that also come into play. Pinto states that it became increasingly apparent that the availability of resources (finances, ecosystems, etc.) was far less significant than the issue of political culture. Her piece elaborates on the political culture of archiving and related issues that framed questions of access differently for experiences of students, historians, librarians and government authorities.

Conceived as a way to enhance student access to library resources, the Archive and Access website addressed the absence of online catalogues of archives and libraries in India and the exclusion of historians from archival decision making. Rochelle Pinto cites the critical efforts of ALF (Alternative Law Forum) and CIS (Center for Internet and Society) in Bangalore to supporting open access via legal and technological support. Like in the case of Pad.ma and Indiancine.ma, Pinto's reminder that archives have diverse users underscores why open access is essential for a public presentation of connected history.

Even if such control has been superseded by crowdsourced efforts, as in Sahapedia, nowhere is this control to access more dominant in contemporary times than in the case of spatial data. The spatial humanities is still an emerging discipline in India, but one that is also a markedly contested terrain. Despite limitations to open access, its increasing relevance to cartography, geography, history, and environment, as well as pedagogy is noteworthy. The chapter by Karan Kumar and Rahul Chopra seeks to explore the "possibilities" of the spatial humanities to understand why the urgency of the method is linked to improving public access in India. It describes the different inquiries that are currently made possible through the spatial humanities and crowdsourcing and also describes the efforts of different agencies, such as the Kalakriti archives, in attempting to create a "space" for GIS thinking in the Indian classroom and beyond.

Digital institutions and pedagogies

In this spirit, the element of outreach that Joyoti Roy's account speaks of underlines the need to engage wider publics and diverse audiences. Given how much bad press Indian museums have received for their poor presentation, the digital turn afforded new possibilities for public connection and access. Roy describes the fascinating story of how the fourteen-point Museum Reform agenda of 2009 drafted by the Ministry of Culture in the Government of India yielded reforms in training, publications, and digitisation from 2011 on. One consequence of this initiative was the Company Paintings Digitisation Project, which aimed at uniting collections across India and the UK (such as those at the National Gallery of Modern Art, Delhi, Victoria Memorial Hall, Kolkata, and the Victoria and Albert Museum, UK) to produce an integrated web catalogue across locations. Roy describes the mechanics of the digitisation project and how the creation of digital surrogates enabled greater access for research. In 2013, the Digital Archive Initiative of the National Museum also planned to create a unique digital platform for Indian museums, and this was developed in collaboration with the Centre for Development of Advanced

Computing or C-DAC and the Art Institute of Chicago. Thus far, the archive has more than 100,000 digital objects and is used for pedagogical access. However, when the Google Cultural Institute arrived in 2011, the platform was directly benchmarked against international standards, bypassing indigenous technological innovation.

Often though the need really is for indigenous solutions that can address the specific needs of Indian archives. As Sneha Ragavan reminds us through the case of the Asia Art Archive – in a sentiment also echoed in Nirmala Menon's experience at IIT Indore's KSHIP – the attention to indigenous context is at the core of what makes the DH story different in India. As Ragavan notes, much art criticism in India pertaining to modern and contemporary art practice has presumed the language of mainstream discourse to be English. Though English is no doubt the language of power, patronage, and pedagogy, the distance between the location of the art works and their commentaries in the field of art and the discipline of art history urges a new view. Consequently, Sneha asks, what constitutes the "vernacular" or "regional," and how might we go about exploring it? What could be the role of the digital with regards to locating and incorporating? Her linking of these questions of location and medium signals the liberatory possibilities of new media that can transcend barriers found in print. In particular, she explores a project undertaken by Asia Art Archive constituting a "Bibliography of Modern and Contemporary Art Writing of South Asia." The project compiled an annotated bibliography of art writing in the form of a digital, searchable, online database of more than 12,000+ texts in more than twelve languages. Instancing this Bibliography Project as a case study, Ragavan asks how critical bilingualism offers ways in which languages function as an en-framing device through which certain modes of articulation were made possible. In short, the chapter seeks to argue for the ways in which the digitalisation of art histories are a step towards democratising the field.

Perhaps, it is for this very reason that Nirmala Menon also says in her piece that postcolonial DH is *in* the making. The chapter by her and Shanmugapriya T. make a point of differentiating between technology in the classroom and DH. KSHIP, which aims to be a multilingual publishing project at Indian Institute of Technology Indore, attempts a model at open access for the public. For Menon and Shanmugapriya T., the creation of the platform for KSHIP is itself a DH Project that attempts to put into practice the principles of open access crucial to the philosophy of what the digital humanities hope to achieve. Their chapter underlines the need to reimagine the humanities undergraduate student's curricula to equip the humanities researcher of tomorrow who will tackle book history, archival studies, manuscript studies, and textual narrative – all core to humanities scholarship – differently with digital technology. Though the survey they undertook reveals a current dearth of DH courses in curricula, they identify the high cost of access as the reason for the lack of DH programming in universities. This accentuates the necessity for more open access resources in publishing, databases, as well as open source tools that can initiate scholars on a discovery of these resources and its usefulness in humanities research.

Curation and design are integral to encouraging and acknowledging diversity, and Souvik Mukherjee's chapter also aims to think through the key issues that are relevant to the various DH pedagogical programmes in Indian academia in comparison with global DH programmes. Referencing key questions raised in Brett Hirsch's edited collection on DH pedagogy, such as "Do we teach digital humanities? Do we profess it? Do we profess to teach it?," Mukherjee gives a first-hand experience of conducting DH research on the colonial history of Kolkata through two separate digital archives on colonial cemeteries, where each project involved teams of students from multiple universities in the city. It offers examples of DH courses taught at both undergraduate and postgraduate levels (as a diploma in digital humanities) to comment on the potential of DH pedagogy in India. Mukherjee notes that the multiplicity of digital practices in the humanities globally is a challenge for scholars. In India, where the growth of DH is recent and limited, the directions for future humanities pedagogy will have to also include a narrative of the lack of digital awareness, resources, empowerment, and knowledge-networks. Besides these issues, there is also the need to re-assess the direction in which DH research and teaching (in their connected ways) are moving in Indian academia.

In the Indian context, though these pedagogical goals are often realised outside of university systems too, attention must also be paid to institution building. Padmini Ray Murray's chapter describes the establishment of the first master's-level digital humanities programme in India, as well as a digital humanities research agenda that contextualises and embeds such work in an Indian environment. Ray Murray demonstrates how *critical making* is a particularly useful mode of inquiry in a context where DH work is relatively nascent, in order to supplement and inform a narrative of the history of what might be considered digital humanities in India. She discusses the shift effected by the Indian context, in terms of moving away from modelling such work on pedagogical paradigms established in Anglo-American institutions. Her work focuses on the creation of a locally reflexive practice that responds more appropriately to Indian conditions. Ray Murray historicises these arguments, demonstrating how design as a discipline is implicated in the work of colonialism, and how the praxis of critical making (as formulated by thinkers such as Matt Ratto and Garnet Hertz) can contribute both to decolonising design and, more broadly, humanities scholarship in India.

Subaltern digital humanities

We are keenly cognisant of the fact that "critical making" is the key to decolonising Indian education. Yet, Padmini Ray Murray notes that "to lay the very foundations of new humanities work in India, there needs to be training, infrastructural support, but most importantly an attitudinal shift towards making as a form of knowledge making." And it is for all these reasons that she said at the 2015 Digital Diversity conference, "Your DH is not my DH." As she says in this volume, "We should be using DH in India as a jumping-off point and tactical mode for enlarging the scope of the humanities in general, in order to prise open institutional resistance to accommodate and legitimize essential research in fields such as Dalit, feminist, indigenous studies. These interrogations of received knowledge must operate on different terrains – primarily, ontologies, epistemologies, praxis, archives, pedagogies, histories and technology."

Towards contouring what such a field could entail, we call the section on community archives "Subaltern DH." Taking seriously the challenge to imagine frameworks for a new humanities, the provocations of Ambai, Ramanujam, and Sarkar offer some inspiring templates for a meaningful DH pedagogy.

The interview with C. S. Lakshmi, or Ambai, as she is popularly known, brings to the fore what can be called tactics of subaltern DH. Ambai's concern pertains to the privacy of subjects who constitute her archive SPARROW (Sound and Picture Archives for Research on Women). This is instantiated in the case of the film *Degham*, that used source material on the trans community and so urges an ethics in viewership. In this case, the archivist is akin to a "native" curator, and sensitivity in designing this archive is also reflected in the selective granting of access.

For similar reasons, Niruj Mohan Ramanujam underlines the need for an LGBT archive since at the time of writing, section 377 remained on the books. The fact that the queer community continues to be vulnerable renders a queer archive a record of disenfranchisement. Such an archive could well serve as a record of the dehumanisation of this community, capturing the violations, atrocities, and injustices committed on citizens of India, in addition to documenting the changing chapters of queer generations. The archive writes Ramanujam would not only serve as a memoir of the traumas of the LGBT community but also constitute a sort of archival justice.

Ray Murray's point about critical making and activism comes to life in Ramanujam's work. While queer archives usually catalogue books, magazines, newspaper articles, photographs, letters, and so on, he writes that in the context of "Queer Archiving = Queer Activism," such an archive can be designed as well as maintained in order to serve activist aims. He focuses on building an "Archive of Feeling," as articulated by Ann Cvetkovic, and discusses a few ongoing archiving projects, frameworks, and the application of tools to analyse archives and inform activism. Paradoxically, the privacy of the queer community needs visibility, along with a sensitivity afforded to contributors to grant them legal protection. In this case, archiving itself is activism, and hence the design and access policies of this curation needs to be dynamic, with varied levels of access that respond to contemporary needs.

Surajit Sarkar's chapter similarly offers a model of sensitive participatory pedagogy. In a digitised and interconnected world – where the boundaries between contexts are blurred and where our understanding of humanity is mediated – it asks if one can recover the oral, the direct, and the analogue in the digital age. Who can be known across digital spaces? How do we ask them to present their worldview or want, desire, or discomfort to us, and in what ways in which these can be (re)presented?

Since it is in the making that there is reflection, critical making is also the subject of Sarkar's chapter. In the context of community archives, Sarkar describes the use of a feedback loop between the content recorded and the affordances of digital form. While recordings are done on field, the digital object functions as a sort of mirror in the field. The form provokes analytical reflection on the lines of *Muktir Kotha*.[9] Sarkar sees this as a form of returning knowledge back to the community and by exhibiting recordings, allowing the recording to itself become a part of the self-definition of the community.

Digital tools create many ways of seeing, knowing, and communicating, and in the process contribute to new modes of distributing resources, ideas, and information, and new interfaces for interaction among diverse human communities. Sarkar argues that awareness of the two aspects of digital humanities, the computational and qualitative, allow us to design and engage with human diversity in an open and transparent way. A locally engaged digital humanities programme, located at the intersection of digital practice and human diversity, can also interrogate the abilities and constraints of methodological tools. Oral history and documentation are a method and tool for pushing beyond entrenched knowledge of the letter. In the realm of the digital, we are afforded the possibility to conceive of the community as a partnership. By employing what Sarkar calls the "epistemic privilege" of the insider, the feedback loop of the post-interview performs a "critical orality." Sarkar states this has the potential to level the playing field for diverse languages, communities, regions, and individual user-makers, who make and curate their frames of knowledge through new media.

Digital practices

Media and technology are inextricably linked to DH in India. Media is at a critical juncture of inquiry for DH, as are its concomitant industries. The chapters in the section on digital media practices interrogate the challenges brought to the news and entertainment industry with the advent of digital modes of making, consuming, and disseminating creative work.

Xenia Zeiler's chapter notes that the impact of digital media on society is an important part of DH. Her chapter looks at the sphere of gaming in India as it interacts with questions of design thus reflecting the world at large. She argues that DH as an academic discipline of study must develop digital methods for researching humanities material but in a wider understanding that also entails the study of digital media and their interrelation with culture and society. Video games today actively contribute to construct perceptions of values, identities, and, in general, society. Game development and production practices are complex and highly reflective processes. Currently in India, especially "indie" (independent) gaming companies successfully develop games, for international and regional audiences, that are based on regional contexts. Zeiler's chapter specifically discusses examples for Indian video games that make use of cultural heritage elements from Indian backgrounds. She looks at aspects of cultural heritage and aesthetics in games such as *Hanuman: Boy Warrior*, *Sky Sutra*, *Antariksha Sanchar*, *Agni*, and so forth, which include representations of mythology, architecture, music, and dance as they interact with game development. She asks how cultural heritage is implemented, interpreted, and constructed in these games, and how specific aspects such as history, art, and architecture are depicted.

Similar to games, Indian newspapers have also upped their stakes in the digital realm. In the same vein, Dhrubo Jyoti and Vidya Subramniam, who worked at the digital desk of the newspaper *Hindustan Times*, ask similar questions of news media. *Hindustan Times'* transformation into a digital newsroom has had an immense impact on the making, curating, and framing of the news. Dhrubo Jyoti and Vidya Subramaniam try to understand digital journalism in the Indian context: Is it elitist in a country where Internet penetration is deeply classed, casted, and gendered? Or is digital journalism the bold dream for the future, where freer and less censored content shall find its way to sections of people who had little access to formal media? *Hindustan Times'* digital desk is at a fundamental moment of formation – if the challenges facing journalists and editors in going "digital first" open up to a better synchronised news network that works efficiently in print and the digital world is something that is yet to be seen. What is certain, however, is that the online and offline avatars of journalism are both jostling to co-exist.

In comparison to the news, in the case of radio the niche content created by podcasters and user driven curation has led to a rebirth of radio. Here, unlike news, a surprising development has been the rapid monetisation of niche markets in the Indian context.

Mae Mariyam Thomas's chapter underlines the fact that unlike the centralised reading experience of news delivery, how we listen to audio is now more individualised and customisable. In this regard, we cannot discount the fact that the Internet feeds off commercial possibility and must also account for how this shapes the digital ecosystem. By all accounts, the digital entertainment industry will see exponential growth in the near future – especially in the context of cheaper data and mobile technologies.

Conclusion: the future of DH in India

These chapters all evidence the fact that the impact of the digital is accelerating in all spheres in India – from the classroom to the museum, from games to the news, from radio to mapping, all human activity has to contend with the digital, and the texts that are produced as a consequence of this will be the texts of tomorrow for DH. As Nishant Shah, Professor of Digital Media at Leuphana University and co-founder of the Centre for Internet and Society reminds us, if the aim is to build an inclusive, diverse and representative database, then the collaborations in media studies, oral histories, cultural archives, and cultural analytics invite a re-thinking of pedagogy.[10]

Such a re-thinking will be prompted not least by what Google has dubbed India's "next billion users." If 90 per cent of Indians don't understand the language of the Internet today, there is no doubt that the changing nature of the digital will be accompanied by a change in language too.[11] Given the regional language users will account for 75 per cent of the country's Internet user base by 2021, the interest of global business in catering to India is now focused on creating products and experiences for Indian language Internet users.[12] If the digital is thought of as an inevitability, it also needs to be understood as possessing potential beyond the monetising possibilities of commerce. The cultures of DH are agentic – whether in the classroom or as an audience that participates in making the object.

In this regard, querying the digital will be a necessary part of all education. Just as a sound humanities education urges an examination of the human condition, a relevant and fundamental education will entail an examination of the digital life. Reflections on subjectivity, digitality, and alterity accompany questions of history, archives, memory, and the imagination. Today, just as we need to ask, "Is e-governance really aiding democracy or is it reinscribing inequality by making the digital divide invisible?" tomorrow, we may need to defend our right to forget or be forgotten. Today's critiques to Aadhaar that stem from these invisibilising effects of digital governance might morph into new challenges when surveillance is framed as a public health measure. Now, we can view, on the one hand, the right to information as a feature of Web 1.0, the read-only web, which was made possible because of a newfound ability to capture data (just as many digital governance schemes are also possible because of the aggregating powers of big data). Correspondingly, we can view the recent right to service legislation as a possibility generated by Web 2.0 and understand its varied application across many Indian states.[13] Classically in this distance between 1.0 and 2.0, the user has become more agentic and gone far beyond being the mere object of interest.

By extending questions of the digital beyond "Digital India," we hope to frame relevant curricula through DH and produce more responsive scholarship for an expanded public sphere. Now more than ever, in a post COVID-19 world, our collective future depends on our ability to forge a digital public sphere – by listening to each other, collaborating by making together and remembering what humanity has meant before this time, even as we stare into our socially distant screens.

Notes

1 Devy, G.N. *The Crisis Within: Knowledge and Education in India*. New Delhi: Aleph, 2017, 72.
2 Shah, Nishant. "Beyond Infrastructure: Re-Humanizing Digital Humanities in India", in *Between Humanities and the Digital*, edited by Patrick Svensson and David Theo Goldberg. Cambridge: MIT Press, 2015, 106.
3 http://bichitra.jdvu.ac.in/about_bichitra_project.php; http://dutchcemeterybengal.com; www.bl.uk/projects/two-centuries-of-indian-print; https://iitikship.iiti.ac.in/; https://indiancine.ma/; https://pad.ma/.
4 http://digitalindia.gov.in/. Accessed on May 29, 2018.
5 http://roopikarisam.com/. Comments on remarks from the Colonial and Postcolonial DH roundtable at the College of William and Mary's, *Race, Memory, and the Digital Humanities Conference* on October 27, 2017. Accessed on May 29, 2018.
6 www.hastac.org/initiatives/hastac-scholars/scholars-forums/decolonizing-digital.

7 http://manifesto.humanities.ucla.edu/2009/05/29/the-digital-humanities-manifesto-20/, which defines DH as an array of convergent practices. In point 12, IT defines the digital as "the realm of the open source." Point 42 says, "Digital Humanities deconstructs the very materiality, methods, and media of humanistic inquiry and practices," noting in point 40 that knowledge assumes multiple forms, point 43. The theory after theory is anchored in *making*.

8 Appadurai, Arjun. 2006. "The Right to Research," *Globalisation, Societies and Education*, 4:2, 167–177, doi:10.1080/14767720600750696. Accessed on May 29, 2018.

9 Catherine and Tareque Masud's *Muktir Kotha Muktir Kotha* follows a group of young men and women who began traversing the far corner of Bangladesh projectionists from 1996–1999, showing *Muktir Gaan*, a documentary on the 1971 Bangladesh Liberation War. "The film screenings prompted ordinary villagers to share their own stories of wartime suffering and resistance. Often the projection space would be spontaneously transformed into a folk concert. Through these interactions with village audiences, the young projectionist came to 'relearn' the wider history of the Liberation War, and the continuing struggle of ordinary people for a more just and democratic society." From https://en.wikipedia.org/wiki/Muktir_Kotha. Accessed on May 29, 2018.

10 http://indianexpress.com/article/technology/social/digital-native-face-off-5058464/. "Digital Native: Face Off" by Nishant Shah. Accessed on May 29, 2019.

11 https://assets.kpmg.com/content/dam/kpmg/in/pdf/2017/04/Indian-languages-Defining-Indias-Internet.pdf.

12 https://timesofindia.indiatimes.com/india/vernacular-users-to-be-75-of-internet-user-base-by-2021/articleshow/62710873.cms.

13 Since Madhya Pradesh enacted this in 2010 and many states followed suit, it continues to await national promulgation via the draft bill, Right of Citizens for Time Bound Delivery of Goods and Services and Redressal of their Grievances Act, 2011.

PART I

Digital histories

1

DIGITAL INFRASTRUCTURES AND TECHNOUTOPIAN FANTASIES

The colonial roots of technology aid in the Global South

Dhanashree Thorat

Introduction

> The point is not where you reside, but where you dwell.
> – Walter Mignolo, in *The Darker Side of Western Modernity*

This project on digital infrastructures in the Global South was written into being while I am, in fact, quite far from the geopolitical locus of my work; in Lawrence, Kansas instead of India. A bustling college town steeped in the counterculture movement of the 1960s and surrounded by sprawling fields of wheat and corn, Lawrence is likely unknown to my Indian interlocutors. I bring up my emplacement in the United States to reflect on my distance from the digital humanities (DH) community in India as well as offer some affordances of my current position in forging connections and alliances between different DH communities. I wish first to acknowledge my distance from India, both geographically and from the lived reality on the ground. Short visits, virtual calls, and transcontinental digital collaborations do not quite make up for the sensory and multilayered experiences evoked by *home*. As a postcolonial scholar and person, I understand this distance partially as a loss, removed as I am from the heart and context of my work. I also intend, however, to use my position and draw linkages between transnational colonial histories of infrastructural violence, and advocate, above all, for alliances between marginalized and formerly colonized people doing digital humanities work in the Global South and the Global North. I begin by tracing these colonial roots of infrastructural projects, then examining the case study of Facebook's technological intervention in India, and concluding with recommendations for digital infrastructural projects in the Global South.

My writing on this project was punctuated by the shrill whistle of trains passing by Lawrence each night, and this sound was a daily reminder of the violence that historically undergirded infrastructural projects. The story of the railways in the American Midwest is one of settler colonial violence and native dispossession. The Kansas Pacific Railroad, which passed through Lawrence, like the better-known Transcontinental Railroad connecting the two American coasts, was connected to a broader settler colonial imperative of opening up the American heartland for white settlers, and the economic, military, and communication needs of the Union. Construction on the Kansas Pacific started in 1855, amidst tensions in the then Kansas Territory about what stance it would adopt on slavery and whether its allegiance lay with Abraham Lincoln and the Union, or with the pro-slavery Confederate South. These infrastructural projects were premised upon the dispossession of native tribes, whose lands were seized by the government, acquired through violence or war, or obtained fraudulently by private companies, so that the railway lines could be built and white settlers could establish towns along the lines.

The Kansas Pacific passed through Lawrence, and surrounding areas, after acquiring lands in the Delaware Reservation and the Pottawatomie Reservation at severely undervalued prices, and some of the tribes never received even that monetary compensation. David G. Taylor explains that acquiring the Indian lands was not solely about "right of way" so the Kansas Pacific could be built. Rather, promoters for the line saw the Indian lands as a means of financing railroad construction; they intended to sell parts of the land they had acquired and use unsold parts "as collateral for loans" (Taylor). Such underhanded, fraudulent schemes by private companies were backed by the Union in the form of treaties, federal funding, and military support.[1] Indian tribes opposed to the theft of their lands for railroad projects were met by the Union military which camped along the expanding railway lines. The railroad infrastructure in the American Midwest thus not only emerged from the violence of settler colonialism, but also served to perpetuate it and it received the full backing of the nation-state.

The railway depot in Lawrence has found itself on the periphery of the town today, but the whistle of the trains passing through should serve as a clarion call to remember this troubling history of railway infrastructure. This instance in American history is also repeated in other colonial contexts where transportation and communication infrastructures were built. The British undertook railway construction in Kenya to counteract Germany's colonial ambitions in Africa, and relied on Indian indentured labourers to perform the gruelling work with high mortality rates. The Panama Canal, intended to connect the Pacific and Atlantic for a faster trade route, was similarly constructed with high mortality rates among the Caribbean labour which built the canal under French, and later American supervision. In India, too, the recent history of transportation and communication infrastructures is steeped in colonial objectives. Bogart and Chaudhary explain that the "initial advocates for developing railways in India were the mercantile interests in London and Manchester" because the railway system would allow for the export of Indian raw materials like cotton, and the import of finished projects from Britain (Bogart and Chaudhary 2). Railway infrastructure developed rapidly after the Indian War of Independence in 1857, but British authorities had long recognized the strategic military and political importance of the railways to the colonial administration.[2] Aside from the railways, the telegraph system built by the British in India also served a similar political and military purpose.

Although both these technologies and their infrastructures would later be subverted by the Indian struggle for independence, their original purpose as a means of control should not be forgotten. These technologies were not intended to benefit the natives, despite their use today by colonial apologists to show that British colonialism aided the sub-continent. Moreover, the inequalities in these original systems are transferred into contemporary communication networks; the contemporary submarine cables,[3] which bring the Internet to the world, are overlaid over extant networks like that of the telegraph cables. Just as the West was better connected through telegraph lines yesterday, countries in the Global North have more robust submarine cable networks than the Global South today. This network is so precarious in the Global South that damage to just two cable systems in 2008 led to disruptions in Internet access to 70 per cent of Egypt, 60 per cent of India, and in at least ten other countries (BBC News). In 2012, a ship anchor severed cables between East Africa and the Middle East and caused disruptions in nine countries (Curt Hopkins).

To understand these imbalances in the submarine cable network, and the resultant *precarity* of the Internet infrastructure in the Global South, we must first address the fact that these submarine cables follow pre-existing sites of power. As Manuel Castells writes, the digital network doesn't spread through the world arbitrarily. Rather, this network "diffuses selectively throughout the planet, working on the pre-existing sites, cultures, organizations, and institutions that still make up most of the material environments of people's lives" (25). As a result of this material undergirding, some actors wield more power in the global network. Castells frames this in the context of value. He argues that dominant institutions, by virtue of possessing power, continue to produce, define, and regulate value, and this leads to politics of inclusion and exclusion. In this regard, the "network society does not innovate" over older or existing social networks.

By invoking this historical and transnational scope of infrastructural projects, I align my work with what Lisa Lowe has called "the intimacies of the four continents" (Lowe 1). Lowe's seminal work argues for situating transnational forms of biopolitical settler violence in proximity, and pushing back against "a global geography that . . . conceives in terms of vast spatial distances" (18). On the one hand, colonial practices in disparate places in the four continents are interlinked, residual, and persistent, and they cannot be studied in isolation from each other. On the other hand, attention to intimacies between the continents also enables us to better discover "less visible forms of alliance, affinity, and society among variously colonized peoples beyond the metropolitan national center" (19). It was in the interest of colonial power to separate colonized people to hinder them from connecting their shared conditions of oppression and forming alliances based on that connection.

Lowe's work is particularly relevant in the context of digital infrastructures given the global colonial history of infrastructural projects in formerly colonized

nations, and the troubling encounter that the colonized had with Western modernity. As Mignolo has stated before, any conversation about "global modernities"
necessarily implies "global colonialities" (3). Digital infrastructures remain steeped
in the rhetoric of progress and development that conditions Western modernity.
I argue that attempts to build digital infrastructures in India (and the Global South)
remain rooted in technoutopian and colonial ideologies, thus advancing the notion
that technological progress with Western aid will address the social, political, and
economic problems vexing the Global South. While my focus in the rest of this
chapter will be on India, the context for my critique remains transnational in the
hope that we can identify emergent technological alliances and resistances among
peoples in the Global South and historically marginalized and dispossessed groups
in the Global North.

Digital infrastructure as a technological problem

In the last several years, government agencies, international organizations, corporations, and scholars alike have been invested in conversations about a global digital
divide. The digital divide generally references disparities in Internet access within
countries and internationally. The most direct evaluation metric for the digital
divide is connectivity, but other factors, such as speed and the device used to access
the Internet, are also taken into account.[4] The policy level solutions to the digital
divide are often framed in technological terms. One report by UNESCO, for
example, outlined five recommendations, mostly to do with Internet infrastructure, and government policy changes related to Information and Communications
Technology (ICT). One section recommends that "bridging the digital divide
needs a combination of complementary technologies" and advises using "satellite
networks, fibre-optic cable and terrestrial wireless systems" together (The State
of Broadband 62). The UNESCO report exemplifies a broader trend in public
discourse on the digital divide. Cultural specificities are briefly mentioned (in this
report, pertaining to a gendered digital divide), and colonial histories are seldom
evoked in such reports. As I show shortly, race, class, gender, and other facets of
social identity are known to affect Internet access, but these facets are treated as secondary issues (after the technological) and addressing social inequities falls outside
the purview of infrastructure building. Rather, improved digital infrastructures are
hoped to address these social inequities so that they don't need to be discussed at all.

This framing of the digital divide as a technological problem, rather than a historical, political, or social problem is important because it sets the terms of inter/
national discourse, and limits the kind of solutions proposed to address it. In my
work, I use the term "infrastructure" to denote both "technical systems and the
social networks" that form around them (Anand in Larkin 331). As sociotechnical assemblages, infrastructures encompass material presence, bureaucratic log-
ics, and ideological orientations. More recently, Alan Liu has argued that digital
humanities[5] must focus critique on infrastructure because infrastructure is, today,
"the mise-en-scene of culture" – infrastructure not only enables an experience of

culture, but it is part of our cultural experience today (Drafts for *Against the Cultural Singularity*). Interestingly, the Telecomm Regulatory Authority of India (TRAI), which played an important role in the Facebook debacle that I describe later, does define infrastructures as socio-technical, although it remains unclear how this conceptual framing translates into policies and practices.[6] While discussing the Digital India initiative, TRAI appears to delineate "digital infrastructures" as a separate interest area from "digital empowerment," with the former encapsulating technical advances and the latter focusing on the human element (TRAI).

To illustrate the problems inherent in this technological perspective of digital infrastructures and the digital divide, I turn to Facebook's unsuccessful attempt at offering the Free Basics initiative in India and examine the colonial paradigms about modernization, progress, and equality evoked by this initiative. While Facebook is one of many foreign tech companies operating in India, it is also one of the most popularly visited websites in the country (Alexa).[7] WhatsApp, the mobile messaging service owned by Facebook, also finds its biggest market in India – the country has the highest number of WhatsApp active users. Not only does Facebook have a vested interest in maintaining its market share in India, but also scholars need to examine the impact of Facebook's operations in India, given their potential vast impact. Facebook's international scope also makes it an appropriate site for studying digital infrastructures in the Global South. Citing the "evident dominance" of just two companies, Google and Facebook, as the most visited sites globally, Graham and De Sabbata refer to the digital scene today as the "Age of Internet Empires" (Internet Geographies). This overrepresentation is significant as "the territories carved out now will have important implications for which companies end up controlling how we communicate and access information for many years to come" (Internet Geographies). Thus, we need to keep extending the kind of postcolonial and decolonial critique that Roopika Risam and Adeline Koh called for when they noted that digital humanities must be attentive to decolonizing digital spaces and "disrupting salutary narratives of globalization and technological progress" (#dhpoco).[8]

The Free Basics initiative launched by Facebook purports to bring Internet access to underserved communities in the Global South. The scheme is grounded in the understanding that mobile phones, rather than computers or tablets, are access points to the Internet for many countries in the Global South. As such, Facebook partners with local telecommunication companies to offer selected online content for free to customers. This online content varies from country to country, but it is supposed to be localized and include a mix of websites delivering essential content, including news, health, jobs, government services, and so on. Customers don't need wifi to access these services, and the sites have a low bandwidth load. Service providers who wish to make their online services available on Free Basics have to go through a vetting process controlled by Facebook. Not surprisingly, Facebook is one of the free services offered as an essential on this platform. Internationally, the scheme is now available in sixty-three countries, mostly in the Global South, and claims to have twenty-five million users worldwide.[9]

In India, for a two-year period from 2014 to 2016, Facebook aggressively conducted a campaign on behalf of Free Basics. Partnering with the Indian telecommunication company, Reliance, Facebook recruited a number of Indian companies to offer their content through the Free Basics platform and sought buy-in from the Indian public to use Free Basics. This campaign might largely masquerade under the rhetoric of advertising and marketing, but it should be seen as a biopolitical maneuver to shape the technosocial infrastructure and imaginary of the Indian sub-continent. The campaign was replete with colonial tropes, bringing together troubling narratives about technological primitivism and the white man's burden. The India framed in the campaign was a simultaneous space of spiritual enlightenment, a new frontier for the digital empire of Facebook, and the testing site for techno-capitalist schemes that could be taken elsewhere if they were successful. India was the sixth country where the initiative had officially launched, and it was the first one in Asia, and conquering the digital frontier of India would have eased the adoption of Free Basics globally.

The advertising campaign received much publicity when Mark Zuckerberg met Indian Prime Minister Narendra Modi as part of latter's tour of Silicon Valley in 2015. Courting the Indian Prime Minister in Silicon Valley became one of the high profile moves that Facebook would make on behalf of Free Basics, and one of the reasons why their campaign was interpreted in colonialist terms. As Deepika Bahri explained, by "partner[ing] with local elites and vested interests," Facebook operated on a colonial model of intervention in the Global South (Bahri in Lafrance).[10] At a town hall event hosted by Facebook for Modi, Zuckerberg announced that his investment in India was personal because India had a part in inspiring him in the early days of Facebook. In 2008, while under pressure to sell the company, Zuckerberg had been advised by Steve Jobs, the Apple CEO, to visit a temple in India "to reconnect to what I believed was the mission of the company" (Annie Gowan – Independent). Zuckerberg did spend a month in India in 2008 and later declared that the trip allowed him to find some spiritual rejuvenation as it "reinforced for me the importance of what we were doing" (Annie Gowan – Independent).

Indian spiritualism has long been co-opted into the American counterculture movement of the sixties and seventies, with gurus, meditation, and yoga offering a path to a transcendent state of mind. And for Silicon Valley technocrats steeped in the counterculture, India is configured as a space where white Westerners visit for spiritual enlightenment, and to escape from the hypermodern, urban landscape of Silicon Valley.[11] This leitmotif of India as a mystical and spiritual place evoked by Steve Jobs and Mark Zuckerberg is part of the older Orientalist discourse of colonialism. If the Orient was framed as a mystical or mysterious site, it absolved colonizers from parsing through cultural specificities and placed these cultures in an otherworldly realm beyond the rational logic of Enlightenment thinking.[12] The Orient, Said observes, "was overvalued for its pantheism, its spirituality" and "such overesteem was [inevitably] followed by a counterresponse," in which the Orient was also framed as backward, barbaric, and so on (Said 150).

Facebook's Free Basics was launched in India against this backdrop of Orientalist discourse, and Zuckerberg's early words already anticipate the emergence of an "Other" subject to which Western aid will be extended. The richness of India's spiritual traditions form the contrast to the abjectness of its technological scene. Indeed, declaring Internet access as a fundamental human right, and framing Facebook as a humanitarian agent, Zuckerberg announced at this town hall that Facebook was working to bring Internet access to four billion people in the world. I use the verb "bring" with the many implications of that term in this context: there is a sense of a unilateral decision made by Facebook on behalf of the people of the Global South; there is an element of "bringing around" or "bringing about," of persuading people about Facebook's mission; and there is an implicit notion that Indians must be brought to the digital panacea promised by Facebook because they are in a space of technological deprivation. This is why Mignolo argued that the "rhetoric of modernity is a rhetoric of salvation (by conversion yesterday, by development today" (xxiv).

To bring the Indian public about, Facebook launched a massive marketing campaign premised on technoutopian fantasies; by this, I mean the notion that technological advancement is a necessity for improving human lives and human rights. The advertisements, publicity material, and op-ed pieces published by Facebook in late 2015 paralleled colonial ideologies touting Western modernity. A two-page advertisement appeared in *The Times of India*, one of the major national newspapers in India, in December 2015.

The advertisement makes several extravagant promises about what Free Basics offers to the Indian poor, ranging from the idealistic (digital equality, connectedness) to the concrete (jobs). The ad also communicates the notion that Free Basics is absolutely essential for the future of the nation. Rhetorical appeals about national development are repeated in a number of phrases: "opportunities online," "better future," "digital equality," and progress, and most strongly, "move India forward" (*TOI* ad). What these terms mean or any specific details about this future are not offered, leaving the reader to imbue these terms with a meaning suitable to the reader's own interests, desires, and (possibly) marginality. Above all, this advertisement makes an argument based on absence: what the reader is supposed to fill in is the negative of these utterances: that a nation lacking in digital infrastructure supported by foreign investment cannot progress, that it lacks a good future, and that it fails to provide opportunities for its citizens. (I am less interested here in the truth value of these statements then their presentation as rhetoric.)

This language of progress and modernization used in the advertisement is far from innocuous because to say that Free Basics will move "India forward" is also to say that India is currently backward. This notion is reinforced by the visuals of the advertisement, which are rich in traditional and cultural symbols (the henna, bangles, and traditional outfits) and frame both the young women as traditional subjects who have embraced Western modernity. Such imagery, particularly of young girls and women, recurs in other Facebook ads on Free Basics and represents the only (and very limited) attempt made by the company to discuss the gendered dimension of the digital divide. Painted within this picture of dearth, Facebook is presented as an altruistic entity rather than a multinational corporation that stands to gain much by staking a claim on the Indian market. The ad also attempts to convince readers that Free Basics is the first step towards digital equality – a disingenuous move which suggests that there have been no prior attempts at digital equality in India and that Facebook's initiative is an appropriate first response, in a series of responses to digital inequality in India.

These technoutopian promises about the affordances of technology, particularly the claims about equality, opportunities, and rights, predate the digital era and are at least as old as the British colonization of India. From a postcolonial perspective, Facebook's intervention in India is reflective of a colonial pattern, of Western attempts to bring technologies into India to supposedly help the sub-continent "develop." Inevitably, this development happens on the terms of a Western agent, and involves a profit-making scheme for this agent. (The railway and the telegraph system I discussed earlier are both classic examples of this scheme.) This rhetoric of development is premised on the understanding that colonized people were pre-modern, primitive, lacking in technology and technological know-how, and it was the responsibility of the colonial empires to advance their barbarian subjects. Rudyard Kipling, the English writer who lived extensively in India, called this the "white man's burden."[13] Facebook's Free Basics falls into this same paradigm of thinking when it posits that access to technology will solve the political, cultural, and economic problems that vex the Global South.

This technoutopianism rests at the very core of Western modernity, and its recurrence as a colonial and neocolonial motif is unsurprising. Brian Larkin notes that it is "difficult to disentangle infrastructures from [such] evolutionary ways of thinking" because infrastructural development has its roots in Enlightenment thought and an idea of a world grounded in circulation and progress (322). Of course, these ideas about circulation and progress are problematized when transposed against colonization and the transatlantic slave trade. The connectedness and ease of circulation brought about by infrastructural development, and the purpose of infrastructural development, also enabled the transatlantic slave trade. The logic of circulation might enable the circulation of ideas (or data, more contemporaneously), but it also references the extraction of resources from colonized places and the introduction of finished products imported from England to the colonies. As a project of Western modernity, infrastructure building is tied to technoutopian fantasies and colonial ideologies, and it must be detangled from these conceptions.

Facebook's Free Basics campaign was eventually unsuccessful. While the colonialist undertones of the campaign certainly played a role, the campaign met its demise in a policy violation. The initiative had been persistently called out for violating net neutrality; given the limited access to the Internet it allowed users. Moreover, Facebook retained substantial control over which services would be offered at all, as content service providers had to follow developer rules outlined by Facebook. In February 2016, TRAI (The Telecomm Regulatory Authority of India) finally banned the service in India on the grounds that it violated principles of net neutrality. The ban came on the heels of a massive uproar, particularly in Indian cities, about Facebook's perceived highhandedness in running the campaign. Many Indian Facebook users felt imposed upon when Facebook added a link to their Facebook profiles and encouraged them to send an automated email to TRAI on behalf of Free Basics. By pushing users so blatantly to make a decision that supported itself, Facebook inadvertently uncovered the ideological underpinnings of its own platform.

Moreover, Facebook's decision to attack Indian net neutrality activists who had been protesting Free Basics was not well received. In one op-ed piece penned by Mark Zuckerberg in *The Times of India*, he decried net neutrality activists who he accused of peddling "fiction" and false claims about Free Basics (Zuckerberg).[14] The op-ed again conjures an image of technological backwardness, offering up the example of a "farmer in Maharashtra called Ganesh" who used Free Basics to "prepare for [the] monsoon season" and eventually started "investing in new crops and livestock" (Zuckerberg). Zuckerberg then asks, "How does Ganesh being able to better tend his crops hurt the Internet?" The success story allows Zuckerberg to misdirect attention away from Facebook's ethics, because the ensuing pathos laden rhetorical question only has one moral answer in the limited terms of discourse set by Zuckerberg. That there might be other models for providing Internet access and building digital infrastructures in India, and in the Global South, goes unacknowledged. At least, unacknowledged by Facebook, but not so by Indian net neutrality activists who adeptly challenged these assertions. As Nikhil Pahwa asked in a competing op-ed, "why hasn't Facebook chosen options that do not violate Net Neutrality?" (Pahwa). Pahwa's question reframes the conversation by bringing up the possibility of an "open, plural, and diverse web" and refocuses the attention on Facebook and its responsibilities in India. Facebook's attacks on Indian net neutrality activists roused anger particularly because Facebook had spoken strongly in favor of net neutrality in the United States. There was a perception of a double standard: that Facebook was attempting to exploit lax digital laws in the Global South in a way that it was prevented from doing in the West.

The TRAI ban was not entirely surprising, given this furor, and it sent out a strong message that we not accept the self-serving benevolence of neocolonial tech corporations. While there is certainly a need to develop digital infrastructures in the Global South, this development cannot be entrenched in colonial ideologies which are ultimately harmful to peoples affected by colonial projects. Yet, the outcomes of this particular episode were not entirely satisfactory: although this was a setback to Facebook (which has never since revived Free Basics in India), the initiative did expand to many neighbouring countries and other parts of the world. Facebook, moreover, is not alone in its ambitious desire to shape infrastructural development around the world. Google, the other Internet empire, has its own such projects, and one of them, Project Loon, was recently approved for testing in India. Such technocratic successes and experiments point to the need for constant vigilance, and for the need too, of imaginative decolonial projects that can envision critical and liberatory forms of digital infrastructures. The Global South cannot be a haphazard laboratory for IT companies in the West to test out temporary schemes for providing Internet access. Such temporary, stop-gap, or limited schemes cannot ultimately benefit the people they purport to serve.

In closing, I would like to offer three recommendations for (digital) infrastructural projects in the Global South:

First, we must move away from the idea of digital infrastructures as apolitical systems, and as systems which offer inherent benefits like equality and progress. As my early example of the railways in Kansas and in India indicates, infrastructures can perpetuate colonial violence against marginalized people, and actively work against the political, economic, and social interests of marginalized people. Given this colonial history, we must ask who defines the terms on which the so-called Third World is being developed, and what ideologies are inherent to the infrastructures and technologies developed by IT companies in the First World. I am not recommending here that the Global South turn away entirely from foreign investment in digital infrastructure. Rather, we must continue to hold technology companies (both native and foreign) accountable, particularly for technological solutions to social inequalities. As Philip and colleagues remind us about postcolonial computing, we cannot "escape from the political nature of technocultural practice. . . [and hence, find] located, always ambivalent engagements" instead (15). Instead of reifying native technologies and infrastructures, we can consider approaches that generate "reflective and provocative engagements and more questions" (15).

Second, we need to articulate richer definitions of Internet access to ground our conversations on the digital divide and digital infrastructures. In particular, defining Internet access as a yes/no binary limits the technosocial imaginary and fosters technoutopian fantasies about digital technologies solving the problems that vex the Global South (*if only* people could access the Internet). Instead, Adam Banks advises that we move towards different kinds of "access', including experiential, critical and transformative access. Framing technology as a site of struggle for marginalized people, Banks asks how digital technologies can be constructed with marginalized people as collaborators, consultants, and partners rather than simply as end-users (42). Technologies and infrastructures must be relevant to people on the ground, and attentive to local conditions. While Banks's work is developed in the context of Black technology practices in the US, this context again illustrates the possibility of transnational alliances on digital technologies and infrastructures among marginalized people in the Global North and Global South.

Third, despite my critical take on Facebook's interventions in India, I don't recommend a techno-pessimistic outlook towards infrastructural development. As Ruja Benjamin puts it, "we need to recruit androids into our struggle" so that we are not situating technology in opposition to human and postcolonial life (Benjamin keynote address). Digital solutions will not resolve social inequalities, but they can be powerfully leveraged by marginalized people in their own lives, and in movements for social and racial justice. In terms of infrastructural development, we can take up Alan Liu's call to "pragmatically [guide], the agencies and factors in [infrastructural] making and remaking" (Alan Liu, Drafts for Against the Cultural

Singularity 2016). Framing digital infrastructures as a sociotechnical endeavour creates space for humanists to intervene in and shape conversations and projects pertaining to infrastructure development. While this particular chapter has been primarily invested in postcolonial critique, we must also imagine and articulate new conceptions of postcolonial design, code, technologies, and infrastructures.

Notes

1 Richard White observes that Congress was so sold on the transcontinental railroad projects that it authorized a "profusion of stocks, bonds, and other favors, that between 1862 and 1872 railroads received grants the size of small and medium states" (White).

2 In a minute on the railway issued by Lord Dalhousie in 1853, he writes that a "single glance cast upon the map recalling to mind the vast extent of the Empire we hold . . . will suffice to show how immeasurable are the political advantages to be derived from a system of internal communication" (Railways India). Dalhousie's minute goes on to spell out the military advantages (especially speedy movement of troops within the sub-continent and the dissemination of intelligence reports), political, and economic advantages.

3 Submarine cables are undersea fibre-optic cables used for telecommunication purposes. The use of satellites in the global Internet network remains minimal, and the submarine cables essentially reflect the predominant material infrastructure of the Internet today.

4 See Ragnedda and Muschert's discussion of the digital divide. They explain that the concept is "typically measured via access to the Internet (versus non-access), number of sites at which the Internet is accessed, users' skill at using the Internet, amount of time spent online, and the variety of activities carried out digitally" (2). Their work calls for attending to the " nuances to the digital divide, [the] ones which add finer gradients to the discussion" beyond binary classifications of access/no access (2).

5 Patrik Svensson has also written extensively on digital infrastructures in the context of the digital humanities. In one of his articles, he traces a three-layered model for developing humanities infrastructures which incorporates conceptual infrastructures (the epistemic undergirding), design principles, and actual (material) infrastructures (Svensson).

6 In a presentation at the Symposium on "Collaborative Regulation for Digital Societies," TRAI offered the following definition of digital infrastructure: A " collection of technological and human components, networks, systems and processes that contribute to the functioning of an information system" (TRAI, drawing on Braa et al., Tilson et al.). http://trai.gov.in/sites/default/files/presentations_&_cv/Day-3_25Aug2017/Session2_Digital%20world/Digital%20Infra_Rajesh%20Sharma.pdf.

7 Alexa has consistently ranked it in the top five of most visited sites in India.

8 Risam and Koh are writing, as I am too, in an older research arc that spans science and technology studies. Kavita Philip and colleagues, for example, defined a field of inquiry called "Postcolonial Computing," which "proposes a rubric under which to examine this new global configuration of technology, cultural practices, economic relations, and narratives of development" (21).

9 Facebook was reported to be talks to bring Free Basics to underserved communities in the US in 2016, but nothing concrete has materialized out of these talks.

10 Bahri offers the following criteria that define Free Basics as a colonialist project: "1. Ride in like the savior, 2. Bandy about words like equality, democracy, basic rights, 3. Mask the long-term profit motive, 4. Justify the logic of partial dissemination as better than nothing, 5. Partner with local elites and vested interests, 6. Accuse the critics of ingratitude" (Lafrance).

11 Another Silicon Valley figure who visited the temple explained its draw by saying that "everybody in the world wants to go and see this place. . . . It's a combination of 'Eat Pray Love,' know thyself and change the world" (Gowan).

12 At the same time, however, there was great interest among the colonial scholars of the Orient in the rationalist project of "dispelling mystery and institutionalizing even the most recondite knowledge" in order to open up the Orient for "European scrutiny" (Said 83).
13 In an imperialist poem of the same name, which responds to the American colonization of the Philippines.
14 One sample statement from the op-ed is as follows: "Instead of wanting to give people access to some basic Internet services for free, critics of the program continue to spread false claims – even if it means leaving a billion people behind" (Zuckerberg).

References

Alexa. 'Top Sites in India.' *Alexa*. 1 April 2018. Web.

Banks, Adam. *Race, Rhetoric, and Technology: Searching for Higher Ground*. Mahwah, NJ: Lawrence Erlbaum. 2006. Print.

Benjamin, Ruha. 'Keynote Address at the Data4BlackLives Conference.' 17 November 2017. Web. 20 March 2018. https://youtu.be/TrEiEjjt7v4

Bogart, Dan, and Latika Chaudhary. 'Railways in Colonial India: An Economic Achievement?' *SSRN Electronic Journal*. (2012): 1–39.

Castells, Manuel. *Communication Power*. Oxford: Oxford University Press. 2009. Print.

'Critical Infrastructure Studies Special Panel at MLA 2018.' 6 January 2018. Web. 30 March 2018. https://criticalinfrastructure.hcommons.org/session-description/

Gowan, Annie. 'Kainchi Dham: The Indian Ashram Where Silicon Valley's Finest Go to Discover Themselves.' *The Independent*. 3 November 2015. Web. 20 March 2018.

Graham, Mark, and Stefano De Sabbata. 'Age of Internet Empires.' *Information Geographies at the Oxford Internet Institute*. 2014. Web. 20 March 2018.

Hopkins, Curt. 'Ship's Anchor Cuts Internet Access to Six East African Countries.' *The Christian Science Monitor*. 29 February 2012. Web. 20 March 2018.

Kipling, Rudyard. 'The White Man's Burden: The United States & The Philippine Islands, 1899.' *Rudyard Kipling's Verse: Definitive Edition*. Garden City, NY: Doubleday. 1929. Print.

Koh, Adeline, and Roopika Risam. *Postcolonial Digital Humanities Website and Blog*. Web. 20 March 2018. http://dhpoco.org/

Lafrance, Adrienne. 'Facebook and the New Colonialism.' *The Atlantic*. 11 February 2016. Web. 25 March 2018.

Larkin, Brian. 'The Politics and Poetics of Infrastructure.' *Annual Review of Anthropology*. 42 (2013): 327–343.

Liu, Alan. 'Drafts for *Against the Cultural Singularity*.' 2 May 2016. http://liu.english.ucsb.edu/drafts-for-against-the-cultural-singularity/

Lowe, Lisa. *The Intimacies of the Four Continents*. Durham: Duke UP. 2015. Print.

Mignolo, Walter. *The Darker Side of Western Modernity: Global Futures, Decolonial Options*. Durham: Duke UP. 2011. Print.

Pahwa, Nikhil. 'It's a Battle for Internet Freedom.' *The Times of India*. 28 December 2015. Web. 20 March 2018.

Philip, Kavita, et al. 'Postcolonial Computing: A Tactical Survey.' *Science, Technology, and Human Values*. 37.1 (2012): 3–29.

Ragnedda, Massimo, and Glenn Muschert. *The Digital Divide: The Internet and Social Inequality in International Perspective*. London: Routledge. 2015. Print.

'Railways (India): Copies or Extracts of Any Correspondence Received by the Last Mail from the Governor-General in Council in India, Relative to Railways Undertakings in That Country.' East India House. 18 July 1853. Print.

Risam, Roopika. 'Diasporizing the Digital Humanities: Displacing the Center and Periphery.' *International Journal of E-Politics*. 7.3 (2016): 65–78.

Said, Edward. *Orientalism*. New York: Pantheon Books. 1978. Print.

'Severed Cables Disrupt Internet.' *BBC News*. 31 January 2008. Web. 20 March 2018.

Star, Susan Leigh. 'The Ethnography of Infrastructure.' *American Behavioral Scientist*. 43.3 (1999): 377–391.

'The State of Broadband 2017: Broadband Catalyzing Sustainable Development.' *UNESCO and ITU*. September 2017. Web. 20 March 2018.

Svensson, Patrik. 'From Optical Fiber to Conceptual Cyberinfrastructure.' *Digital Humanities Quarterly*. 5.1 (2011). Web.

Taylor, David G. 'Thomas Ewing, Jr., and the Origins of the Kansas Pacific Railway Company.' *Kansas State Historical Society*. 42.2 (1976): 155–179.

TRAI. 'Digital Infrastructure in India.' Symposium on Collaborative Regulation for Digital Societies. 25 August 2017. Web. 20 March 2018. http://trai.gov.in/sites/default/files/presentations_&_cv/Day-3_25Aug2017/Session2_Digital%20world/Digital%20Infra_Rajesh%20Sharma.pdf

White, Richard. 'The Origins of the Transcontinental Railroad.' *The Gilder Lehrman Institute for American History*. Web. 20 March 2018. http://oa.gilderlehrman.org/history-by-era/development-west/essays/origins-transcontinental-railroad

Zuckerberg, Mark. 'Free Basics Protects Net Neutrality.' *The Times of India*. 28 December 2015. Web. 20 March 2018.

2

A QUESTION OF DIGITAL HUMANITIES IN INDIA

Puthiya Purayil Sneha

The 'digital turn' has been one of the significant changes in fields of interdisciplinary research and scholarship in the last couple of decades. The advent of new digital technologies and the growth of networked environments have led to a rethinking of the traditional processes of knowledge gathering and production, across an array of fields and disciplinary areas. The field of digital humanities (henceforth DH) has emerged as yet another manifestation of what in essence is this changing relationship between technologies and the human being or subject. The nature and processes of information, scholarship and learning now produced or mediated by digital tools, methods or spaces have formed the crux of the DH discourse as it has emerged in different parts of the world so far. It has been variously called a phenomenon, field, discipline and a set of convergent practices – all of which are located at and/or try to understand the interaction between digital technologies and humanities practice and scholarship. DH in the Anglo-American context has seen several changes – from an early phase of vast archival initiatives and digitization projects, to now exploring the role of big data and cultural analytics in literary criticism. Some of the early scholarship in the field illustrates the problems with defining and locating it within specific disciplinary formations, as the research objects, methods and locations of DH work cut across everything from the archive to the laboratory and social networking platforms. Largely interpreted as a way to explore the intersection of information technology and humanities, DH has grown to become an interdisciplinary field of research and practice today. However, DH is also clearly being posited as a site of contestation – what is perceived as doing away with or reinventing certain norms of traditional humanities research and scholarship.[1] A specific criticism within more recent debates around the origin story of digital humanities in fact has been its Anglo-American framing, drawing upon a history in humanities computing and textual studies, and located within a larger neoliberal imagination of the university and academia.[2] As a result, it has largely been framed within the existing narrative of a crisis in the humanities, highlighting the more prominent role of technology, which is now expected to resolve in some way questions of relevance and authority that seem to have become central to the continued existence and practice of the humanities in its conventional forms.

The problem of definition

The question of what DH means has been asked many times, and in different ways. Most scholars have differentiated between two waves or types of DH – the first is that of using computational tools to do traditional humanities research, while the second looks at the 'digital' itself as integral to humanistic enquiry.[3] However, as is apparent in the existing discourse, the problem of definition still persists. As a field, method or practice, is it a found term that has now been appropriated in various forms and by different disciplines, or is it helping us reconfigure questions of the humanities by making available, through advancements in technology, a new digital object or a domain of enquiry that previously was unavailable to us? These and others will continue to remain questions *for* the digital humanities, but it would be important to first examine what would be the question/s *of* digital humanities. Dave Parry (2012) summarises to some extent these different contentions to a definition of the field when he suggests that 'what is at stake here is not the object of study or even epistemology, but rather ontology. The digital changes what it means to be human, and by extension what it means to study the humanities.'

Some speculation on the larger premise of the field, with specific reference to its emergence in India, is what I hope to chart out in this study. This is not in itself an attempt at a definition, but sketching out a domain of enquiry by mapping the field with respect to work being done in the Indian context. In doing so, these propositions will assume one or the other (if not all three) of these following suggested threads or modes of thought, which also inform larger concerns of the DH work at Centre for Internet and Society (CIS):

1   The first is the inherited separation of technology and the humanities and therefore the existing tenuous relationship between the two fields. As is apparent in the nomenclature itself, there seems to be a bringing together of what seem to have been essentially two separate domains of knowledge. However, the humanities and technology have a rather chequered history together, which we can locate with the beginning of print culture. As Adrian Johns points out in the *Nature of the Book*, 'any printed book is, as a matter of fact, both the product of one complex set of social and technological processes and the beginning of another' (Johns, 1998, 3). The larger imagination of humanities as text-based disciplines can be located in a sense in the rise of printing, literacy and textual scholarship. While the book itself seems to have made a comfortable transition into the digital realm, the process of this transition, the channels of circulation and distribution of information as objects of study have been relegated to certain disciplinary concerns, thus obfuscating and making

invisible this 'technologised history' of the humanities. Whether DH can be an attempt to uncover such a history and bridge these knowledge gaps would be a question here.

2   The distance between the practice and the subject. How does one identify with DH practice? While many people engage with what seem to be core DH concerns, they are not all 'digital humanists' or do not identify themselves by the term. While at one level the problem is still that of definition and taxonomy – what is or is not DH – at another level it is also about the nature of subjectivity produced in such practice – whether it has one of its own or is still entrenched in other disciplinary formations, as is the case with most DH research today. This is apparent in the emphasis on processes and tools in DH – where the practice or method seems to have emerged before the theoretical or epistemological framework. One may also connect this to the larger discourse on the emergence of the techno-social subject[4] as an identity meditated by digital and new media technologies, wherein technology is central to the practices that engender this subjectivity.

3   Tying back to the first question is also the notion of a conflict between the humanities and DH. This comes with the perception of DH being a version 2.0 of the traditional humanities, a result of the existing narrative of crisis and the need for the humanities disciplines to reinvent themselves to remain relevant in the present context, and one way to do this is by becoming amenable to the use of computing tools. DH has emerged as one way to mediate between the humanities and the changes that are imminent with digital technologies, but it may not or even need not take up the task of trying to establish a teleological connection between the two. The theoretical pursuits of both may be different but deeply related, and this is one manner of approaching DH as a field or domain of enquiry; the point of intersection or conflict would be where new questions emerge. This narrative is also located within a larger framing of DH in terms of addressing the concerns of the labour market, and the fear of the humanities being displaced or replaced as a result. Parry's objective of studying DH works with and tries to address this particular formulation of the field.

Locating these concerns in India, where the field of DH is still at an incipient stage comes with a multitude of questions. For one the digital divide still persists to a large extent in India, and is at different levels due to the complexity of linguistic and social conditions of technological advancement. It is difficult to locate a field that is so premised on technology in such a varied context. Secondly, the existing discourse on DH still draws upon, to a large extent, the given history of the term which renders it inaccessible for countries in the Global South, especially from a postcolonial context, and with a sufficiently intersectional perspective.[5] Another issue that is not specifically Indian but can be seen more explicitly in this context is the somewhat uncritical way in which technology itself is imagined. In most spaces, technology is still understood as either 'facilitating' something, either a specific kind of research enquiry or as a tool – a means to an end, and as being value or culture neutral. However, if we are to imagine the digital as a condition of being as Parry says, then technology too cannot be relegated to being a means to an end. Bruno Latour indicates the same when he says, 'Technology is everywhere, since the term applies to a regime of enunciation, or, to put it another way, to a mode of existence, a particular form of exploring existence, a particular form of the exploration of being – in the midst of many others' (Latour, 2002).

DH then in some sense takes us back to the notion of technology or more specifically the digital realm as being a discursive space, and a technosocial or cultural paradigm that generates new objects and methods of study. This has been the impetus of cyber culture and digital culture studies, but what separates DH from these fields is another way to arrive at some understanding of its ontological status. At a cursory glance, the shift from content to process, from information to data seems to be the key transition here, and the blurring of the boundaries between such absolute categories. More importantly, however, does this point towards an epistemic shift – a rupture in the given understanding of certain knowledge formations or systems is also a pertinent question of DH. There are several questions, therefore, for DH – in terms of what it means and what it could do for our understanding of the humanities and technology. However, the questions of DH still need to be made explicit. This mapping exercise will attempt to explore some of these thoughts a little further. Through discussions with scholars and practitioners across diverse fields, we will attempt to map and generate different meanings of the 'digital' and DH. While we can expect this to definitely produce more questions, we also hope the process of thinking through these questions will lead to an understanding of the larger field as well.

The problem of the discipline

Much has been said and written about DH as an emergent field or domain of enquiry; the plethora of departments being set up all across the world, well mostly the Western world, is testimony to the claimed innovative and generative potential of the field. However, as outlined in the introduction, the problem of definition still persists and poses much difficulty in any attempts to engage with the field. While the predominant narrative seems to be in terms of defining what DH, or to take it a step back, what the 'digital' allows you to do, with respect to enabling or facilitating certain kinds of research and pedagogy, a pertinent question still is that of what it allows you to 'be'. DH has been alternatively called a method, practice and field of enquiry, but scholars and practitioners in many instances have stopped short of fully embracing it as a discipline. This is an interesting development given the rapid pace of its institutionalization – from being located in existing Humanities or Computational Sciences and Media Studies departments it has now claimed functional institutional spaces of its own, with not just interdisciplinary research and teaching but also other creative and innovative knowledge-making practices. The field is slowly gaining credence in India as well, with several institutions pursuing research around core questions within the fold of DH.

So is the disciplinary lens inadequate to understand this phenomenon, or is it too early for a field still considered in some ways rather incipient? The growth of the academic discipline itself is something of a fraught endeavour, as debates around the scientific revolution and Enlightenment thought have established. To put it in a very simple manner, the story of academic disciplines is that of training in reason.[6] Andrew Cutrofello says, 'In academia, a discipline is defined by its methodological rigor and the clear boundaries of its field of inquiry. Methods or fields are criticized as being "fuzzy" when they are suspected of lacking a discipline. In a more straight-forwardly Foucauldian sense, the disciplinary power of academic disciplines can be located in their methods for producing docile bodies of different sorts' (1994, 116). The problem with defining DH may lie in it not conforming to precisely this notion of the academic discipline, and changing ideas of the function of critique when mediated by the digital, which is of primary concern for the humanities. DH has in many spaces also emerged as a manifestation of increasing interdisciplinarity and the blurring of boundaries between traditional disciplinary concerns.[7]

However, a prevalent mode of understanding DH has been in terms of the disciplinary concerns it raises for the humanities themselves; this works with the assumption that it is in fact a newer, improved version or extension of the humanities. The present mapping exercise too began with the disciplinary lens, but instead of enquiring about what DH is, it tried to explore what the 'digital' has brought to, changed or appropriated in terms of existing disciplinary concerns within the humanities and more broadly spaces and process of knowledge-making and dissemination. This thought stems from the premise that if we have to posit the digital itself as a state of being or existence, then we need to understand this new techno-social paradigm much better. Prof. Amlan Dasgupta, at the School of Cultural Texts and Records at Jadavpur University in Kolkata, sees this as a useful way of going about the problem of trying to arrive at a definition of the field – one is to understand the history of the term, from its inherited definition in the Anglo-American context, and distinguish it from what he calls the current state of 'digitality' – where all cultural objects are being now being conceived of as 'digital' objects. In the Indian context, the question of digitality also becomes important from the perspective of technological obsolescence – where there is a great resistance to discontinuing or phasing out the use of certain kinds of technology, either for lack of access to better ones or simply because one finds other uses for it. Prof. Dasgupta interestingly terms this a 'culture of reuse', one example of this being the typewriter which for all practical purposes has been displaced by the computer, but still finds favour with several people in their everyday lives. The question of livelihood is still connected to some of these technologies, so much so that they are very much a part of channels of cultural production and circulation, and even when they cease to become useful they have value as cultural artifacts. We therefore inhabit at the same time, different worlds, that of the analogue and digital, or as he calls it, 'a multi-layered technological sphere'. The notion of the 'digital' is also multi-layered, with some objects being 'weakly digital', and others being so in a more pronounced manner. The variedness of this space, and the complexities or 'degrees of use' of certain technologies or technological objects is what further determines the nature of this space and makes it all the more difficult to define. DH itself has seen several phases in the West, but has seen no such movement or gradual evolution in India, where these phases exist simultaneously, he says.[8]

This further complicates the questions of access to technology or the 'digital divide' that have been and still are some of the primary approaches to understanding the pervasiveness of technology, particularly in the Global South. The need of the hour therefore is to be able to distinguish between this current state of digitality that we are in, and what is meant by the 'digital humanities'. It may after all be a set of methodologies rather than a subject or discipline in itself – the question is how it would help us understand the 'digital' itself much better, and more critically, and the new kinds of enquiries it may then facilitate about this space we now inhabit. This, Prof. Dasgupta feels, would go a long way in arriving at some definition of the field.

One of the important points of departure, from the traditional humanities and later humanities computing as mentioned earlier, has been the blurring of boundaries between content, method and object/s of enquiry. The 'process' has become important, as illustrated by the iterative nature of most DH projects and the discourse itself which emphasises the 'making' and 'doing' aspects of the research as much as the content itself. Tool-building as a critical activity rather than as mere facilitation is an important part of the knowledge-making process in the field (Ramsay, 2010). In conjunction with this, Dr. Moinak Biswas, at the Department of Film Studies at Jadavpur University, thinks that the biggest changes have been in the form of the collaborative nature of knowledge production, based on voluntarily sharing or creating new content through digital platforms and archives, and crucially the possibility of now imagining creative and analytical work as not separate practices, but located within a single space and time. He cites an example from film, where now with digital platforms and processes, 'image' making and critical practice can both be combined on one platform, like the online archive Indiancine. ma[9] or the *Vectors* journal,[10] for example, to produce new layers of meaning around existing texts. The aspect of critique is important here, given that the consistent criticism about the field has been the ambiguity of its social undertaking – its critical or political standpoint or challenge to existing theoretical paradigms. Most of the interest around the term has been in very instrumental terms, as a facilitator or enabler of certain kinds of digital practice. While the move away from computational analysis as a technique to facilitate humanities research is apparent, the disciplinary concerns here still seem to be latched onto those of the traditional humanities. Questions about the epistemological concerns of DH itself therefore remain unanswered.[11]

While reiterating some of these core questions within DH, Dr. Souvik Mukherjee at the Department of English, Presidency University and Dr. Padmini Ray Murray, at the Centre for Public History, Srishti School of Art, Design and Technology, speak of the problem of locating the field in India, where work is presently only being done in a few small pockets. The lack of a precise definition or location within an established disciplinary context are some reasons why a lot of work that could come within the ambit of DH is not being acknowledged as such; conversely, it also leads to the problem of projects on digitization or studies of digital cultures/ cyber cultures being easily conflated with DH. Related to this is the absence of self-claimed 'digital humanists', which makes it all the more difficult to identify the boundaries of their research and practice. More importantly, the lack of an indigenous framework to theorize around questions of the digital is also an obstacle to understanding what the field entails and the many possibilities it may offer in the Indian context. This they feel is a problem not just of DH, but in general for modes of knowledge production in the social sciences and humanities that have adopted Western theoretical constructs.[12] One could also locate in some sense the present crisis in disciplines within this problem. Sundar Sarukkai and Gopal Guru explicate this issue further when they talk about the absence of 'experience as an important category of the act of theorising' because of the privileging of ideas in Western constructs of experience (Guru and Sarukkai, 2012). This is also reflective of the bifurcation between theory and praxis in traditional social sciences or humanities epistemological frameworks which borrow heavily from the West. DH, while still to arrive at a core disciplinary concern, seems to point towards the problem of this very demarcation by addressing the aspect of practice as a very focal point of its discourse.

Dr. Indira Chowdhury, oral historian and director of the Centre for Public History, who is also a faculty member at the Srishti School of Art, Design and Technology, Bangalore, sees this as a favourable way of understanding how the field as such has emerged and what its various possibilities could be in terms of different disciplinary perspectives. She is uncertain of its emergence as a response to a 'crisis' in the humanities as such. She recalls an instance of one of her students who went on to work on hypertext in Canada, several years ago, which for her seemed to be the first instance of something close to DH. The IT revolution in the early 2000s was a significant change, and there were several things that it enabled people to do, in terms of concordance, cross-referencing and getting around texts in certain ways. However, whether key questions in the humanities really changed, whether they were taken any further, is something yet to be explored because it is still such a new field, and one can only be speculative about it, she feels. It perhaps pushes for a new level of interdisciplinarity and a different kind of collaborative space that the digital enables. What is significant and exciting for her as a historian, however, is that if history has to survive as a discipline, not only in schools but also in terms of public spaces and discourse, it should actively engage with the digital. This not only presents significant challenges, in how to represent the past in the digital space, (in short problems with method) but also opens up new possibilities, for example with oral history and the advent of digital sound. The definition of the field will also evolve, as people define it from different spaces of practice and research, which Dr. Chowdhury feels is crucial to keeping it open and accessible by all.[13]

In the last few years there have been few digital initiatives in India that have tried to engage with some of these questions opened up by DH, or rather the possibilities offered by the Internet and digital technologies terms of mediating new digital objects, platforms and experiences. One of the earliest instances include Bichitra,[14] a digital variorum of Rabindranath Tagore's works developed at the School of Cultural Texts and Records (SCTR), Jadavpur University, which hosts a comprehensive collection of Tagore's work across several genres in English and Bengali, and uses a unique collation software, Prabhed, to access the collection in unique ways tracing its various changes across editions. Two other recent projects that raise similar questions are the Scottish cemetery project at Presidency University, Kolkata,[15] an online archive of narratives which offers a comprehensive collection of images, stories and historical information on the cemetery and Scottish heritage, and tools for data analysis of the collection; and Two Centuries of Indian Print,[16] a pilot project by the British Library and other partner institutions in India which aims to digitize four thousand early printed Bengali books and explore how digital research methods and tools can be applied to this digitized collection.

Indiancine.ma and Pad.ma[17] are two examples of online archives of film and video, which offer users diverse ways to engage with cultural content by working with them in multiple video and audio formats and themes, and through edits, annotations and referencing. Another instance of an interesting open-access publishing platform here is KSHIP at the IIT Indore,[18] which seeks to promote an open-access publishing model for academic work in Indian languages, by publishing original research monographs in Humanities, Social Sciences, Sciences and Engineering, and hosting peer-reviewed journals from academic societies primarily in India. Apart from this, universities have also been offering courses on DH or related areas that have engaged with a critical exploration of the digital within existing disciplinary frameworks of media studies, oral histories, cultural archives, design and informatics, for example. Even as the uptake of DH as a term may be slow, this is not an exhaustive list of efforts in the field, however, with new projects and initiatives emerging in different kinds of institutions, within academia and often at its margins or in creative practice, indicating therefore the inherent fluidity of this developing field.

Even from diverse disciplinary perspectives, at present the understanding of DH is that it facilitates new modes of humanistic enquiry, or enables one to ask questions that could not be asked earlier. As Prof. Dasgupta reiterates, it is no longer possible to imagine humanities scholarship outside of the 'digital' as such, as that is the world we inhabit. However, while some of the key conceptual questions for the humanities may remain the same, it is the mode of questioning that has undergone a change – we need to re-learn questioning or question-making within this new digital sphere, which is in some sense also a critical and disciplinary challenge. While this does not resolve the problem of definition, it does provide a useful route into thinking of what would be questions of DH, particularly in the Indian context.

[This chapter was originally published in Mapping Digital Humanities in India, *authored by Puthiya Purayil Sneha, as part of the Centre for Internet and Society (CIS) Papers Series. The text has been slightly edited and reformatted for the present publication.]*

Notes

1 For more on this, see Stanley Fish, 'Mind Your "Ps" and "Bs": The Digital Humanities and Interpretation', *New York Times*, January 23, 2012; Stephen Marche, 'Literature Is Not Data', *LA Review of Books*, October 28, 2012; Adam Kirsch, 'Technology Is Taking over English Departments', *The New Republic* (eMagazine), May 2, 2014.
2 See Allington, Daniel, Sarah Brouillette, and David Golumbia. 2016. 'Neoliberal Tools (and Archives): A Political History of Digital Humanities', *Los Angeles Review of Books*, May 1, 2016.
3 For a more detailed overview of the different phases of DH, see Patrik Svensson, 'Landscape of Digital Humanities', *Digital Humanities Quarterly*, 4, 2010.
4 For more on the nature of the technosocial subject, see Nishant Shah, 'The Technosocial Subject: Cities, Cyborgs and Cyberspace' (PhD diss., Manipal University, 2013).
5 See Roopika Risam, 'Beyond the Margins: Intersectionality and the Digital Humanities', *Digital Humanities Quarterly*, 9, 2015.
6 Interview with author. December 16, 2013. School of Cultural Texts and Records, Jadavpur University, Kolkata.
7 This is rather simple abstraction of ideas about discipline and reason as they have stemmed from Enlightenment thought. For a more elaborate understanding, see Immanuel Kant, *Conflict of the Faculties*. Translated and with and introduction by Mary J. Gregor. Lincoln: University of Nebraska Press, 1978; and Michel Foucault. *Discipline and Punish*. Translated by Alan Sheridan. New York: Vintage, 1995.
8 See <https://indiancine.ma/>, accessed May 28, 2018.
9 See <http://vectors.usc.edu/issues/index.php?issue=7>, accessed May 28, 2018.
10 Interview with author. December 17, 2013. School of Cultural Texts and Records, Jadavpur University, Kolkata.
11 Interview with author. December 17, 2013. Presidency University, Kolkata.
12 Interview with author. December 12, 2013. Centre for Public History, Srishti School of Art, Design and Technology, Bangalore.
13 See <http://bichitra.jdvu.ac.in/index.php>, accessed May 28, 2018.
14 See <http://scotscemeteryarchivekolkata.com/>, accessed May 28, 2018.
15 See <www.bl.uk/projects/two-centuries-of-indian-print>, accessed May 28, 2018.
16 See <http://indiancine.ma/> and <https://pad.ma/>, accessed May 28, 2018.
17 See <https://iitikship.iiti.ac.in/site/about/>, accessed May 28, 2018.
18 As an indicative list see courses offered at Jadavpur University (https://sctrdhci.wordpress.com/about/the-course/), Presidency University (http://dhgenedpresi.blogspot.in/) and Srishti School of Art, Design and Technology (http://srishti.ac.in/programs/pg-program-ma-in-digital-humanities).

References

Allington, Daniel, Sarah Brouillette, and David Golumbia. "Neoliberal Tools (and Archives): A Political History of Digital Humanities." *Los Angeles Review of Books*. May 1, 2016. Accessed November 15, 2016. <https://lareviewofbooks.org/article/neoliberal-tools-archives-political-history-digital-humanities/>.

Cutrofello, Andrew. "Practicing Philosophy as a Discipline of Resistance." In *Discipline and Critique: Kant, Poststructuralism and the Problem of Resistance*, 116–135. Albany: State University of New York Press. 1994.

Guru, Gopal, and Sundar Sarukkai. *The Cracked Mirror: An Indian Debate on Experience and Theory*. New Delhi: Oxford University Press. 2012.

Johns, Adrian. *Introduction to the Nature of the Book: Print and Knowledge in the Making*, 1–57. Chicago: University of Chicago Press. 1998.

Latour, Bruno. "Morality and Technology: The End of the Means." Translated by Couze Venn. *Theory Culture & Society*, 19: 247–260. 2002.

Parry, Dave. "The Digital Humanities or a Digital Humanism." In *Debates in the Digital Humanities*, edited by Mathew K. Gold. Minneapolis: University of Minnesota Press. 2012. <http://dhdebates.gc.cuny.edu/debates/text/24>

Ramsay, Stephen. "On Building." Author's blog. January 11, 2011. <http://lenz.unl.edu/papers/2011/01/11/on-building.html>

3

HISTORIANS AND THEIR PUBLIC[1]

Rochelle Pinto

The Archive and Access project (www.publicarchives.org and www.publicarchives.wordpress.com) was conceived of at the former Centre for the Study of Culture and Society, Bangalore, where my then colleague Aparna Balachandran and I worked in 2009. The project was funded by the Sir Dorabji Tata Trust, and its aims converged with some of the initiatives of the Centre, which had pioneered interventions in the field of higher education in India in different directions, prior to our joining it.[2] One of these interventions was an exemplary library (now at the Azim Premji University in Bangalore, which also hosts the project website), that was pioneering not only for the scale of reading in the social sciences that had helped give the library its dimensions in a short span of time, but for the online catalogue, with the contents page of each text available to anyone who accessed it, allowing researchers in different parts of the country to put in requests for material; for the classroom readings and syllabi that could be downloaded, and for the online archive of materials that had been collated through the research projects of students. These were uses of digital technology that students of the humanities in India could scarcely conceive of before they appeared on the Centre's website, with the exception of institutions such as the CSSS in Kolkata and the Roja Muthiah Library in Chennai, and a few others which begun work on cataloguing and creating repositories of digital material.

Such endeavours spoke of the desire to maximize student access to resources without the intervention of either faculty or librarians, and not merely of the availability of technology and expertise. One could say that this converged historically with the global expansion in the use of digital technology for pedagogy and research and preceded the Indian state's acquiescence to the need to perceptibly manifest the use of digital technology.[3] In the field of pedagogy, digital technology provided some escape from intense control around intellectual resources through the gradual unrolling of quasi-state initiatives such as Inflibnet, Delnet and Shodhganga, which, whatever their technical and other drawbacks, were distinct signs that projects of scale were conceived of and implemented with visible success by government and quasi-government institutions.

Perhaps the controls around library and archival systems would not have been as noticeable if we had not recently encountered, through the years of research outside the country, libraries in which texts from the sixteenth and twentieth century sometimes arrived within an hour of each other at our desks, as they did at the British Library in London, and where offsite holdings had even more books that could be made available, should we need it. Or, if we had not discovered that a student or teacher in a small town in the Midwest in the US, could avail of the inter-library loan whose efficiency significantly diminished the difference created by library budgets in different universities. When told that the inter-library loan extended to prisons, allowing inmates to pursue degrees while they served time, it brought a realization of what a systematic democratization of all the appendages of higher education could achieve. It also raised the question of what, other than fewer resources, impeded even the partial replication of such structures.

There was of course, no absolute difference between Indian and other library contexts, and the experience of finding out that India had a library movement, and that it was possible to pursue a degree in prison, revealed our position of privilege, and more pertinently, the absence of any collective intervention by universities in facilitating access to archives and libraries.[4]

On the question of access and democratization, it was serendipitous that members of the Alternative Law Forum in another part of the city actively explored technological and legal mechanisms to counter the exclusive hold of capital and copyright law over intellectual production, particularly film, music and academic texts, excluding authors from decisions over distribution, pricing, and ownership of their work.[5] The Centre for Internet and Society likewise offered both technical and institutional support to projects that explored how digital technology generated new questions within political and social research.[6] This institutional conjunction emphasized the political dimensions and possibilities of what were otherwise seen as the simple replacement of obsolete with new technology.

The potential use of digital technology in the context of the archive unfolded uneasily in India alongside a culture of secrecy and control around knowledge repositories. At the same time, it exceeded this culture with unexpected speed, replacing closely guarded catalogues with open access digital ones in a manner that outstripped any desire or potential for control. That these issues are not restricted to India is evident from the perceptible changes in policies of the British Library, where even catalogues were once unavailable online. In recent times, however, a Flickr account makes historical images from the library available for public use.[7]

While the difference between libraries elsewhere and in India is self-evidently a difference of resources, it is also more than apparent that a lack of political interest is the primary reason for uneven and even arbitrary rules of access. The availability of full-text repositories made available by institutions in Brazil and in various other countries that have been not always been seen as resource-rich is an indicator of this.[8] Likewise within India, the School of Public Texts and Records, run by the Department of Comparative Literature, Jadavpur University, is an exemplary instance of what it is possible to achieve in a state university with limited funding.[9] The history of library movements shows that there was and is no dearth of individuals who devoted time and resources to building local and national library movements, but as with many such questions, what could be interventions by sections of society are more often heroic and costly exercises by individuals.[10] Thus, though there have been individual projects around literacy and libraries in India, the scale and regularity of access to public libraries can by no means be taken for granted, and the functioning of prison libraries, as a study on Himachal Pradesh makes apparent, is not a priority or a guarantee in most places.[11]

Aims of the project

The Archive and Access website was designed by Siddhartha Chatterjee and Anitha Balachandran of theSeeChange.com, with assistance from Mahiti.org via Sunil Abraham and Nishant Shah of CIS, to fulfil two objectives. It occurred to us that there was no collective mapping of the many small or large historical collections in the country, and that this information lay with the individuals who had researched particular histories. See Change addressed this by designing a directory page that listed archives and libraries in four regions of the country. Contributors could post information on collections they knew of by filling in a form on the page. The information we received could be added to the list. To complement this list, we also created a blog (publicarchives.wordpress.com), inviting historians to discuss their experiences of the archive so as to publicize perspectives on archives and information that could be useful to future users.

To address the absence of interaction between librarians, technology providers and users, the project held workshops on legal and political questions of access. Our familiarity as researchers with areas such as Goa and Tamil Nadu determined our initial focus, though this was subsequently broadened to Bangalore, Kerala, West Bengal, Assam, Delhi and Pune. In general, the contrast between the kinds of technology that library science graduates are exposed to, and the anxiety among custodians of the libraries over open access, are at odds with each other. A persistent anxiety that goes unaddressed among librarians is the potential loss of visitors and loss of value attached to the library if the contents are placed online.

The creation of a joint online catalogue was a response to the fact that initiatives of the state were still predominantly restricted to state institutions. Projects such as the INFLIBNET initiative for instance target state colleges and universities. While this heralds an era of availability of resources to colleges that are otherwise underfunded and lack exposure to national intellectual resources, it does not address private institutions that face similar issues. The website www.publicarchives.org hosted a joint catalogue of twelve to fifteen libraries from different parts of India. It had the potential to involve more libraries that already possessed a computer typed catalogue in the form of an excel file. To date, the project has uploaded the catalogues of libraries that were already digitized or were available as a computer file.[12] This joint catalogue project hoped to address private libraries that may not have the resources to buy and maintain an online catalogue or software that follows professional standards.

The choice of the software Koha was made after learning that small libraries often used locally modified software supplied at a low cost by firms. By the time the software developed problems or needed to be upgraded, small firms had often closed down or moved away. As the modified software often did not follow international standards, the data could not be transferred and libraries had to invest considerable amounts of time retrieving the data or generating it again manually. The project offered these basic services free of cost to participating libraries. The data collected for the online catalogue could in turn be imported into the existing library system if the library needed the catalogue locally. The online catalogue, we hoped, would enhance the public profile of the participating institutions.

The website primarily addressed what was then a complete lack of systematic online information about archives and library collections in India. This meant that researchers usually worked by word of mouth and had to travel to libraries if they did not already have information about their holdings, just to find out the nature and extent of their collection. In some libraries, the absence of a catalogue often means that some works are not accessed at all unless the librarian and researcher have prior knowledge of their existence.

Historical libraries and public archives

There are two differences between questions of access as they affect public libraries and as they impinge on archives, beyond the issue of care of fragile documents, which may require monitored access. Archives are technically open to the public, but their contents are linked to the workings of government both in the past and in the present. The Public Records Act, which makes the archives the custodian of the records of government, simultaneously signals that public access, by the fact that it is legally guaranteed, needs to be guarded and curtailed for the political threat it poses. The link with the colonial government and, potentially, governments prior to the colonial state also transforms the public into a threat not just to physically fragile documents but also to the hold of government over the secrets of the past, and over its interpretation.

The second point of difference is that while librarians and archivists have formal and informal platforms of communication, and have explored questions of access to libraries and technological advances, historians are absent from any public conversation about the state of archives or their future.[13] In a field replete with people with specialized knowledge, there is an absence of collective discussion and decision-making over the public nature of archives, allowing the government a nearly uncontested domain of control. Once again, many individuals have attempted to address these questions, but for a body of highly educated people across two or three academic disciplines that have a direct interest in archives and libraries, and even accounting for the resistance to intervention in the functioning of the archives by the state, our ability to generate a public discourse around these institutions over issues of public access is unimpressive.[14]

Two further questions qualify these differences. The first is that the manner in which the public library and the archive are legally constituted does not entirely define the antiquity of their holdings, aside from the fact that the archive holds documents of government and libraries hold printed texts. Researchers may find sixteenth-century texts in the public library in Goa, just as citizens may find land documents in the state archives, but they do not ask for these because of their historical value. Not everyone who enters the public library has a need or desire to read contemporary documents, and not everyone who enters the archive has an interest in history. This makes the absence of a public discourse that would help these different kinds of users even more regrettable. With the growing use of digital technology by many archives, the need to ensure minimal levels of access, to catalogues for instance, and to a few full texts could be expected to diminish. Irrespective of the complexity of issues of public access or rights, the mandate for digitization has diluted the control that can be possibly exercised, unless the possibilities of the technology are deliberately curtailed to prevent access. The government of India is not known to be shy about the latter.[15]

To reiterate, even with the changing relationship that archives have to technology, historians have not been able to use their position to link questions of pedagogy, government control and public interest through a public forum. No public discussion exists for instance on the state of historical material that has been digitized by various well-funded organizations at their expense, but not made available for public access. International protocols set by UNESCO do put in place quasi-legal directives around which strategies of acquisition are shaped, and which are reminders of unanswered political questions about the claim on archives.

Who owns the archive?

In our conversations with interested historians, librarians, and custodians of the archive, it became obvious that archives around the country housed several valuable collections, not all of which will survive time or be preserved. The significance of many of these collections does not lie in their capacity to enhance national history, but in the way they symbolize evidence of joint histories and connections between processes, communities and territories that have been erased, or are simply not about the nation. Some among these historians have begun conversations with government officials and ministries towards preserving collections, or towards bettering the terms of exchange with foreign institutions.

While researching a jointly written monograph funded by the Centre for Internet and Society, Aparna Balachandran and I found that archives had diverse users.[16] Our own predilection as academics was to endow the archives with the values attributed to objects and spaces that are viewed as a part of the national heritage, despite the awareness of the relations of power that constitute the archive and the ways in which it continues to be a mechanism of political control protecting the future of the state. The fragility and potentially ephemeral nature of the archives contributed substantially to this feeling. If the only response to the state of the archive were to extend the expression of mourning in anticipation of loss, it would also perpetuate what Arjun Appadurai termed as our tendency to sacralize the archive 'as the site of the past of some sort of cultural collectivity (often the nation), which is seen as sacred by definition'.[17] Appadurai's other observations continue to inform relations to the written document, such as the tendency to see it as the objective material trace of the spirit of the past, whose value is reinforced by its enclosure and control within the state archives. From Michel Foucault on, theorists of history and politics have since detailed how the archive by the fact of being embedded within discourses of state and bureaucratic power reproduces and extends them.

To evade the tendency to fetishize the archive through the singular lens of cultural loss, the attempt was to inquire into the structures that linked the archive to the contemporary, to users other than historians, and that defined its relation to the state and its public. Both Derrida and Achille Mbembe point to the structures of authority and the obsessive search for origins that mark our relationship to the archive.[18] The anxiety about cultural loss when associated with the archive as an amorphous and undifferentiated object, tends to reinstate the state as the proper inheritor of the collective past, a possibility that we evoke by default if we suspend inquiry into who else can possibly own the archive and what forms it can take.

Two aspects became apparent when we moved beyond anxieties of preservation. Archives had a growing stream of visitors looking for land documents, (sometimes a thriving business for translators and those who can mediate the legal interpretation of these documents), suggesting that the question of preservation and digitization could also be driven by popular and contemporary use, as much as antiquity. Further, Aparna Balachandran noted that archivists in different regions made decisions about exchanges and acquisitions based on how they valued different sections of their collection. Often, a particular kind of document, or a particular period in history, was valued because of its significance within regional or state or community histories.[19] Thus, antiquity alone did not determine what was seen as most valuable in the archive, but depending on how the archive was constituted in relation to different histories, it could be seen as the threatening repository of political truths to be burnt down, or as the repository of manuscripts that added symbolic weight as a founding object to the claims of a regional cultural history.

The archive is therefore not an object on its own, but acquires its shape in conjunction with the nature of the quest for documents. This has emerged in the challenges that historians pose to the understanding of the archive as a set of transparent records about the past, through questions that are shaped by their methodological stances. Though as a physical object, a place and a secure epistemological ground for a history, the archive seems self-contained and self-justifying, Ann Stoler suggests that we resist this assumed position the archive occupies as the beginning point for a written history.[20] This is echoed differently by Anjali Arondekar's *For the Record*, which cautions us about going to the archive to find and thereby create new seemingly sovereign subjects. Her inquiry into how sexuality, excess and deviance are discursively positioned shifts the beginning point of research to an inquiry into what becomes archiveable; what transforms practice into an archival object?[21] On the other hand, for a historian excavating a post-apartheid state, the archive carries the mark of violence and, as Achille Mbembe suggests, of death.[22] Mbembe emphasizes that the status of the archival document is always linked to rituals that govern its production and reception, rituals of secrecy, control and the sense of time past and present that the archival document encases. He also notes that the primary status of the archival document is that of its materiality, that it must be touched and seen as evidence that something happened; that there was a life that produced the document and an event whose existence it secures.

This is not identical to and in fact in opposition to the state-approved consciousness of ourselves as the inheritors of history which infuses our presence, vision, and handling of the document with the momentousness of history come alive. Despite recent critiques, for those of us still schooled into seeing ourselves as the subjects of history, the sight, but more importantly, the sensory privilege of being able to touch an old document makes us the last in a relay of touch beginning with the one who produced the document to each reader along the way. This is akin to Appadurai's characterization of our relationship as a Cartesian one, where touch is subordinated to the idea of spirit or collective historical consciousness, which does not inquire into the criteria that determine who is primarily invited to participate in it and those implicitly excluded or unimaginable as subjects of history.[23]

Documents and distrust

Matthew S. Hull's *Government of Paper: Materiality of Bureaucracy in Urban Pakistan* narrates his discovery of how the circulation of official documents in contemporary Pakistan has a political function of its own, linked to, but also independent of, the intentions or grand design of the bureaucracy. In fact, the relative autonomy of these objects occasionally undermines the thrust of bureaucratic control. Pakistanis, he notes, simply refer to their state institutions as 'the bureaucracy'.[24] Whatever the differences between the two states, this instinctive recognition of the structure of the bureaucracy, seems to be common to citizens of India and Pakistan.

Hull makes two significant points; the first is to draw our attention to the fact that minute record-keeping as a mechanism for seizing and regulating power began with the East India Company and was then absorbed into colonial governance as a way of ensuring control over long temporal and spatial distances. He states, 'Three decades before Thomas Hobbes famously argued that the lack of a final, absolute authority led inevitably to a war of all against all, the company had worked out mechanisms for the accountability of all to all'.[25]

The other point he emphasizes is that one should not assume that this mechanism continues seamlessly into the postcolonial era. Hull points out that while it is assumed that bureaucratic writing controls the relation between words and things, in

Islamabad, in fact 'documents are known to be easily and frequently manipulated'. Yet, 'they nevertheless remain an essential basis for action. How can this be?' he asks.[26]

Documents, he suggests, are frequently tools for building coalitions or oppositions. Artifacts precipitate and graphically represent the formation of shifting networks and groups of functionaries and clients. In alerting us to the fact that 'graphic artifacts are not simply the instruments of already existing social organizations', Hull highlights a symptomatic feature of the relationship to paper in the realm of politics in the sub-continent.[27] A distrustful relationship to paper marks the shift from the colonial to postcolonial usage of documents and archives.

The vesting of truth by the British in the visual and physical form of the document, termed document Raj by Bhavani Raman in her book by the same name, fused the notion of legal truth with tangible evidence and with formalized codes of writing. This, as is well known, successfully undermined other norms of arbitration, record-keeping and dispensation of justice. Documents, claimed Raman, 'not only became pre-eminent artifacts of knowledge, but acquired a punitive power'.[28] This situation is akin to what David Dery calls 'papereality', according to her, where documents become 'real' in as far as they have to be taken into account by everyone, and are the binding intermediaries to the relationship between state and citizen.[29] This 'document raj' became the overdetermined sign of the reach of the colonial state.

One could say that aside from exceptions, the official document by and large, was granted a relatively stable political space. It could order and discipline the colonial subject as well as the colonial officer. Due process, that is, may not have been fair, or just, or equitable, but there was in a sense, a consistency to its language, a presumed correspondence between what the document set out to say and do, and how it was received by those who read it or filed it or signed it, at least within the world of the lettered. That this relationship came apart frequently in the hands of those unaccustomed to the world of letters is also well known, and therefore marks the limits of what could be achieved by the bureaucratic process.

There is a range of reasons for the state's complicated relationship to official documents, from the fact of inequitably empowered linguistic diversity to other issues. Perhaps the more pertinent among these is that the political processes through which power is managed cannot be legitimized or recorded by the state's documentary practices. These illegitimate but real practices are the context to the mechanism that Hull points to, which is that the paper trail in itself is an active agent that can be wielded so that the relationship between state, public, and evidence is negotiated strategically. As a result, the words in an individual document are sometimes evacuated of meaning or diminished in significance. The wording of an official document has to be coherent in itself, but the document works as a whole as a kind of template, understood as activating another process in a chain of processes. How, when and where that document circulates is more or as determining than what the words on the page connote. Hull also notes this when he comments on the way in which documents acquire a different status as their surface accumulates signatures, stamps and seals that turn it into what he calls a graphic artifact.

This rewiring of the place of the document in the political process perhaps occurs when the political system of democracy and its accompanying bureaucracy are partially functioning political grammars, that can neither contain nor permit other mechanisms of power. The perception by the state, that the political present is a constantly proliferating threat that must be contained by it, extends to a dread of the recent past, and the possible legal meanings that could be activated by documents about the Emergency, for instance.

These studies help explain why the idea of historical consciousness has such limited significance outside of state-mandated feelings and the near involuntary aura that a small fraction of the educated attach to the archive. The indifference to archaeological sites and the defacement of antique sculpture may not be unlinked to the earlier discussions. These studies also suggest that the archival document, like the bureaucratic one acquires its status from the mandate of the different institutions housing it, such as public libraries, municipal libraries or state archives. While the archive works as a special kind of document and institution in relation to the state, we need to view it in a continuum with other state documents, subject to the laws and anxieties governing secrecy and publicity. If political power is controlled or activated by the timely placing of a document or hiding it or shredding it, not every paper-bearing institution is under the scrutiny of the state.

The archives and the present

The self-description of the national archives simply says that it came into being in 1891 and that it stores non-current papers of government. The Public Records Act of 1993 mandates that the NAI is the custodian of all non-current records of the Union Government of India and its predecessor bodies, British residencies and princely states.[30] Through the time frame of the 'non-current', the National Archives of India not only marks its continuity as the record-keeper of both the colonial and postcolonial state, but decisively pulls away from the monumental staging of its collections as a repository of tradition – as a non-current repository, its commitment is firmly to the present.[31]

The different institutions that oversee different kinds of documents help us understand how the state organizes its imperatives towards the past and the present. A separate National Mission for Manuscripts, for instance, was established in 2003 under the Ministry of Culture and Tourism and officially handles manuscript documents, framing subjects for longer temporal, and different cultural intervals.[32] Meanwhile, The Ministry of Culture's Working Group on Art and Culture for the XI five-year-plan clubs its plans for public libraries and archives together.[33] In its report, libraries are the vehicles for dissemination, education, inculcation of reading habits and useful information, and archives are distinct as the repositories of tradition. This report also mandates that the NAI must receive and store de-classified documents from various ministries and prepare them to be viewed by the public and subsumes this under the tradition-supporting work of the archive.

The Ministry of Culture's plan is the only place where these two poles of activity are unobtrusively thrust together. If at its origin, the archive promises a glimpse into Raj glory, colonial oppression or national tradition, its ties to the present thrust it into a political equation that exceeds its control of the past. The Public Records Act, the Right to Information, the Official Secrets Act – the legal brackets that secure the archive to the political present – have focused attention on the relationship between state secrecy and its repositories in the contemporary.

All three acts either enable or control the scrutiny of the public. This taut relationship with the public is embodied by documents such as the Emergency papers, which have just been released into the archives, to be catalogued and prepared for public use. News reports unsurprisingly reported how they were declared lost and then found after RTIs were used to extract them. Equally unsurprising is the absence of any public comment by historians, leaving the question of the archive's accountability to the recent past to journalists.

Achille Mbembe tells us that the archival document is the initial point from which the historian constructs time as a totality, as a spectre around which other historical entities are constructed. We can use Mbembe's formulation to suggest that in the tussle for documents that the state guards with dread against the demands of the citizen, it is the spectre of democracy that is summoned each time a document is asked for in the name of public rights. An unpublished thesis examining 'technologies of witness' in the staging of democracy during and after the Emergency of 1975 in India suggests that the threat of democracy summoned by the RTI act is pacified through judicial symbolism.[34] Rather than evacuating these rituals of democracy of their political potential, however momentary, we could suggest that the demand made to the state is manipulated into being the gesture that restores the state to its position of power as the notional dispenser of justice, without the need for any actual fulfilment of this promise.

The threat of democracy

If controlling access is one way in which the state manages its anxiety about archiving and the mechanics of democracy as an ongoing practice, the public is also included in some processes of decision-making, revealing the ambiguity over what the document is supposed to do in the relationship between citizen and state. On one occasion, the National Archives invited Naved Masood, an IAS official, and the historian Shahid Amin to prepare critiques of the Public Records Act of 1993 in anticipation of its reformulation by a committee. Their statements to this committee are interesting as they link the archive's relation to the past with that of the present but by defusing the charge of antiquity.

Masood for instance reminded the government that the successes of modern Indian history were in part a result of acts that permitted access to documents.[35] Likewise, Amin ended his own critique with the ironic reminder that the now almost defunct Indian Historical Records Commission was instituted by the colonial state to release pre-censored and 'safe' material into the hands of native historians. So if Masood presses the point that national history is enabled by public access, Amin shows us a former colony kept at a distance from public records, like their contemporaries under a free state.[36]

As an IAS officer speaking to the state, Masood deliberates his own position in relation to the national archives: even a government official, he states, has to register as a scholar to gain access – 'the odd government functionary keen to know what transpired in his sphere of work in the past', should have access to the archives, he argues.[37] Aside from the compulsions of the Ministry of Defense, it appears that inertia or indifference prevents the passage of papers from Ministry to archive. Masood reveals quite alarmingly that the colonial state could be considered exemplary in its record-keeping. In contrast, the numbers of records entering the archive have fallen off sharply after 1947, leaving a scanty trail for historians of the contemporary. He asserts that records of the last sixty years may reveal processes that are both the 'causes' and 'outcomes' of aspects of government functioning and the government should consider it crucially important that papers be preserved. Masood's note is addressed to the government as the agent of preservation and the keeper of records. He also addresses the government functionary as the final user. It is worth noting then that though his appeal is an intra-governmental one, it reads like any other unheard and sometimes unfiled citizen's appeal. The fact that the functionaries of the state have no control over the state is not new, and the degree to which conscientious archivists rely on public complaint and public outcry to shift what should be the regular machinery of governance, is another symptom of how democratic functioning is seen as a parallel system that could hopefully disrupt regular realpolitik. Democracy is again the spectre that is summoned in the hope that it acts as a motor for good governance. Equally unsurprisingly, Matthew S. Hull, who was quoted earlier, notes in relation to Pakistan, 'As it turned out, it was much easier for me to read what are called 'current files', that is, not archives, but active files and other documents that were currently in use'.[38]

'Current files, not archives' – constituting libraries

The public library is intended, by act of government, to dispense state bulletins and newspapers, and sometimes incidentally valuable historical material to enhance the political literacy of a generalized public. It has a benign denotative value. Far from summoning a challenge to the state's sovereignty, or contributing to a monumental tradition, it denotes the power of a municipal kind, a library that houses newspapers and children's reading rooms, the meeting place of the educated unemployed and the amateur historian.

Those seeking land records are the most regular users of the Delhi State Archives, and it therefore gets constituted as a place that does the routine work of a government office. Similarly, the Central Secretariat Library, which is housed within the Secretariat complex in New Delhi, sees itself as a repository, but not as a historical, moral or political guardian of government records and documents. It is primarily open to government employees by right, for any research they may want to conduct. Regardless of content dating from the colonial period, this institution views itself as a quasi-public library and there is not much anxiety over making older books and documents available. A student working in the northeast, for instance, will find it cumbersome to enter the National Archives and to access maps of the region which may be far more easily traced in the Central Secretariat Library.[39]

We could say that the form of the state that the historian most often encounters is not the state that censors documents before they enter the archive, but the bureaucratic offices in which demands for maps may be arbitrarily refused or granted, where women researchers may be refused pornographic texts and where offices shut early and texts are lost.[40]

This seeming dispersal of state power can make institutions amenable to use, as well as multiply the points of contact at which rights and access are denied. In the case of land records that both litigants and officials see as a mundane request, the government agency and its visitors are already inserted into a legal routinized system for collecting and issuing documents. Once the work of the archive has been routinized, negotiations of various sorts, from bribes to being allowed to view damaged and hidden documents, become possible. These avenues remain to be explored by projects that try to find points of contact with and maximize the usage of public institutions such as prison libraries which are notionally public institutions but whose existence and use cannot be taken for granted.

Archives and libraries are thus constituted more by mandate than by content, and by both the past and the present. They symbolize mundane as well as monumental power. As the state retreats from the norms of democratic functioning at a day-to-day level, the nation's history and the historicity of the archive are singularly telescoped to serve the present by appropriating the past, and irrespective of the nature of government, the absence or denial of access to prison libraries, however mundane their existence, can become symbols for the daily exercise of authoritarian power.

Notes

1 Some of the ideas in this chapter were initially developed in Aparna Balachandran and Rochelle Pinto, 'Archives and Access,' in *Histories of the Internet in India*, Centre for Internet and Society, n.d., https://cis-india.org/raw/histories-of-the-internet/blogs/archives-and-access/archives-and-access.pdf. I thank the Advanced Centre for Women's Studies, TISS, Mumbai, and CAMP: Properties of the Autonomous Archive, 2011, http://pad.ma/AJV/info and the Department of English, Delhi University, where these ideas were initially presented.
2 We were assisted in the initial part of the project by Abhijit Bhattacharya of the Centre for Studies in Social Sciences, Kolkata.
3 Preservation projects by the Indian government have obviously preceded the use of digital technology by decades.
4 For a wide ranging comparison of library legislation and movements in different parts of the world and in India, see Anupama, 'Library Services to the Prisoners in Himachal Pradesh a Study and Proposed Model,' University, December 31, 2001, http://shodhganga.inflibnet.ac.in:8080/jspui/handle/10603/80137.

5 Lawrence Liang, 'Guide to Open Content Licenses,' accessed July 10, 2017, http://archive.org/details/media_Guide_to_Open_Content_Licenses. 'Pad.ma,' *Pad.ma*, accessed July 10, 2017, http://pad.ma/.

6 'Histories of the Internet,' *The Centre for Internet and Society*, accessed July 10, 2017, https://cis-india.org/raw/histories-of-the-internet/histories-of-the-internets-main.

7 'The British Library,' *Flickr*, accessed July 10, 2017, www.flickr.com/photos/britishlibrary/.

8 http://bndigital.bn.gov.br.

9 http://granthsouthasia.in.

10 B. Pratapa Reddy, 'Finances of Public Libraries in Anantapur District,' University, December 31, 1990, http://shodhganga.inflibnet.ac.in:8080/jspui/handle/10603/64697. 'Library Movement in India – Free Online CBSE UGC NET Guide Book June 2016,' accessed July 8, 2017, www.netugc.com/library-movement-in-india.

11 Anupama, 'Library Services to the Prisoners in Himachal Pradesh a Study and Proposed Model.'

12 Currently, though the project is housed at Azim Premji University, the catalogue page has not been revived.

13 See, among others, www.lislinks.com/forum/topics/university-library-network-in-india-is-known-as.

14 For interventions and responses to the question of public records and the functioning of the archives, in particular by Naved Masood and Shahid Amin, see https://publicarchives.wordpress.com/state-of-the-archive/.

15 http://economictimes.indiatimes.com/news/politics-and-nation/mobile-internet-services-suspended-in-kashmir/articleshow/58871234.cms.

16 Aparna Balachandran and Rochelle Pinto, 'Archives and Access.'

17 Arjun Appadurai, 'Archive and Aspiration,' in *Information Is Alive – Art and Theory on Archiving and Retrieving Data*, eds. Joke Brouwer, Arjen Mulder, and Susan Charlton, Rotterdam: V2_NAi Publishers, 2003, 15, http://v2.nl/publishing/information-is-alive.

18 Jacques Derrida, *Archive Fever – A Freudian Impression*, trans. Eric Prenowitz, *Literature and Literary Criticism*. Chicago: Chicago University Press, 1996; Achille Mbembe, 'The Power of the Archive and It Limits,' in *Refiguring the Archive*, eds. Carolyn Hamilton et al. Dordrecht and Boston: Kluwer Academic Publishers, 2002.

19 See in particular, Aparna Balachandran's discussion of the Tamil Nadu Archives in comparison to the Delhi State Archives, https://cis-india.org/raw/histories-of-the-internet/blogs/the-cyborgs/tamil-nadu-archives.

20 Ann Laura Stoler, *Along the Archival Grain: Epistemic Anxieties and Colonial Common Sense*. Princeton: Princeton University Press, 2009.

21 Anjali R. Arondekar, *For the Record: On Sexuality and the Colonial Archive in India*, Durham, NC: Duke University Press, 2009, https://catalyst.library.jhu.edu/catalog/bib_3504069.

22 Achille Mbembe, 'The Power of the Archive and It Limits.'

23 Arjun Appadurai, 'Archive and Aspiration.'

24 Matthew S. Hull, *Government of Paper: The Materiality of Bureaucracy in Urban Pakistan* (Berkeley: University of California Press, 2012).

25 Ibid., 7.

26 Ibid., 22.

27 Ibid., 21.

28 Bhavani Raman, *Document Raj: Writing and Scribes in Early Colonial South India*. Chicago and London: University of Chicago Press, 2012.

29 David Dery, '"Papereality" and Learning in Bureaucratic Organizations,' *Administration & Society*, January 1998; 29, 6; ABI/INFORM Global, p. 677.

30 As per the mandate of Public Records Act of 1993, NAI is the custodian of all non-current records of the Union Government of India and its predecessor bodies as also the former British Residencies in the erstwhile Indian princely states. Its holdings are occupying 40 kms (approximately) of shelf space and are in regular series from 1748.

31 National Archives of India is an attached office of Ministry of Culture. It was formally known as the Imperial Records Department and was established in March 1891, at Calcutta, and shifted to Delhi in 1911 with the shifting of the capital city. After independence in 1947, the Department was renamed as National Archives of India on 30 August 1947, and the Head of the Department was designated as Director of Archives and as Director General of Archives since June 1990.

32 The National Mission for Manuscripts was established in February 2003, by the Ministry of Tourism and Culture, Government of India.

33 http://planningcommission.gov.in/plans/planrel/fiveyr/11th/11_v2/11th_vol2.pdf.

34 Maya Dodd, ' "Archives of Democracy": Technologies of Witness in Literatures on Indian Democracy Since 1975,' Stanford University, n.d.

35 https://publicarchives.wordpress.com/2011/01/19/a-note-on-the-difficulty-of-accessing-post-independence-records-in-india-by-naved-masood/.

36 https://publicarchives.wordpress.com/2011/01/19/response-to-proposal-to-amend-the-public-records-act-by-shahid-amin/.

37 https://publicarchives.wordpress.com/2011/01/19/a-note-on-the-difficulty-of-accessing-post-independence-records-in-india-by-naved-masood/.

38 Hull, Government of Paper, 28.

39 This section initially appeared in Aparna Balachandran and Rochelle Pinto, 'Archives and Access.'

40 The phrase 'banality of power', of Mbembe's coinage, should have been the most appropriate characterization for this phenomenon. However, Mbembe's article, which draws strongly from Bakhtinian conceptions of power and resistance in their carnivalesque excesses, does not address itself to what is an exercise of power with an aesthetic if any that inverts the carnivalesque.

References

Anupama. "Library Services to the Prisoners in Himachal Pradesh a Study and Proposed Model," *Panjab University*, December 31, 2001, http://shodhganga.inflibnet.ac.in:8080/jspui/handle/10603/80137.

Appadurai, Arjun. "Archive and Aspiration," in *Information Is Alive – Art and Theory on Archiving and Retrieving Data*, eds. Joke Brouwer, Arjen Mulder, and Susan Charlton, Rotterdam: V2_NAi Publishers, 2003, http://v2.nl/publishing/information-is-alive.

Arondekar, Anjali R. *For the Record: On Sexuality and the Colonial Archive in India*, Durham, NC: Duke University Press, 2009.

Balachandran, Aparna and Rochelle Pinto. "Archives and Access," in *Histories of the Internet in India*, Centre for Internet and Society, n.d., https://cis-india.org/raw/histories-of-the-internet.

Bhavani, Raman. *Document Raj: Writing and Scribes in Early Colonial South India*, Chicago, London: University of Chicago Press, 2012.

Derrida, Jacques. *Archive Fever – A Freudian Impression*, trans. Eric Prenowitz, Literature and Literary Criticism, Chicago: Chicago University Press, 1996.

Dery, David. " 'Papereality' and Learning in Bureaucratic Organizations," *Administration & Society*, January 1998; 29, 6; ABI/INFORM Global.

Dodd, Maya. "Archives of Democracy: Technologies of Witness in Literature on Indian Democracy Since 1975," unpublished PhD dissertation, Stanford University, 2006.

Hull, Matthew S. *Government of Paper: The Materiality of Bureaucracy in Urban Pakistan*, Berkeley: University of California Press, 2012.

Liang, Lawrence. "Guide to Open Content Licenses," accessed July 10, 2017, http://archive.org/details/media_Guide_to_Open_Content_Licenses.

"Library Movement in India – Free Online CBSE UGC NET Guide Book June 2016," accessed July 8, 2017, www.netugc.com/library-movement-in-india.

Mbembe, Achille. "The Power of the Archive and It Limits," in *Refiguring the Archive*, eds. Carolyn Hamilton et al., Dordrecht and Boston: Kluwer Academic Publishers, 2002.

Press Trust of India. "Mobile Internet Services Suspended in Kashmir," *The Economic Times*, 27 May, 2017, accessed 10 July, 2017. https://economictimes.indiatimes.com/news/politics-and-nation/mobile-internet-services-suspended-in-kashmir/article-show/58871234.cms.

Reddy, B Pratapa. "Finances of Public Libraries in Anantapur District," *Sri Krishnadevaraya University*, December 31, 1990, http://shodhganga.inflibnet.ac.in:8080/jspui/handle/10603/64697.

Stoler, Ann Laura. *Along the Archival Grain: Epistemic Anxieties and Colonial Common Sense*, Princeton: Princeton University Press, 2009.

4

MAPPING CHANGE

Possibilities for the spatial humanities in India

Karan Kumar and Rahul Chopra

Maps, for the longest time, have inhabited our imagination, and our lives. While they represent a cartographer's point of view, they are simultaneously pivotal to our understanding of the world and construct cartographic realities as world views for the map's users. Cartographers and historians of cartography tend to often stress the importance of a 'map' in understanding the way historical communities perceived their environment, orientation, and culture, and determined the most fitting way to communicate this perception to communities with other cultural, sociological, linguistic, and historical contexts. Often, the map also served as a bridge between worlds that are known and unknown.[1] Finally, all maps served to visualize a reality in spatial terms.

The 'map,' as we know it today, has changed from its earlier significance in imagining new worlds. While its essential function may still pertain to navigation and location, the variance in method, practice, perception, and skill has furthered what maps can now achieve. Historical maps, such as Ptolemy's *mappa mundi*, and Google Earth, as an example of digital mapping platforms, are united in their ways to understand the world despite their seeming differences. Even as we know the physical landscape of the earth we inhabit has not changed to a great extent over the last two thousand years, what has changed is our perception of the world itself.

From maps to GIS: the journey to the spatial humanities

The beauty of this interrogation, however, has been the output that it has created, from software to projection, dimensionality to comprehensibility, and much more. In the late 1960s, the first iteration of what we now know as a 'geographical/geospatial information system', or GIS, led cartographers into a new era (Murrietta-Flores et al. 2017, 1). The limited dimensionality of a 2D physical map was challenged, giving way to an age where now anybody can, on his or her computer or smartphone, begin an exercise in cartography of a region somewhere across the world. This inherent power in the idea of an accessible, definable, modifiable map recently spurred interest in a community of humanists and geographers, who created what we know today as the spatial humanities.[2] What is interesting to note about the spatial humanities is that it is an added arm almost, to the exploration of 'space' with a humanist lens.

The promulgation of GIS as an accessible and widely usable software is a fairly recent phenomenon, yet we have seen examples of the use of spatial data to solve multiple issues and aid research across disciplines from the early 1850s. John Snow, in 1854, created a map of the Soho area in London to determine the point of origin of the cholera outbreak earlier in the year (Bynum 2013). The academy is flush with examples across history that have emphasized the use of spatial data, historic data, and other sets of theoretical perspectives to build, support, and link arguments to reach a cohesive conclusion.

However, the explicit adoption of spatial and historic data in interdisciplinary research and studies did not 'take place' until the late 1960s; with the advent of the spatial turn. The spatial turn, embodied the uncovering of the critical knowledge of 'how' and 'why' certain phenomena took place, by interrogating the space in which they took place.[3] As Warf and Arias note, 'Geography matters, not for the simplistic and overly used reason that everything happens in space, but because where things happen is critical to knowing how and why they happen.' (2009, 1). Time and again, spatial humanists have argued that GIS 'lies at the heart of [the] spatial turn' because of its ubiquity and sheer ability to uncover hidden patterns and dimensions of texts and other bodies of knowledge that mere reading cannot (Bodenhamer et al. 2010, vii).

For the purpose of this chapter, the definition of 'GIS' is not limited to the software itself, but also the analytical process of using geographical data in a structured inquiry across disciplines. The possibility of bringing together different sets of data on a map gave GIS an impressive foundation to build scholarly perspectives on. Practitioners who worked with large-scale spatial data and attempted to create interdisciplinary analyses through GIS-based inquiries understood the vast potential that GIS held, and still holds in the practice of social science and the humanities. The biggest obstacle, however, to unlocking this potential was the need for technical knowledge to coexist with critical theory in the humanities and social sciences, and in instances where such amalgamated knowledge was available, the possibilities were endless for three key reasons:

1   The accessibility of spatial data and the ability to cull spatial data points from other texts and bodies of knowledge;
2   The infinite virtue of the data and analyses itself that computers and the power of computing offered;
3   The ease of interpretation that visualized data offered when compared with dense textual and numerical data sets.

When categorized across time, the history of GIS highlights an increasingly interdisciplinary use. Coppock and Rhind (1991) classify this history and evolution of application into four distinct phases – the pioneering era from the early 1960s to 1975, the experimental era from the early 1970s until 1980, the commercialization era from the early 80s until the end of the decade, and the fourth – current – era, of user-dominated and suited application of the software to multiple efforts. This fourth phase, most often characterized as the spatial turn referred to earlier, is also the most prominent phase in the development of applications for GIS-methods in the humanities and the social sciences. It has initiated the use of GIS technologies as a tool of qualitative inquiries in the spatial humanities. As Bodenhamer et al. note:

> Questions drive humanities scholarship, not hypotheses, and the questions that matter most address causation: why matters more than whom, what, or when, even though these latter questions are neither trivial nor easy to answer. The research goal is not to eliminate explanations or to disprove the hypothesis but to open the inquiry through whatever means are available and by whatever evidence may be found.
>
> *(2010, xiii)*

Thus, GIS became a tool with which a humanist could ask, and attempt to answer multiple questions, using data from across disciplines and through a framework rooted in causation.[4]

Studies that use GIS in historical, cultural, and literary studies are currently disparate and application-driven. However, there has been a recent emergence of the spatial studies to the digital humanities as a field through efforts such as the use of GIS-like technologies and tools to better understanding the role of space and place within disciplines in the humanities. Historical GIS stands as a good example of spatial humanities, which can be classified as a subset of the digital humanities (Gregory and Geddes 2014). Historic data often includes cultural, literary, sociological, political, environmental, physical and cartographical data from different disciplines. These may include the writings of ancient travellers and scholars; works of fiction and non-fiction that present a spatial perception to the reader; scholarly endeavours in documenting communities, movements, practices, and people, as well as historic maps of the world and its places, amongst others.

Multiple institutions across the world use historic data in GIS-based inquiries. For example, the Stanford University Center for Spatial and Textual Analysis (CESTA)[5] and their work in historical GIS and the spatial humanities. Some of their projects include mapping oral histories, documenting geomorphological change through text-based data projections and visualizations, using GIS to trace the development and spread of ideas in human history. Historical data has also been used in projects and the creation of atlases that are open access, through the Electronic Cultural Atlas Initiative (ECAI), a global consortium of spatial humanists and scholars from other disciplines and backgrounds aimed at creating a virtual repository of cultural information and data from across the world 'with a time and place interface' ('About ECAI').

Spatial humanities in India

The official source of maps and geospatial data in India is the Survey of India.[6] They have a large body of antique and contemporary maps, but none which are GIS-ready are available for download to the public. In fact, at the time of writing this chapter, the Survey of India site restricted downloads of scans of three maps a day, and that too only when one provided Aadhaar card details. Significantly, no official outline map of India with administrative boundaries even at the district level is available in a GIS-ready format from their website. That means there is no official map of the country in a GIS-ready format with official boundaries to plot data spatially at the district level. India specific satellite data and some GIS data is available for download for free and to all from Bhuvan,[7] Indian Space Research Organisation's portal. Other sources of satellite data of India include EarthExplorer[8] (United States Geological Survey) and GIOVANNI[9] (National Aeronautics and Space Administration), amongst others.[10]

Whose geospatial data is it anyway?

There exists an asymmetry of access to geospatial data of India. The utility of this data as a tool of governance is unparalleled; however, citizens and practitioners are left wanting. The state is using these tools in its governance, as an example digitizing land records, and using geospatial data to ease land administration. Yet, these records are not available in the public domain. The opacity of and limited access from the state is intriguing. To address this limited access, practitioners often generate their own geospatial data sets.

Interestingly, most of this work is created to aid research and analyses of issues of large scale relevance to India, but unavailable in the public domain. For instance, if one were to map the administrative boundary of a city to assess phenomena such as internal migration, expansion, development and progress, or even access to resources – the lack of publicly available and accurate administrative boundaries makes the work of the researcher extremely difficult. Alternatives such as mapping districts, assembly constituencies, and local government area-extents have been used, and these alternatives exist in the public domain due to efforts by individuals and communities of Indian data scientists and cartographers, such as DataMeet.[11]

Not only is data limited, but there have been further attempts to control the use of Indian geospatial data through bills such as the draft of the proposed Geospatial Information Bill of 2016.[12] This is 'a bill that controls the acquisition, dissemination, publication and distribution of geospatial information in and outside India. . . . [It will] make your daily use of maps illegal by requiring a 3 month vetting and approval process for any use of mapping' (Savethemap.com). A group of data enthusiasts, cartographers, and 'cartophiles' got together when the draft was released for advocacy of freer use of Indian geospatial data, and created a movement called 'Save the Map' (STM).

While STM is an effort that is commendable, the people that got together for it are of relevance to this chapter. Designers, cartographers, GIS developers, scholars, and other practitioners who have for the past few years been working on different aspects of the spatial studies, such as the use of GIS technologies in scholarly and governance efforts, the use of historical maps in tracing infrastructural and physical development, land use – land cover change, assessment trackers for public schemes and local urban governance.

Challenges and possibilities: examples of Indian spatial humanities work

In India, as mentioned earlier, the spatial humanities is still an emerging discipline. This is because there was inadequate access to training in the usage of geospatial tools and technologies across disciplines and due to proprietary and expensive GIS software. Some web portals have emerged that enhance ease of use for researchers who are thus far untrained in working with geospatial data. One example is the Environmental Systems Research Institute's (ESRI) 'Story Maps' web portal. Story Maps allows users to integrate narratives into maps that can be created through simple guided tutorials that can be found on the web page.[13] The resource allows anyone to use an existing text or create a new one, and superimpose the narrative onto a map.

One project that truly highlights the potential of Story Maps, is National Geographic's 'On Foot in the Path of the Silk Road'.[14] The project is a highlight of various points along the fabled silk road, as they are today, with narratives and descriptions of these points culled out of multiple travelogues, ranging from the writings of Marco Polo, to ibn Sina and al Biruni – to name a few.

Moving onto software – most GIS software tends to be proprietary and expensive. On the other hand, open source softwares such as QGIS[15] and GRASS GIS[16] have the same computing power and ability as the commercial software. It is possible to use such open source softwares for research and pedagogical use even at the undergraduate level.

The potential it holds for Indian academia, as well as scholars whose research is India-centric is vast. Our own initial work in the field has highlighted multiple areas where the spatial humanities and its methods can create deeper, meaningful analyses through simple visualisations of geographic components within research.[17] For instance, the simple act of georeferencing a map can change the way we view a particular landscape. Georeferencing, is a process that takes a historical or any map with a different coordinate reference system, and reprojects it to align it to a known system so it can be analysed, modified, and queried along with other geographical data.[18]

Over the past few years, working on methods in the spatial humanities and with a large number of publicly available historic maps of India[19] – we were able to uncover multiple crowdsourced platforms that housed a growing collection of historic maps of India. Mapwarper,[20] for instance, is an online georeferencing tool that allows users to upload their collections of historic maps, georeference them, and then make them available to other users on the platform to use and modify.

Mapwarper has a growing collection of historic maps specific to India, from different parts of the world and from different points in time – making the act of viewing and juxtaposing historic renditions of landscapes to current landscapes extremely intriguing. Georeferencing, while an inherently geographic and scientific process, is a stepping-stone to engage in humanities research within a historical context. For instance, by georeferencing an old map of a city, one can attempt to understand spatial perceptions of the community that inhabits the place as well as others that have experienced it.

Apart from this, there are also other repositories of historic maps of India, and the world – that can be found on a website that hosts the data set of the 'Mountains of Central Asia', called Pahar.[21] The website is home to a plethora of data on the Himalayas and its surrounding ranges – that is available to the public free of cost, for non-commercial use. The collection hosts a range of material from books, to journals, maps, and photos. While Pahar is dedicated to historic material on the Himalayas and other mountains from Central Asia, there are other university libraries and collections, such as those of the University of Chicago,[22] MIT,[23] and Stanford University,[24] that house a vast collection of historic maps of different parts of the world. These are archives that exist in the public domain, accessible by different people and used for different purposes.

Small-scale efforts across Indian universities, as well as centers of learning across the globe have attempted to research Indian contexts using methods in the spatial humanities. For instance, researchers at Hamilton University have been working on a project in the spatial humanities that seeks to understand the ideologies and underlying philosophies of advertisements in two cities in North India, namely Delhi and Varanasi.[25] The project, by mapping out locations of the advertisements and then annotating them with the type, the language, the script, and other features – seeks to archive the range of advertisements for educational institutions and understand the ways in which they market themselves to prospective students and their parents. Another interesting example of work from researchers outside of India is focused on mapping the dialogical relationship between texts and material culture, as well as its impact on the historical landscape of two religious sites in India that the project terms 'Sacred Centers'.[26] These sacred centers are the Hindu Gaya and the Buddhist Bodhgaya, both places of pilgrimage for their respective religious communities.

Maps of India in private archives and collections are often inaccessible, unless requested for research and analyses. One such instance is offered by the Kalakriti Archives. Based in Hyderabad, India, The Kalakriti Archive's collection of historical maps of India is one that has allowed for the creation of interdisciplinary conversations around the various aspects of certain maps in the collection. Housing one of the largest private Indian map collections in South Asia, the archive has multiple sets of maps that represent a wide range of ideas and afford a variety of inquiries. Maps from the collection for example, have been used to study the historico-religious underpinnings of Hindu cosmology and its cartographic representation, as well as the development of the city of Hyderabad – among other projects and curatorial efforts (Nanda and Johnson 2015).

The Leonard Munn Maps for example, a collection of more than 500 maps from the 1915 Survey of Hyderabad housed at the Kalakriti Archives, have been used to create pedagogical tools, uncover sites of historic relevance, such as step-wells, and trace the cultural and historical development of the city of Hyderabad. Often one assumes, a map that is over a century old will have little to no relevance in today's world.[27] Efforts in the spatial humanities, with specific reference to the Munn collection at the Kalakriti Archive, have constantly challenged that assumption and contributed to scholarly and other efforts to date. A local heritage conservation organization, for instance, runs walking tours and historical city tours using knowledge gleaned from the Munn maps; a design forum dedicated to heritage conservation utilized the maps to uncover the locations of step-wells to create a repository of knowledge on the historical architecture of the newly formed state of Telangana. Scholars who have worked with the maps have also been able to study shifting land-use practices in the city of Hyderabad, and practitioners have been able to create pedagogical tools out of processes used to cull information from the maps themselves.[28] The maps are highly detailed, and house extremely interesting points of information such as a prevalence of 'plague houses' near entry points to the city and transportation infrastructure within its bounds. The maps could potentially be used to investigate the reason for the existence of 'plague houses', in a John Snow-esque manner, or even to understand climate change and urban planning in the context of Hyderabad's history and landscape.

Conclusion

The spatial humanities thus, emerges as a discipline that attempts to bridge this knowledge gap where geography is the 'link' between disciplines due to its focus on studying subjects and objects that are common to multiple disciplines. Bodenhamer et al., quoting Stanley Brunn, the geographer, note, '[Geography] is the discipline most concerned with studying the relationships between the human and physical phenomena.' Geographers 'are both exporters and importers of knowledge' and thus geography serves as a sturdy bridge crossed by many disciplines' (2010, 2). GIS technologies serve to broaden our horizons, by helping uncover correlations and causations that might otherwise be unobserved. They create a universal visual language that represents a culture along with its complexities and contradictions (Bodenhamer et al. 2010, 87). What this means is that GIS has the potential of becoming the tool for the humanities to analyze history, culture, space, and so on.

Reaffirming Warf and Arias's point about the importance of geography in understanding events: if we are to begin deeper and more meaningful explorations in the spatial humanities within the Indian context, maps need to be made more accessible. The should be accessible by publics across fora, and the knowledge and tools required to use them in inquiries need to be made available. The spatial humanities makes us broaden the understanding and use of tools such as GIS to propagate a new form of interdisciplinarity.

There is vast potential for the spatial humanities across different avenues of research, thought, and practice. It is a constant effort that creates new archives of material that has meaning and context, and is representative of the 'complexities and contradictions' of cultures. It affords an opening of inquiry and allows for different kinds and types of evidence to come together under one research statement.

Two critical perspectives thus emerge that are relevant to the spatial humanities. The first is an acknowledgement of 'what exists' in terms of a physical, geographical reality. And the second is a realisation of 'how we *understand* that existence' – in terms of our perception of that reality and its manifestation in human thought and expression.

Notes

1 Read more on the construction, perception, and practice of space and place in Meredith Cohen and Fanny Madeline's *Space in the Medieval West: Places, Territories, and Imagined Geographies*. The anthology provides insight into how space was perceived and mapped in the Middle Ages and the historiographical context of the study of such spatial construction.

2 Mark Monmonier's seminal work *How to Lie with Maps* from 1991 is additionally insightful in terms of understanding how maps and data can be manipulated to visually project data, as well as how the use of maps can open up the boundaries of the ability to query information and phenomenon with a critical lens.

3 A deeper understanding of the spatial turn and perceptions of space and place within the context of geography can be found in Charles W. J. Withers, 'Place and the "Spatial Turn" in Geography and in History'. *Journal of the History of Ideas* 70. 4 (2009): 637–658.

4 The work of Michael Brown and Larry Knopp also supports the idea that GIS, coupled with the right questions and theoretical lens can also drive interdisciplinary work such as efforts rooted in bringing "a spatial epistemology to queer urban history, and a cartographic one to queer geography." Read more on their work 'Queering the Map: The Productive Tensions of Colliding Epistemologies', *Annals of the Association of American Geographers* 98.1 (2008): 40–58.

5 To know more about the projects and research at CESTA, visit their website, <https://cesta.stanford.edu/>.

6 For more on Survey of India, check their website, <www.surveyofindia.gov.in/>, accessed on 30 May 2018.

7 To view the data sets available through Bhuvan, see <http://bhuvan.nrsc.gov.in/gis/thematic/index.php>, accessed on 30 May 2018.

8 To view more, go to <https://earthexplorer.usgs.gov/>, accessed on 30 May 2018.

9 For more on GIOVANNI, see <https://giovanni.gsfc.nasa.gov/giovanni/>, accessed 30 May 2018.

10 P. L. Madan's *Indian Cartography: A Historical Perspective* also provides an overview of the development of cartography as a discipline and practice in India, and it gives insight into the ways in which maps can be interpreted to understand not only spatial data but also social, economic, and political information.

11 Please see, <http://datameet.org/>, accessed 30 May 2018.

12 Note that this highlights the situation at the time of writing. As of 2019, the bill was not passed, debates had stagnated, and the bill was not introduced to the house after comments were invited in 2016. Reports indicate that the government officials are

considering merging certain provisions of the bill with the proposed Data Protection Bill that under the guidance provided through the recommendations of the Justice BN Srikrishna Committee.

13 Find more at <https://storymaps.arcgis.com/en/>, accessed on 30 May 2018.

14 See more on the project at <www.nationalgeographic.org/projects/out-of-eden-walk/media/2018-02-on-foot-in-the-path-of-the-silk-road/>, accessed on 30 May 2018.

15 For more information, see <www.qgis.org/en/site/>, accessed on 30 May 2018.

16 See <https://grass.osgeo.org/>, accessed 30 May 2018.

17 To understand the context of India's geography further, and also as additional reference material, refer to Sanjeev Sanya's, *Land of Seven Rivers: History of India's Geography*. London: Penguin, 2012.

18 Read more about georeferencing at <https://support.esri.com/en/other-resources/gis-dictionary/term/georeferencing>, accessed on 30 May 2018.

19 Some maps can also be found in Aisha Khan's *A Historical Atlas of India*. New York: The Rosen Publishing Group, 2004. The authors have also referred to Manoshi Lahiri's *Mapping India*. New Delhi Manohar Publishers & Distributors, 2011, to analyse and explore historical maps of India.

20 See more at <https://mapwarper.net/>, accessed on 30 May 2018.

21 For the Pahar project, see <www.pahar.in>, accessed on 30 May 2018.

22 See more at <www.lib.uchicago.edu/collections/maps/>, accessed on 30 May 2018.

23 See MIT's website, <https://libraries.mit.edu/>, accessed on 30 May 2018.

24 To see the Stanford collection, see <http://library.stanford.edu/rumsey>, accessed on 30 May 2018.

25 See more on the project at <www.dhinitiative.org/projects/landscape>, accessed on 30 May 2018.

26 See more on the project at <www.dhinitiative.org/projects/scaredcenters>, accessed on 30 May 2018.

27 For further reading, refer to Matthew Edney's *Mapping an Empire: The Geographical Construction of British India, 1765–1843*. Chicago: University of Chicago Press, 2009, which illustrates how spatial perceptions of India have been constructed over time and underpins the problematics of such spatial construction while also noting the importance of the colonial mapping efforts that were central to the British Empire's governance and administration.

28 See more on the project at <https://gisdev.in/Hyderabad_1915/>, accessed on 30 May 2018; this is a project that is still in the making, and the website thus is hosted on a private server and only provides a glimpse of the kind of work that is currently underway.

References

'About ECAI'. *Electronic Cultural Atlas Initiative*. n.p., 2018. Web. 5 May 2018.

Bodenhamer, David J., John Corrigan, and Trevor M. Harris [Editors]. *The Spatial Humanities: GIS & The Future of Humanities Scholarship*. Bloomington: Indiana University Press, 2010. <https://books.google.co.in/books?id=eb7wAAAAQBAJ.>

Bynum, W. F. 'In Retrospect: On the Mode of Communication of Cholera'. *Nature* 495 (2013): 169–170.

Coppock, J. Terry and David W. Rhind. "The History of GIS." In *Geographical Information Systems: Principles and Applications*, Vol. 1, edited by D. J. Maguire, M. F. Goodchild, and D. W. Rhind. London: Longman Scientific & Technical, 1991.

'GIS'. Web. 3 May 2018.

Greogy, Ian N. and Alistair Geddes [Editors]. *Toward Spatial Humanities: Historical GIS & Spatial History*. Bloomington: Indiana UP, 2014.

Murrietta-Flores, Patricia, Christopher Donaldson, and Ian Gregory. 'GIS and Literary History: Advancing Digital Humanities Research Through the Spatial Analysis of Historical Travel Writing and Topographic Literature'. *Digital Humanities Quarterly* 11.1 (2017).

Nanda, Vivek and Alexander Johnson. *From Cosmology to Cartography*. New Delhi: National Museum, 2015.

Warf, Barney and Santa Arias. *The Spatial Turn: Interdisciplinary Perspectives*. 1st edition. London: Routledge, 2008.

PART II

Digital institutions and pedagogies

5

MUSEUM COLLECTIONS IN INDIA AND THE DIGITAL SPACE

Joyoti Roy

How have we arrived where we are?

India has more than a thousand museums, most owned by the government and others run by private trusts and individuals.[1] The amount of art objects across these collections is innumerable, and there has been no specific attempt to list these, but it is estimated that collections with national museums range from two Lakh to five Lakh, and smaller museums have a few thousand. The collections include archaeological finds, sculptures in stone, wood and metal, ethnographic collections, costumes and textiles, paintings and photographs, jewellery and ceramics.

When the museums were set up, some before Independence such as the Indian Museum[2] in Kolkata, and several others after 1947 including the National Museum[3] in New Delhi, these institutions were hubs of deep intellectual activity. Sadly, though, there were inherent barriers which only enabled intellectuals to engage with objects and collections. Museums were systematic libraries of collections rather than aesthetic displays to be enjoyed. Labels were abridged and so jargonized that an ordinary visitor would hardly recognize the importance or value of the object. Unfortunately, these trends continued for decades together and while the cultural experiences in other fields, namely film, music, theatre and art, were rapidly changing and evolving in the presence of technology, museums held on to their exclusive, 'temple of knowledge' idea and didn't really open up. Occasional exhibitions would draw attention, and when Indian collections were shown abroad, they would get a breath of fresh air in interpretation and presentation. Even national forums such as the Museum Association of India were unable to offer enough warning that these rich institutions would disappear into oblivion if not contemporized in their presentation or critiqued for their relevance.

To make the situation more difficult, museum-going did not, and still does not, come naturally to Indians, and each museum struggles to bring in audiences through their programmes, exhibitions and value-added services such as audio guides, talks, workshops and curated tours. The lack of adequate museum training institutions also led to this situation. Only a handful of organizations/universities, such as Aligarh Muslim University,[4] the National Museum Institute[5] and the University of Calcutta,[6] offered training and poor publicity of these courses added to the misery. Even until a few years back, museums only had professionals from two generations ago and hardly any new recruitments were taking place. Thankfully the situation improved at the turn of the twenty-first century.

In 2009 the Ministry of Culture, Government of India, took up a survey of various museums under its aegis and made an appraisal of their public programmes and infrastructure.[7] The research drew up the Fourteen-Point Museum Reform[8] that, when implemented, would bring about a positive change in the Indian museums that were suffering in the hands of severe competition from other cultural experiences, lack of human resources and most of all lack of imagination in public engagement.

The Museum Reform Points highlighted many issues – Collection and Stores Management; Proper Scientific Display of Artefacts; Information, Signages, Floor Plans and Visitor Facilities; Museum Shops and Souvenirs; Multi-media, Audio-Visual and Guide Facilities; Attracting Various Audience Segments Including Students and Children; Image Building, Publicity and Cultural Events; Visiting and Traveling Exhibitions; Expansion and Acquisition of Collections; Professional Development of Museum Personnel; Implementation of Plan Schemes and Special Projects; Security (Modern Techniques); Conservation and Restoration; and Interaction between Academics, Archaeologists and Artists.

From among the fourteen points, the point on Multi-media, Audio-Visual and Guide Facilities encouraged the design, and continuous update, of website and information systems; introducing museum-related activity cum technical research blogs; digitizing important stored artefacts for 'virtual guides', CDs and websites; introducing/improving audio guides; working on time-bound plans; setting up LCD panels to display digitized artefacts on videos and PowerPoint presentations; introducing 3-D holographic projections, simulated images and virtual reality; and setting up interactive sound and talking trees, musical clocks and other attractions. It was a very ambitious list.

The archives, particularly private archives, had plunged into digitization before the museums did, although with every international collaboration, new ideas and techniques emerged in presenting collections in museums. In a way, one could say that the Indian archives and museums made a transition into the digital world at the turn of the twenty-first century, and it was only towards the end of the first decade that results were beginning to appear.

One of the first in the field of archival digitization was the American Institute of Indian Studies (AIIS) in Gurgaon, who had digitized more than three thousand views of Indian temples (sketches and photographs) in the late 1990s, and researchers could go and access them on appointment.[9] They did the same with films and sound bites in their Centre for Ethnomusicology. Perhaps simultaneously the Alkazi

Foundation for the Arts in Delhi[10] was preparing to open its archive to Indian scholars and organized itself to make accessible more than 100,000 photographs, prints and maps from their collection for researchers. I had the opportunity to work as its Chief Archivist in 2010, and found the archive to be extremely organized and well documented. It not only listed the common data about photographs (date, medium, photographer, description, etc.); it also had a section that had cited where the image was published or talked about in the public domain. First organized in the New York office of the Foundation, the Alkazi digital archive was several steps ahead of similar archives existing in museums at the time. Other interesting archives had managed to establish themselves: the Intach Documentation Centre in Delhi had started collecting images from their surveys and listing projects, begun in 1993; the Center for Studies in Social Sciences (CSSS)[11] in Kolkata had a fully functional archive; and the private archive of Indian visual culture CIViC in Delhi was also beginning to digitize and archive its collections.

In 2011, the Ministry of Culture asked one of its organs, the National Culture Fund, to take up three aspects of the Museum Reform Programmes – training, publications and digitization. It was done under the aegis of a memorandum of understanding that had been signed between the Ministry of Culture and UK Cultural institutions, namely the British Library, the British Museum and the Victoria and Albert Museum. The collaborations aimed particularly at digitization of shared heritage and, in this case, the Company Paintings. Various aspects of the Museum Reform Programmes were very successful while some did not take off. Nevertheless, at least twenty to twenty-five government museums benefited from these and a ripple effect is still evident.

The Company Paintings Digitization Project of the National Culture Fund

The eighteenth and nineteenth centuries saw a proliferation of European patronage of Indian art under the aegis of the East India Company. This patronage facilitated the production of a special kind of Indian painting executed for the Europeans and heavily influenced by their taste, in both subject and technique. Popularly called the Company Paintings, they were an attempt by Indian artists to work in a mixed Indo-European style, which would appeal to the European officers who were employed by the various East India Companies in India. Illustrations of Indian professions, castes and tribes, mannerisms, customs and festivals, monuments and sites, flora and fauna were among themes of this semi-documentary painting style which evolved and flourished in many parts of India – Andhra, Trichinopoly, Madras, Madurai, Malabar, Coorg and Mysore in the South; Murshidabad, Patna, Calcutta and Puri in the east; and Oudh, Benaras, Agra, Delhi, Rajasthan and Punjab in the north. Examples of Company Paintings from Sri Lanka, Burma, Nepal and Malacca also exist in this genre.

The Company Paintings were often heavily influenced by the local styles of paintings in these regions as well. Although Indian artists shifted from using the opaque gouache and tempera colours to the more translucent watercolours in their execution of Company Paintings, occurrences of local stylistic patterns in individual regions and use of local materials is also prevalent. While most Company Paintings are on paper supports, examples on cloth, canvas, glass, ivory and mica have also been found.

Today sizeable collections of Company Paintings exist in the National Gallery of Modern Art, Delhi and the Victoria Memorial Hall, Kolkata. There are several other private collections within the country, which own small but important collections of Company Paintings. A much richer ensemble exists in the museums of United Kingdom, particularly in the British library's India Office collections and the Victoria and Albert Museum, London.

The Digitization Project aimed at bringing all these collections spread across India and the UK on one digital platform. This would not only allow for a seamless experience of the paintings sitting in different sites for the viewer/researcher but also address in some manner the constant concerns that majority for Indian collections fill European museums and Indian audiences are kept bereft of a chance to see them.

The main challenges that presented themselves during the project were on the actual act of digitization and producing metadata. Each painting had to be carefully photographed and by following certain specific protocols – particularly taking care that high-intensity light should not potentially damage the natural colours. The responsibility of coordinating the project came upon me as I had been recently employed as the Project Coordinator for the Museum Reform Programmes, and where I managed to put together a guideline for the digitization project.

More important was to understand who would assemble the digital platform, and what kinds of information it would hold about the collections. The collections from the National Gallery of Modern Art, Delhi, were indeed digitized, and their existing catalogue entries became the information entered about them: a simple list with the title of the work, the region where it was produced, its medium and dimensions, and finally a short description of what it showed.

The digitization project would also, in the course of its development, enrich the cataloguing of the paintings, thereby adding, classifying and streamlining metadata about each individual object. This process of cataloguing was to be facilitated through dedicated research by competent research assistants under the guidance of the academic consultants to the project. The digitization project would aid the creation of digital surrogates of preservation quality of collections, which will be available for a myriad of applications in times to come for their host museums. The digitization project was also imagined as a preservation exercise as it could drastically reduce the physical handling of Company Paintings, thereby protecting them passively. The digital surrogates could never replace the originals but would suffice for research purposes that do not require actual handling of the original material.

One of the most important procedures within a digitization project is the creation of digital surrogates. Creation of digital surrogates must primarily serve the digitization initiative; however, since it is often a time-consuming exercise, if the creation of digital surrogates is carried out with a long-term vision, it can serve many peripheral purposes such as the possibility of future publications, production of facsimiles and giclee prints by the museums, and can also be made available to researchers for reference/publication if the museums agree. The imaging exercise will undergo the following steps:

1 Pre-imaging preparations were made for preparing the original artworks before they could be photographed. The Conservation Departments of the museums were involved in assessing their condition and it had to be ensured that all the paintings were digitized within safe limits of handling, were as flat as possible and were not actively deteriorating.

2 Paintings were placed on neutral coloured acid-free, paper-based backing boards, in order to carry out imaging. The specifications and attributes for the digital surrogates were set. Imaging was carried out at two levels – master files and access files. While the master files were used as digital archival material for the long run, the access files will be uploaded along with the web catalogue. The master files included images with 7304 pixels by 5478 pixels, 16-bit, 1998 RB colour space. The Victoria and Albert Museum were using uncompressed TIFF files created with the specifications, 5440 pixels by 4080 pixels, 16-bit, 300 pixels per inch (hereafter ppi), in Adobe 1998 RB colour space, and the British Library was using uncompressed TIFF files created with the specifications, 5440 pixels by 4080 pixels, 16 bit, 300 ppi, in Adobe 1998 RB colour space. The access files were set at compressed JPEG files with specifications of resolution 250 pixels by 312 pixels at 600 ppi at the bit depth of 24, 60 MB weight.

3 Further, the imaging room was temperature and humidity controlled (temperature not exceeding twenty-five degrees centigrade and relative humidity not exceeding 50 per cent). If originals were stored in more stringent conditions, they were brought out and placed in a transitory zone for at least forty-eight hours before bringing them out for digitization. The ambient light in the imaging room was kept between 50 and 70 Lux and no more. The imaging team kept track of the cumulative exposure to light for each original object (in Lux hours). The colour temperature was kept at 5000K. This was important because light exposures to delicate museum objects follow the reciprocity law. The intensity of light and the time of exposure determine the effect of light on objects and can be interchangeable parameters in deriving the cumulative effect. Keeping this in mind, flash photography was done for the creation of digital surrogates in some cases. In such cases, CFL tube flash lamps were used after employing UV filters. To be even safer, in the digitization of Company Paintings, flash photography was permitted, but no more than three frames were photographed in quick succession. The imaging room was also set up carefully, walls had neutral colours, and no brightly coloured posters, notices and so forth were allowed. No sources of glare (mirrors, shiny surfaces) were present in the imaging room.

4   The integrated web catalogue of Company Paintings was to become a search-able web repository of photographs and related information about Company Paintings in the collections of NGMA, Delhi and VMH Kolkata. At a later stage, the catalogue would include collections from other private and semi-government institutions as well.

Other considerations were as follows: (a) The web catalogue would occupy inde-pendent web space. In other words, it should be a separate website. (b) The web catalogue would be linked to the mother websites of the host museums and recipi-ent museums in the United Kingdom. (c) The catalogue would be able to accom-modate all the entries from the offline catalogue. (d) It would have a home page describing the project, its mission and the attributes of the catalogue. It should explain the terms and conditions of use very clearly. (e) The catalogue would be aesthetically designed and be efficiently navigable. (f) The search parameters within the website should be advanced and optimum. There should be ample keyword searches. (g) The entire collection should be categorized first under museums and then under various other themes such as dates, province, medium, subject, and so forth. (h) It should have options of printability, conversion to PDFs and emailing facilitation. (i) Information about the digitization project and its execution must be available online for it to guide other digitization projects.

The project website could not ultimately be set up but the collections from National Gallery of Modern Art, Delhi, and a large number of artefacts from the Victoria Memorial Hall were indeed digitized. The Company Painting Digitiza-tion Project did pave the way something much more dramatic and successful – the Google Art Project. It is interesting to compare the cases of technology developed by the Centre for Development of Advanced Computing, Ministry of Electronics and Information Technology (henceforth CDAC), for the National Museum with the global platform offered by the Google Cultural Institute.

Museums of India – National Portal and Digital Repository of the National Museum and Ministry of Culture

National Museum, New Delhi, being a premier museum of India, houses an impressive collection of artefacts from across the country and the world. It has more than 200,000 art objects, representing 5000 years of Indian art and craftsmanship. The collection includes sculptures in stone, bronze, terracotta and wood, a large collection of miniature paintings and manuscripts, coins, arms and armour, jewel-lery, textile, costumes and anthropological objects. Antiquities from Central Asia and pre–Columbian artefacts form the two non–Indian collections in the museum. The museum is the custodian of the treasure trove of India's multi-layered history and multicultural heritage.

The Digital Archive initiative of the National Museum and all other museums under the Ministry of Culture began in 2013, which was the 150th year of Swami

Vivekananda's birth anniversary. On this occasion, the Chicago Art Institute came forward to host a collaborative programme with the museum. A plan for creating a unique platform for digitizing and archiving the collections of Indian museums was envisaged. Between 2013 and 2015, the Chicago Art Institute worked closely with CDAC, based in Pune, to hone and develop a Digital Platform that could host collections from various art museums under the Ministry of Culture. As a result, the National Museum, New Delhi; Indian Museum and Victoria Memorial Hall, Kolkata; Allahabad Museum; Salarjung Museum, Hyderabad; the National Galleries of Modern Art, Delhi, Mumbai and Bangalore; and the Archaeological Survey of India started digitizing their collections. The joint platform is called *Museums of India – National Portal and Digital Repository.*[12]

The archive is already populated with nearly 100,000 objects from across museums and the National Museum micro-site has 30,000 objects available online to be studied and seen by interested visitors. The site itself is searchable by museum, object type, material, artist or technique.

The building of the archive required meticulous work on the part of the museum. Each Department Curator first carried out photography of objects from their collections with the help of the museum's photography department. Each department has an extension of the back end of the archive, and first the assistant curators or curators make the primary object entries in their departments. Thereafter these entries are studied by staff members (who have been especially employed on the project), and after basic proofreading, they send the entries for the Director General to approve. Once approved by the Director General, an indication is sent to CDAC to make entries online. This cycle can take up to seven to ten days for fifty to one hundred entries. Photography is done carefully of objects to show all sides of the object. This is particularly important for archaeological objects, which often require study from all directions and angles.

This Digital Archive is used by a myriad of scholars, particularly people who write in to ask for permission to use photographs for publications. On average, the National Museum processes more than 2500 requests each year for publishing of photographs in publications and journals. This yields revenue for the museum, and the archive is used frequently.

The archive is also used by college, university and school students for their projects and studies. Aside from its core application, this initiative has also helped the museum develop its own merchandise as objects get digitized and photographed. The initiative also helps in developing publications, workbooks and children's activity sheets.

There are, however, several challenges. The archive interface is not very attractive or aesthetically designed. This greatly diminishes the experience for a lay visitor. A scholar, however, may find it useful. The project has also suffered because the lack of staff at museums often leads to a majority of administrative work being done by curators, and they are left with little time to populate the archive; it also affects the quality of contributions and level of information.

There is also no peer review of the entries, and everything rests on the director general's shoulders to approve. Director generals of the museum for the last several years have been non-technical professionals and not subject experts. Nevertheless, the initiative has brought government museum collections to light in a big way. This would not only increase the accountability of the museums towards their collections; it could allow easier research and engagement, or at least create a starting point for researchers. This is particularly useful for site museums of the Archaeological Survey of India, which are often located in very remote areas.

For a brief period, the CDAC initiative also included 360-degree scanning of small objects to allow for a 3-D viewing experience of objects using special glasses. However, this has remained very gimmicky and does not offer anything more than a spectacle to the viewer.

The Google Arts and Culture Platform

In comparison to the constraints presented by local limitations in the case of CDAC is the tech-savvy and expertise-driven Google Cultural Institute. The Google Arts and Culture Platform is hosted by Google, and therefore museums that do sign up for showing on it need not worry about space. Since it is a not for profit initiative, there are no financial transactions, and Google provides the platform for free; in the initial years, they also offered to digitalize select collections at a very high to medium resolution. They also offered what they called a 'Street View', which was like a 360-degree panoramic view of museum galleries and historic sites. More than one hundred archaeological sites can be street viewed on Google today.

The Google Cultural Institute (earlier called the Google Art Project) arrived in India in 2011. The international project was launched much earlier, and several museums had signed up to share their collections online. In September 2011, I had the opportunity to introduce the Google team (then based in Bangalore) to the Ministry of Culture.

At the time, the team was looking to collaborate with the national museums of India to explore the possibility of them sharing their gallery views and collections online. Google called it their '5 per cent' project. It was a kind of a CSR, but where every employee could give 5 per cent of their work time to develop an idea of their passion. The man behind the Google Art Project is Amit Sood – an Indian-born Google employee who had already made great headway with his 5 per cent project, which was the Google Art Project itself.

By 2014, Google had signed agreements with the National Museum, New Delhi, National Gallery of Modern Art, New Delhi, the Archaeological Survey of India, the Victoria Memorial Hall, Kolkata and a few other museums.

The name of the initiative has changed over a few times now; today it is called the Google Arts and Culture Initiative and hosts thousands of museums across the world and their collections: the Victoria and Albert Museum in London, the Guggenheim Museum in Bilbao, the British Museum in London, the Palace Museum in China, the Tate Gallery in London, the Louvre in Paris, the Museum of Modern Art in New York and many more. In India, more than seventy-five institutions are featured on Google, both government and private, and they include archives, museums and theatres. More recently, craft initiatives, personal archives and thematic collections and stories about India have also been included.

The metadata formats have been developed by Google and are quite thorough. Each museum/archive is given a metadata sheet to be filled, which is ultimately reviewed syntactically and cleared by Google for publishing. The content for each object or story is completely the institution's prerogative, and Google does not interfere. The material also remains the copyright of the institution, and direct downloads of images and text are not allowed from the published platform. In the beginning, the government museums found it very difficult to sign agreements with Google, but given the IT giant's technological solutions and aesthetic for the platform, most agreed in the end.

Two years later in 2014, Google introduced the possibility of curating online exhibitions with objects. I was working at the National Museum at the time, and it gave us a tremendous opportunity to make selections of masterpieces and create online exhibits with objects. The online exhibition tool also allowed for zooming in and out to focus on details, decorations and specific aspects of objects. It was much more meaningful and educative for the online visitor to see objects within curated exhibitions rather than see them in isolation. In fact, when the new jewellery gallery of the National Museum was inaugurated in November 2014, an online exhibition with the jewels made for a remarkable online experience.

Ever since Google has expanded its India team, several museums and organizations are partners with Google. Increasingly, collections across the world are available to search and engage with online. I believe this has been a true contribution to the culture of the world. The Google interface is aesthetic, clean and encourages storytelling. There are many possibilities, as videos can also be uploaded, but most of all, the Google webpages of a museum can be embedded into the websites of the respective museums.

More recently, Google has launched Google Labs, whereby they invest in developing an interactive technology for a museum exhibit. In a recent exhibition titled 'India and the World: A History in Nine Stories', held at Chattrapati Shivaji Maharaj Vastu Sangrahalaya (henceforth CSMVS), Mumbai, the Google Arts and Culture Platform created an interactive exhibit around pot shards and interpreting our past.[13] Intriguingly titled Future Relics, the experience required the viewer to think of words that they thought should be part of history; these words would then get digitally inscribed on symbolic pot shards and get embedded into the software. After three months of showing, the database of what people consider when reflecting on history and culture has emerged as a massive collection of keywords.

Museum collections on social media

Increasingly, Indian museums are using social media for sharing collections. If an individual visits the social media pages of the popular museums of India, it is likely that they will get a substantial idea about their collections. While some museums post images and descriptions of their permanent collections systematically and regularly, others may become more active during temporary exhibitions. In recent years, large international exhibitions such as the Body in Indian Art (2014, National Museum), The Everlasting Flame: Zoroastrianism in History and Imagination (2016, National Museum) and India and the World: A History in Nine Stories (2017, CSMVS, Mumbai) have utilized the platform of social media to share descriptive posts about 90 per cent of their exhibits. Social media strategies focus on sharing beautifully photographed objects with details that attract eyes and also sometimes initiate online debates and discussions. In certain occasions, museums such as CSMVS have also collected information about objects informally through social media campaigns. Social media has gone beyond being a notice board for museums. It has become an active space for learning, reading and interaction.

Why do we need a digital space for experiencing the arts?

Intimacy is at the centre of any arts experience. Surprisingly, digital platforms are able to provide that, even though one is not engaging with a real object. The possibilities of digital photography have now made possible an experience of looking at museum objects in great detail, something that seeing them in museums may not allow. This certainly does not mean that people would stop going to museums, but interested parties would come back to their desks and settle down to see things up close.

The digital platforms also provide a median space between a museum and a book. Text can be moderated, and while the digital space does not impose too much formality, writing on objects can be more personal and lucid, more relatable. The digital space puts museum objects in a different kind of context. Here the interaction between the object and its text is much more seamless. The digital space is also able to single out the viewing span for each object with little distraction and vantage points, angles, good lighting – everything can be controlled to benefit a 'good look'. And why not?

Knowledge production and acquisition have now moved into a phase where self-learning has taken centre stage. In this scenario, the digital space provides an agreeable and convenient platform that can quench the curiosities of young people. The immense trust that people have in the digital space and the variety of information it provides can really help museums get their ideas out there. This, in turn, can increase the relevance of museums as institutions. The fact that many voices can live simultaneously on digital platforms also allows for democratization of information to a certain extent and will hopefully feed into a different kind of history-making in the long run.

Notes

1 For more detail on these museums, please see this report: 'Reimagine Musuems and Galleries: India-UK Opportunities and Challenges', British Council India, October 2014, <www.britishcouncil.in/sites/default/files/re-imagine_museums_india-uk.pdf>, accessed on 26 May 2018.

2 For details, see <https://indianmuseumkolkata.org/home.html>, accessed on 26 May 2018.
3 For more information on the National Museum, please visit their website: <www.nationalmuseumindia.gov.in/index.asp>, accessed on 26 May 2018.
4 Please see the Department of Museology at Aligarh Muslim University for more details: <www.amu.ac.in/departmentpage.jsp?did=41>, accessed on 26 May 2018.
5 For more information, please see <www.nmi.ac.in/>, accessed on 26 May 2018.
6 For details on the department, and their coursework, see <www.caluniv.ac.in/academic/department/Museology.html>, accessed on 26 May 2018.
7 The press release, dated 9 December 2015, on this report can be found at <http://pib.nic.in/newsite/PrintRelease.aspx?relid=132808>, accessed on 26 May 2018.
8 For details on the Fourteen-Point Agenda on Museum Reforms initiated by the Ministry of Culture, please consult the list of achievements of the ministry, dated 15 May 2015, released by the Press Information Bureau: <http://pibmumbai.gov.in/scripts/detail.asp?releaseId=E2015PR1332>, accessed on 26 May 2018.
9 Part of the AIIS collection on Indian temples has since been housed by Google Arts and Culture. The collection is available here: <https://artsandculture.google.com/partner/american-institute-of-indian-studies>, accessed on 26 May 2018.
10 Please consult their website for more details: <http://acparchives.com/>, accessed on 26 May 2018.
11 For details on the archive, consult their website: <www.cssscal.org/archive.php>, accessed on 26 May 2018.
12 Please see the digital archive here: <http://museumsofindia.gov.in/>, accessed 26 May 2018.
13 A preview of the exhibition is available at <www.csmvs.in/india-and-the-world-a-history-in-nine-stories>, as well as <www.indiaandtheworld.org/>, accessed 26 May 2018.

6

PROCESSES OF PLURALISATION

Digital databases and art writing in India

Sneha Ragavan

Much of writing in India pertaining to modern and contemporary art practice has presumed the language of mainstream discourse to be English. This may well be true, considering the general relations of language to power, and modes of patronage and pedagogy. Needless to say, this is more acutely felt in the field of art and the discipline of art history despite the abundance of art writing in several Indian languages since the late nineteenth century. Keeping this in mind, the first part of this chapter presents some preliminary thoughts on the question of the 'vernacular' or 'regional' languages within the domain of art historical writing in India. In conjunction with this, the second part of the chapter explores the limits, extents, and possibilities offered by the digital; in particular, the emergence of digital art history as method. For this, I take as a case study an ongoing project undertaken by Asia

FIGURE 6.1   AAA Bibliography website

Art Archive (AAA), the 'Bibliography of Modern and Contemporary Art Writing of South Asia', which compiled an annotated bibliography of art writing from South Asia in the form of a digital, searchable, online database of 12,000+ texts in more than twelve languages (see Figure 6.1).

Keeping this in mind, the chapter poses a few questions: Does digital art history complicate processes of canonisation within the field? Have there been any paradigmatic shifts in what constitutes research with the availability of digital resources? How do digital art histories open up possibilities of pluralisation of the field of art historical research? Does the digital inherently carry the potential for pluralisation, or does it run the risk of merely reproducing structural hierarchies that persist in the field?

A question of language: art writing in India

The role of multiple linguistic spheres in a complex nation-formation like India is an important site to address and continues to be a point of contestation. Yet, if we take up the field of art historical and critical writing, the contributions of languages outside of English have been overshadowed. Very often, these are marginalised and represented as a supplement, or as 'regional/vernacular' variants, of the national narrative. This part of the chapter attempts to pose a few preliminary questions – to begin with, why we must contend with the multilingual nature of the art writing of India, and what its implications might be for the field at large.[1] What will hopefully emerge is an initial attempt at tracing the literary histories of art writing[2] in India, functioning neither as a clarion call for 'going regional' nor subscribing to a multicultural framework of telling 'one story in multiple languages'. It merely signals the necessity for art historical research in India to pay close attention to the languages of its discourse – including English. This will allow for complicating both the history and historiography of art history as a discipline, its canons of criticism, and modes of circulation; in other words, recognising its multilingualism in all its complexities.

It is well known that English is the language of the national discourse of art history and art criticism in India. At a general level, this has ties to histories of the English language in the nineteenth and early twentieth centuries – its hegemonic status as a language of governmentality, institutionalization and pedagogy, civil society and the bourgeois national public sphere. With regard to the politics, history, and role of language, the emergence in recent decades of disciplines such as comparative literature and translation studies has led to complex articulations moving beyond the familiar 'national-regional' terrain. For instance, this has involved an active reconfiguration of all languages, including English, as 'Indian languages'. We see immense efforts made by various institutions within the domain of literature to bring forth the work of important literary figures from across multiple languages through acts of translation.[3] Even here, however, translation efforts are largely confined within the domain of creative writing (prose and poetry), with the rich culture of literary criticism often overlooked.

There have been vibrant discussions and reflections on aesthetics and art from across multiple Indian languages. But even today, a serious engagement with the 'vernacular'[4] intellectual milieu has remained peripheral to art history and criticism's analytical, methodological, and structural concerns. In the specific context of the field of art, the hegemony of English has ties to the overarching national/international/global framework of its practices and histories, canons of criticism, networks of dissemination, and not to mention, its structural dependence on a market economy where the cultural capital of its members are determined/mediated through English as the global language. However, here we must ask, in any engagement with art writing in the 'vernacular' or Indian languages, do we anticipate a confirmation or refutation of the mainstream national/global narrative? Or do we presume 'vernacularity' itself to serve as a counter-hegemonic narrative to it? Yes and no to both. The absence of acknowledging the 'vernacular' intellectual milieu is more an indicator of the complicity of English and elitism in the very structure of the field of art. Furthermore, while the 'vernacular' could be seen to be oppositional to mainstream discourse, we must bear in mind that it has its own hierarchies.

In other words, any stepping into the 'vernacular' intellectual milieu must necessarily not seek to reinstate the predominance of English, but rather aim at deterritorialising the language sphere itself. Such a task will necessarily involve an engagement with crucial factors such as the interrelationship of languages, their movements across geo-political regions, the emergence of new literary styles and genres based on these movements, and patterns of linguistic and literary innovations. And while one modality through which such enquiries can be undertaken is in the writing of 'specific' histories, this process certainly does not discount commonalities or shared histories and interactions.

Indeed, just as it is no longer possible to write singular histories of modern and contemporary art in India – with the calling into question of both the 'singularity' of such narratives as well as what might constitute its 'Indianness' – so, too, art historical research needs to be underscored by the fact that the language of its historiography has never been singular. Methodologically, however, there are possibilities of writing histories of any aspect of artistic production, dissemination, or institutionalisation in India without a framework that considers the field a sum total of whatever happened in say, Bombay, Baroda, or Calcutta. Only an enquiry that takes stock of the multilingualism of art historical discourses in India can take into account genealogies of languages at various historical moments in their articulation of aesthetic and cultural ideals.

Similarly, the 'global contemporary' has allowed us to draw connections and relations between and across nation-states, with articulations of 'trans-national' or even 'post-national' positions in this field of artistic and cultural production. And criticisms of sub-nationalisms or regional parochialisms kept in mind, it is nonetheless important to think about reasons for the absence of tracing internal movements. Moreover, while the dominant trend has been of placing both art and art writing in India at par with the international/world/global art discourse, it is urgent that we explore the discursive domains that writings on art in various languages within India occupy, and to analyse the genealogies and histories of art writing within and between languages.

In this context, exploring the dimensions of bilingualism is one possible area of enquiry. For instance, many periodicals on art and culture were bilingual or multilingual in nature.[5] We also know of a long-standing practice where artists, art historians, and critics such as Baburao Sadwelkar, Dinkar Kowshik, Asit Kumar Haldar, Mala Marwah, Ram Kumar, P. A. Dhond, Meera Mukherjee, J. Swaminathan, Dnyaneshwar Nadkarni, and Gulammohammed Sheikh, to name a few, wrote in more than one language. This is clearly illustrative of the seriousness with which they engaged the bilingual sphere. Our task as researchers here would be in not merely analysing the similar or differing content of what they wrote in the two or more languages, but also in understanding the ways in which language functions as an enframing device through which certain modes of articulation were made possible. In addition to this would be the work of locating the sites of writing and modes of circulation, the general nature of its discourse and the specific readership it addressed, degrees of pedagogic intent they carried, and so on. In other words, to inquire into the nature of this critical bilingualism would be less about an ability to speak in two or more languages but more about understanding the modalities through which language and its process of meaning-making are inscribed by various socio-cultural, ideological, and political apparatuses (Walsh, 1991, 127). Indeed, to undertake a historiography of art writing bearing in mind such bilingualism will also allow for a re-contextualisation of the history, role, and place of English within its discourse.

Digital art history and its methods

It is against this backdrop of the necessity to engage with the rich multilingualism of art writing in India that I arrive at the second part of the chapter to ask what happens to our understanding of histories of art writing in India, when we introduce digital technologies to the study of art history. By this I am not referring to *digitised* art history, which involves a digitisation of artwork images or personal papers and documents of artists, writers, and institutions. Rather, I refer to *digital* art history which involves, in part, as Claire Bishop notes, 'the use of computational methodologies and analytical techniques enabled by new technology: visualization, network analysis, topic modeling, simulation, pattern recognition, aggregation of materials from disparate geographical locations, etc.'. (Bishop, 2015). As the subject of the pros and cons of digital art history in general have been explored by several scholars (Drucker, 2013; Bishop, 2015; Manovich, 2015), I instead explore a more specific set of questions relevant to the context of art history in India, by means of a case study. I refer here to the 'Bibliography of Modern and Contemporary Art Writing of South Asia' – an ongoing project initiated in 2011 by Asia Art Archive (AAA), a non-profit organisation dedicated to researching the contemporary arts of the region, with which I work as a researcher.

The project has aimed at collating annotated bibliographies of art writing in South Asia across multiple languages, presented in the form of a digital database that would be online, searchable, cross-referenceable, and citable. The aim of the Bibliography Project was to focus on art historical discourses around the visual materials that formed part of the research collections at Asia Art Archive; therefore, a bibliography of published writing for first-hand reference. Notwithstanding the critique of such computational means of amassing data through 'manifestation of the drive for mastery over history and the archive' (Bishop, 2015), the Bibliography Project aimed at facilitating research towards different understandings of the field from multilingual contexts – to focus especially on writing on modern and contemporary art in Indian languages other than English. This, we believed, would not only enable art historical research to question the dominance of English language in the field of art history but also de-centralise English to considering its context-specific iterations. In effect, it meant that through the Bibliography Project, we would direct our attention to the multitude of published writing that already exists but is not consolidated. We asked if there are there strands of writing that are being ignored, and are there strands of writing that question art historical frameworks. By sharing information on publications from libraries, institutions, and personal archives across several cities and languages, the online database aimed to enrich understanding of this field and be useful to students, scholars, researchers, artists, writers, and the arts community at large.

In its first phase, the project began its cataloguing process in India, looking at writing in Assamese, Bengali, English, Gujarati, Hindi, Kannada, Malayalam, Marathi, Odia, Punjabi, Tamil, Telugu, and Urdu. As of the end of 2014, it compiled a bibliography of more than 10,000 texts, including books, book chapters, exhibition catalogues, and articles and essays published in periodicals. By 2015, the scope of this project was expanded to explore the resonant histories of art writing across languages and regions in South Asia, moving beyond the national borders of India to explore art writing in Tamil from Jaffna in Sri Lanka, Urdu from Lahore in Pakistan, and Bangla from Dhaka in Bangladesh. The data set, as it were, varied from language to language, and from researcher to researcher, depending on access to publications in both public institutions and personal archives.

From its inception, the project was conceived as a shift away from the conventional modes of producing bibliographies which were published in book form (or more recently in digital form) as running lists that were categorised alphabetically, chronologically, thematically, or medium-wise. Rather, it explored the possibilities offered by digital tools and technologies for the ways that they would be both compiled and accessed. Therefore, the bibliographies were compiled on spreadsheets, which meant, at the very outset, the breaking down of various components into unitary fields. The advantages of this 'database logic' became immediately known during the cataloguing process itself – as various patterns of writing and publishing began to emerge. In this regard, it would be useful to draw on Lev Manovich's theorisation of the database as that key form of cultural expression for the digital age. He writes, 'As a cultural form, database represents the world as a list of items and it refuses to order this list. In contrast, a narrative creates a cause-and-effect trajectory of seemingly unordered items (events). Therefore, database and narrative are natural enemies' (2001, 225). In other words, by structuring data into fields/collections, the database opens itself up to multiple points of entry and navigation where no one 'narrative' is privileged over the other. This also involves the thinking of metadata as a source of knowledge, and as a structure of knowledge with which it is possible to reconfigure the field differently. So to the question then of whether the Bibliography Project destabilises the canon, yes and no. Canons are formed through a nexus of individuals and institutions with access to symbolic, cultural, and economic capital. To that end, while canons for all intents and purposes continue to be valid in institutions and the ways that art histories are written, the Bibliography Project certainly has extended the canon and, in so doing, opened up the field to the possibility of moving beyond the status quo.

For a bibliography, which even in analogue form lends itself rather easily to a database logic, this meant for us the ability to use keywords to search/mine the database, and potentially discover texts that one did not know existed. It was a reference 'tool', much like an analogue bibliography, except it differed from the latter by not already categorising texts chronologically, thematically, or alphabetically. To further explore the potentials of this function of the bibliography as a digital database, we felt it would be important to present it online not only as a search engine, for which one already has to know what one is looking for, and be able to articulate it accurately to gain precise results. Given this limitation, and working towards a rich, exploratory mode/interface of information seeking, Mitchell Whitelaw makes the case for 'an ethos of generosity'. He writes, 'Search favours expert users, for those who understand a collection's contents and can query it effectively. It is most ungenerous, ironically, to those most in need of generosity: visitors unfamiliar with a collection' (2012). By contrast, through 'combining methodologies from information visualisation with the techniques of web design', Whitelaw presents cultural collections via a set of 'generous interfaces', thereby providing what 'search cannot'. For AAA's Bibliography Project, Whitelaw developed 'generous interfaces' through using techniques of information visualisation. Figures 6.2-6.6 show these interfaces as they appear on AAA's site. Three aspects of the bibliography were selected and presented in the form of visualisations. The first involved people from the Bibliography database – authors and artists – to enable users to see connections between them, discover new texts, see which periodicals specific authors published in, and so on (see Figure 6.3). The second visualisation (see Figure 6.4) drew on the places in the database to explore the geographic coordinates of art writing and publishing in South Asia. The third visualisation (see Figures 6.5 and 6.6) sliced the database by language, place, and publication, represented in a faceted timeline – thus showing both the collection itself and its inadequacies. What this allowed was a way for users to generate patterns that one would lead to newer findings – for instance, to discover patterns of places of publishing in relation to artists about whom texts were being written, noting that a specific thematic became the subject of extensive debate in certain decades, and so on.

Explore the Bibliography

These visualisations provide three different views of AAA's continuously growing bibliographic database. Use them to browse the collection, discover new references, and investigate trends, relationships and patterns. Design and development by Mitchell Whitelaw.

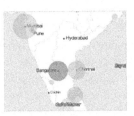
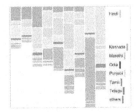

The **People** view focuses on the authors and artists in the database. See the connections between them, who published in which periodicals, and what keywords were used in different languages. Filter by language to focus, compare and contrast.

The **Places** view shows the bibliographic database on a map, revealing the geographic coordinates of South Asian art writing. Focus by location or decade to filter the database.

The **Clusters** view shows the changing profile of the database over time in a faceted timeline. Slice the collection by language, place or publication type and select a segment of the graph to see the bibliography entries.

Select a visualisation to begin

FIGURE 6.2 Data visualisation on the AAA Bibliography website

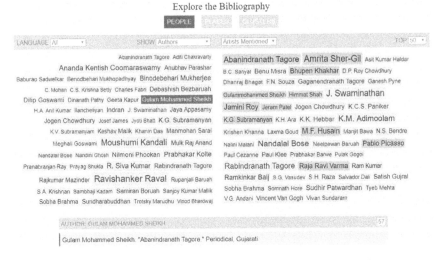

FIGURE 6.3 People view, data visualisation on the AAA Bibliography website

While this is one side of the project, that is the interface and its uses that relate to the digital, the back end is a site that raises questions involving the kind of skills and labour in building the database. The database was a compilation of minor databases built by a team of more than fifteen project researchers, based in different

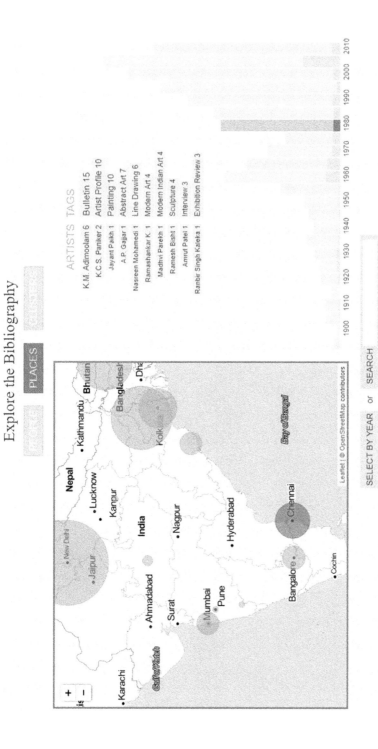

FIGURE 6.4   Places view, data visualisation on the AAA Bibliography website

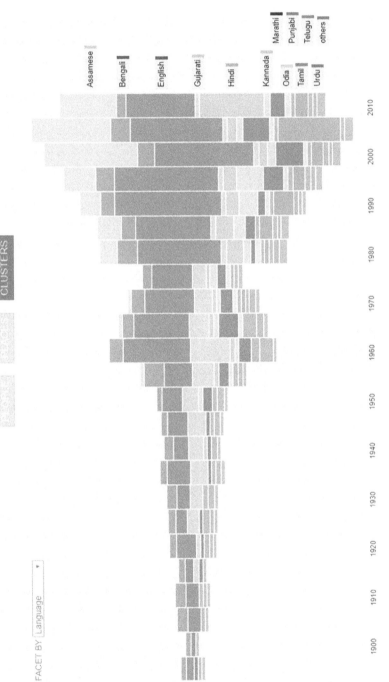

FIGURE 6.5 Clusters view of languages, data visualisation on the AAA Bibliography website

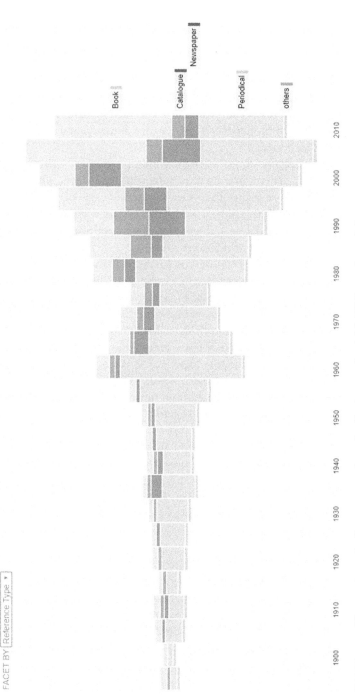

FIGURE 6.6   Cluster view of reference type, data visualisation on the AAA Bibliography website

cities, working to list bibliographies across several languages. Most researchers, it must be noted, were practicing artists, or former artists pursuing higher education. The absence and reluctance of graduates of art history to participate in building this database was starkly noticeable and telling. Several of them hesitated to work on this database for its 'mechanical drudgery', preferring to instead undertake more analytical research that had either scholastic, curatorial, or programmatic outcomes. Rather than seeing these as decisions/positions of specific individuals, the problem is and should be seen as structural – with the discipline of art history and the persistence therein of hierarchies and binaries of mechanical labour and intellect, resource and scholarship.

The Bibliography Project brought within its purview writing of all kinds – academic texts, art criticism texts, popular texts, and so on, with the only common thread between them – that of art. In that sense, one of the claims attempting to be made through this project was to bring such writings within institutional domains because of the near absent engagement with such forms of writing as knowledge production, which were otherwise only considered as equivalent to skill or illustration or descriptive writing, rather than as 'academic work'. In that sense, we note that there was already some kind of hierarchisation in place. One of the main challenges here was to bring academic rigour to documentation itself. Indeed, from experience, we know that databases are hardly objective; they are defined by parameters and fields. These include a confrontation with questions of not just what to include or exclude, but how to translate knowledge such that it conforms to the database logic. For instance, for those researchers enlisting books from languages outside English, since the database was constructed as one, the questions faced ranged from how to transliterate (spellings, debating the use of diacritical marks), how to translate titles and keywords (accuracy over conveying gist), what spellings to devise/invent for authors or artists who had yet not made it to the national/global English art history, and so on. In that sense, these were not value-neutral databases that were being created, nor were they 'mechanical' processes so to speak. Clearly, then, the skills or tools we refer to here do not involve a mindless act of 'repetition', so to speak, but are premised on acts of translation: of their knowledge of the field of fine arts to suit in this instance, a database logic.

So it was important for us that these processes not be random but work with a methodological and historical understanding. As a result of this, we reached out to several students and graduates of art history to be able to bring to this project its necessary rigour. However, the significance of such work in order to expand or problematise the historical configuration of the field was reduced by several art history graduates to the mere fact of some kind of wretchedness of process. Nonetheless, it is also telling in that it speaks of an intellectual refusal to engage with the actual intricacies of knowledge production. This reluctance to engage with hard realities of knowledge also comes from the institutional construction of some kinds of labour as intellectual and others as manual. It would be useful to think through the implications of such divisions, where, for instance, only that which gets produced from institutional or city centres is considered knowledge; anything other is looked at with suspicion. We must note that it is precisely in these ways that vernacular knowledge production is excluded from mainstream Anglo-centric discourses for not being rigorous enough. Where the underlying premise of the Bibliography Project was that every kind of knowledge production is valuable for research, the general assumption being made about vernacular writing by the institutional structures of art history was that this seemingly non-academic or popular writing was not worthy enough, and this came to assume the status of natural fact. It must also be noted that even in history writing, there is a constant reproduction of the division between intellectual and manual labour. Several established scholars' initial response to the Bibliography Project involved an expression of scepticism as to what there was in this vernacular and popular milieu that was worth historical analysis. Such positions time and again seem to reinstate only certain individuals and institutions as producers of history and knowledge, and the reluctance to engage only reaffirms their positions.

To conclude, I would like to reflect briefly on the question of value in the context of digital art history, in light of the Bibliography Project. And here I would like to bring up what we understand today as the network effect, which to quote Bernard Stiegler, is 'an economic mechanism of positive externality, as a result of which the value of goods or services depends on the number of other users' (2016, 261). In the context of immaterials such as information, their value, it seems, is directly proportional to how successful they are in forging a network effect. In the context of the Bibliography Project, it is then, more than analytics or crowdsourcing, the move towards a multilingual art history as it makes its way into art history curricula and research projects that would signal the value of the project – one that is, by these standards, yet to be realised. The question then emerges if the network effect is only one among several means of generating value, or if we can think of others, such as a discursive one, of its role in contributing to shifting the terrains of art writing – one whose impact can only be gauged over a long period of time, and not in immediate results, but one that even so relies on dissemination as a means of preservation.

Notes

1 For an earlier version of this part of the chapter, see Ragavan, 2014.
2 This chapter draws its inspiration from Sisir Kumar Das's seminal work on the history of Indian literature. For more, see Das, 1991.
3 I refer here to the work of institutions such as the Sahitya Akademi and its regional manifestations, various university presses, and publishing houses that translate works from one Indian language to the other, and so on.
4 I use the term *vernacular* consciously here, as the very nomenclature itself is a site of productive tension.
5 *Vrishchik* (Gujarati and English), *Roop-Bheda* (Marathi, Hindi, English), *Desh, Probasi, Visva-Bharati News* (Bengali and English), *Visva-Bharati Patrika* (Bengali and Hindi), *Nunkalai* (Tamil and English), *Srujani* and *Rangarekha* (Odia and English), and *Kala Dirgha* (Hindi and English) are some bilingual periodicals.

References

Bishop, Claire. "Against Digital Art History." *Humanities Futures*. October 20, 2015. Last accessed on 29 May 2018. <https://humanitiesfutures.org/papers/digital-art-history/>

Das, Sisir Kumar. *A History of Indian Literature, Volume I*. New Delhi: Sahitya Akademi, 1991.

Drucker, Johanna. "Is There a 'Digital' Art History?" *Visual Resources* 29:1–2 (2013): 5–13.

Manovich, Lev. *The Language of New Media*. Cambridge, MA: MIT Press, 2001.

Manovich, Lev. "Data Science and Digital Art History." *International Journal for Digital Art History* 1 (2015): 12–35.

Ragavan, Sneha. "A Question of Language: Art History in India," *Take on Art* 4:15 (2014): 14–16.

Stiegler, Bernard. *Automatic Society: The Future of Work, Volume I*. Cambridge and Malden, MA: Polity Press, 2016.

Walsh, Catherine E. *Pedagogy and the Struggle for Voice: Issues of Language, Power, and Schooling for Puerto Ricans*. New York: JF Bergin & Garvey, 1991.

Whitelaw, Mitchell. "Towards Generous Interfaces for Archival Collections." Paper presented at the ICA Congress, Brisbane 2012. Last accessed on 29 May 2018. <http://mtchl.net/towards-generous-interfaces-for-archival-collections/>

7

DIGITAL HUMANITIES IN INDIA

Pedagogy, publishing and practices

Nirmala Menon and Shanmugapriya T.

Diane Jakacki and Katherine Faull point out in their essay "Doing DH in the Classroom: Transforming the Humanities Curriculum through Digital Engagement", "the term Digital Pedagogy has gained traction in the wake of the digital humanities moving from the margin to the center in the academy". They go on to underline the lack of a standard definition for the term, which can mean anything from massive online open courses (or MOOCs) to flipped classrooms to assignments and scaffolded projects. However, as these two authors as well as others have pointed out, the difference between integrating technology to curriculum design and programmes and digital humanities (DH) is the intent of the learning outcomes and objectives for a course. Yet, others have pointed out that the history of DH in different continents have all followed a path of research-intensive centres and groups and some of the first programmes established in the field (King's College, London, for example, and others) were graduate programs with a master's degree or a PhD. Very few DH programmes have begun with an emphasis on undergraduate programmes. We see a similar trend in India, where unlike Jakacki and Faull's assertion, digital humanities are still in the margins of the Indian academy, and with few exceptions, there are very few programmes and courses where students have access to and awareness of opportunities and possibilities in DH work. This, in turn, means that by the time such students become research scholars, there is very little confidence or inclination to understand the impact of the digital on the ways in which their projects can be influenced. In this chapter, we want to argue that if we want to equip the humanities researcher of tomorrow, the humanities undergraduate student's curriculum must be reimagined in substantive ways. Think of some traditional humanities research areas and then wonder if research in those areas can today be imagined without harnessing, engaging and critiquing the digital. If a student is interested in archival studies, are traditional archives different from digital ones? Can a student working in this area understand the field without understanding how digital archives are curated and the role of algorithms and artificial intelligence (AI) in the long-term sustainability and discoverability of that archive? What if he/she is interested in manuscript studies or book history? Even if a student is interested in textual narratives, if the reading, production and consumption of literature have acquired multifaceted digital intricacies, can a literature scholar overlook its impact on the scholarship? If we are studying the philosophy of education, can we overlook the impact of MOOCs and the technologizing of education, not to mention its utilitarian impetus and long-term damaging consequences? The resistance to the digital comes as both anxiety and suspicion. Eileen Gardiner and Ronald Musto ask, "Have old ways of research, writing and publication been supplanted as the digital alters all historical forms and models" (5)? The suspicion stems from a fear that their traditional disciplines will be taken over by the digirati. However, digital humanities can be incorporated into the existing curriculum as a transdisciplinary endeavour, so there are opportunities for students across disciplines of the humanities and social sciences to be trained in available tools. The introduction of digital humanities can, therefore, be an evolutionary process and not a revolutionary one. And that can happen only if we focus on undergraduate curriculum across universities and colleges and take steps to include training in technology, including the rhetoric and theory of technology, as part of their programmes.

In this chapter, we first survey the programmes and courses offered in a few prestigious public universities in India and see if there are any interdisciplinary majors or minors offered that have digital studies or its equivalent as a component. We then emphasize some of the reasons for this lack of diversity in programmes, including the expense of accessing digital tools; we also emphasize the need for more open access resources in publishing, databases as well, as open source tools that can get a young student started on a road to discovery of these resources and their usefulness in humanities research. We give a short but important list of such available tools in a section we call the "Digital Humanities Tool Box". And lastly, we will give a small overview of a digital publishing project[1] at IIT Indore: a digital humanities project that attempts to put into practice the principles of open access, which we believe are so crucial to digital humanities as a discipline and philosophy.

First, we provide a quick sample of curriculum and courses across numerous public universities in India. We have surveyed some well-known institutions' undergraduate and postgraduate humanities courses in order to see the implementation of digital literacy. The universities that we surveyed were Andhra University, Guwahati University, Patna University, Dr. B. R. Ambedkar University, Gujarat University, the University of Kashmir, St. Stephen College, the University of Delhi, Jawaharlal Nehru University, Jadavpur University, Presidency College, Presidency University, North-Eastern Hill University, University of Madras, Pondicherry University and the University of Kerala. The collected data were imported in the RAW online data visualization tool to see the integration of humanities courses in the institutions. A visualization of the data is given in Figure 7.1.

- English
- Economics
- Counseling Psychology
- Disabilities Studies
- Persian
- Women's Studies
- His Eco Spl. Telugu
- Telugu-Eco Philosophy
- Eco-Poli Spl.English
- Social Work
- Buddhist Studies
- Urdu
- Japanese Studies
- Geo
- French
- Kannada

- Hindi
- Quantitative Eco
- Assamese
- Education
- Philosophy
- Arabic
- His-Oriya-Political Sci
- Telugu-Geo-Tourism
- Commerce
- Christianity
- Germanic and Romance
- Arabic and African
- Korean Studies
- Perfoming Arts
- Anthropology
- Malayalam

- Sanskrit
- Adult Continuing Education
- Bengali
- English Language Teaching
- Political Sci
- Maithili
- His Poli C A
- Telugu Poli Sci &Manage
- Arts
- Journl Com
- Linguistics
- Chinese South-East Asian
- Media Studies
- Geology
- Jainology
- Malayalam&Com

- Telugu
- Ancient History Arch.
- Bodo
- Foreign Languages
- Psychology
- Urdu
- His-Poli Sci-Spl. Telugu
- Social Work&Eco-Poli
- Social Sci (History)
- Comparative&Indian Lit
- French and Francophone
- Comparative Lit
- Khasi
- Saiva Siddhanta
- Music

- Special Education
- History
- Com&Jour
- Library Information Sci
- Sociology
- His Eco Political Sci
- Poli Sci -Self Govt.
- Tourism &Geo. Poli Sci
- Islamic Studies
- Development Studies
- Punjabi
- German Studies
- Film Studies
- Tourism
- Vaishnavism

- Applied Eco
- Politics
- Creative Writing &Trans
- Linguistics
- Turkish
- His Eco Rural Industrialization
- Telugu-Eco&Poli Sci
- Tourism –Geo&English
- MassCom Jour
- Arabic
- Russian Studies
- Arts and Aesthetics
- Media&Com
- Tamil
- Indian Music

FIGURE 7.1 Data visualization of humanities programmes from well-known institutions around the country

The data visualization shows that established mainstream courses are occupying large spaces such as English, economics, psychology, politics, philosophy and so forth. Other interdisciplinary courses such as history–economics–political science, political science–history–local self-government, social work–economics–political science, and so forth are pushed to smaller spaces. However, these kinds of interdisciplinary courses have only been recently implemented in a few universities. If we closely analyse the data, we can see some courses are aligned with *computer*, such as history–economics–computer application, history–political science–computer application, and so forth. The graduate students learn fundamental features such as introductions to computers, input and output devices, along with some tools such as Adobe Photoshop, from these courses. Even in the few crossover programmes and courses, we see more of applied humanities and social sciences, and not fields like literature or philosophy or cultural studies. This lack of inclusion of newer research methods in the humanities stems from an instinctive resistance to technology from the framers of curriculum and policy. This resistance, as we have seen in global discourse about digital humanities, is often premised on the suspicion that DH is a sell-out to the science, technology, engineering, and math (STEM) hierarchy in universities, as well as the larger consumptive practices of the university systems, as evidenced by the pre-eminence of point systems and quantitative evaluation models for professors and students alike. We would, however, flip that argument to ask, If humanities scholars are called upon to challenge the changing philosophies of education, learning outcomes and research, can we do so without understanding the modelling metrics of such a system? If we do not equip future humanities students and scholars with the tools necessary to fulfil what has long been the responsibility of such disciplines – critical engagement with humanist subjects – then we are in the danger of further marginalizing our influence in the academy. The integration of technology into the classroom can be helpful for the students "to think critically about media engagement so that they can become better digital citizens" (Jakacki and Faull 2016, p. 359). The digital pedagogy should focus on advanced integration of methodologies, as Hirsch (2012) claims that digital pedagogy needs to be "moved out of marginalization and exclusion, to the fore of the digital humanities" (6).

Bharathiar University,[2] Coimbatore, included "Introduction to Digital Humanities" in their postgraduate syllabus for the academic years 2016–2017 and 2018–2019. Professor Padmanabhan, who introduced this course, says that their goal includes both theoretical and practical learning; however, since they do not have lab facility and lack of access to digital tools, they are unable to teach the advantage and disadvantage of digital humanities methodologies and tools. The theoretical course includes stylistic analysis, authorship studies, electronic scholarly editing, textual analysis, cognitive stylistics and literary imagination, multi variant narratives and speculative computing robotic poetics, etc.

We did a random survey of some of the prestigious programmes that are listed in the data visualization chart (see Figure 7.1). It was seen that, except for Bharathiar University's and Jadavpur University's,[3] there are scattered interdisciplinary courses, such as history–economics–computer application. Other than these minimal examples, there was little or no opportunity for the average humanities students at a public university to be introduced to and familiarised with digital tools that might open their perspectives on new and existing modes of research in the humanities. Is this sufficient for students engaging in larger or smaller projects on topic modelling, text encoding analysis, data visualization, geospatial analysis and visualization, and so forth?

Digitization of analogs, digital-born materials, digital library and digital databases for Indian scholarship[4] have significantly increased in the last few years, thanks to the open access system, which allows the scholarly community to be able to participate in knowledge production and dissemination (Eve 2014, p. x). This digital establishment opens up a new horizon in the landscape of humanities to engage in digital humanities practice in terms of scholarly research by applying digital tools and techniques. However, digital humanities in India still assembles "its necessary resources for the field move from 'emergent' to 'established'" (Borgman 2009). Indian humanities scholars are in the critical moment of transition from traditional humanities to digital humanities experiment and research. Despite the opportunity and resources, they have particular challenges, which include the dearth of access to digital tools, lack of awareness about open sources, and deficiency of technical literacy that blocks them from adopting new research practices of digital humanities. Indian digital humanities scholars, instructors and practitioners are "called to action" (Borgman 2009) with some key defining factors such as access to tools, resources, technical literacy and infrastructure. In the following section, we examine the contemporary challenges in the digital humanities practice of application of tools and techniques for humanities scholarly research.

Kathleen Fitzpatrick says that tools and techniques of digital media bear on traditional humanities questions; at the same time, "it's also bringing humanistic modes of inquiry" to analyse the dearth of digital pluralism and technical literacy (Lopez et al. 2015). There are some digital initiatives in India that unfold the current development of digital society, such as the Digital India Programme, Centre for Internet and Society (CIS),[5] Impacting Research Innovation and Technology (IMPRINT)[6] and so forth. The main vision of the Digital India Programme is digital infrastructure and digital empowerment; similarly, digital pluralism is one of the aims of CIS. Digital humanities is also a part of the domain of Computation of IMPRINT, which recognizes digital humanities as a field for preserving heritage in the country, such as languages, dialects, art forms, architectural structures, social and ethnic practices, which shows a significant growth in the domain of digitization. Nevertheless, humanities scholars still have the deficiency of "access to funding, expertise, and of course adequate and advanced physical and technological infrastructure, such as computational methods often limits the kind of work that can be done with digital artifacts" (Sneha 2016, p. 4). The lack of access to digital tools is one of the major issues for humanities scholars. It is difficult for individuals to access payable software or tools for their works. There are scattered attempts to facilitate the application of digital tools throughout the country, such as the

TDIL Project, Digital Village, Digital Libraries Project[7] and so forth, but digital materials and the Internet still face "the problem of access, and more importantly *quality of access*" (Sneha, p. 8), which might be one of the causes of the deficiency in accessing digital tools. However, digital humanities scholars and practitioners are actively engaged in arguing for and supporting open sources. As Spiro says, "We can see openness at work throughout the digital humanities community, such as in open source software, freely accessible digital collections and open access journals and books" (p. 24). There are many web technologies, digital tools and pieces of software freely available on the Internet. The scholars can select the tool that is appropriate for their data analysis.

These open sources can offer an excellent start for understanding the digital environment for scholarly activities. Nevertheless, humanities scholars have typically overlooked the openness of computational methods for their research due to the following reasons: (1) They are not aware of the existing open sources, and they are uncomfortable with using digital tools, as they trained using the traditional humanities research method. (2) The notion of text as data is unfamiliar as a concept, as is the way in which technology can push the envelope on research possibilities, along with and complementing current practices of research. However, a fundamental understanding of available digital tools and possible types of analysis is imperative. Many mainstream humanities scholars in India perform research by using traditional techniques such as text analysis, pattern analysis, stylistic analysis and so forth. However, these techniques easily can be done through the use of digital humanities methods. Patrick Juola, in his essay "Killer Applications in Digital Humanities", discusses how the broader humanities community neglects the practice, method, results and tools of digital humanities:

> People who do not participate in a field cannot be expected to be aware of the developments it creates, an expectation sadly supported by recent survey data. In particular, (Siemens et al., 2004; Toms and O'Brien, 2006) reported on a survey of "the current needs of humanists" and announced that, while over 80% of survey respondents use e-text and over half use text analysis tools, they are not even aware of "commonly available tools such as TACT, WordCruncher and Concordancer." The tools of which they are aware seem to be primarily common Microsoft products such as Word and Access.
>
> *(74)*

As Juola says, if we closely observe some of the traditional humanities theses in the database *Shodganga: A Reservoir of Indian Theses*,[8] there is clearly an apparent neglect of participation in digital scholarship. Some are not even aware of "commonly available tools" (Juola 2007, p. 74) which would not require much technical skill to use. For instance, Mohan Kumar is a doctoral researcher in a private university who shares his experience during a small project which he has undertaken in his postgraduate studies. In his project, "Naked Is Not to Ignore But to Explore: A Semiotic Study on Khalil Gibran's *The Prophet*", he focused on a particular word which was used in a different context in the novel. He could have used some text analysis tools which are freely accessible on the Internet. However, he did text analysis manually. In his words, "I manually did my text analysis, because I wasn't aware of any digital tools which would have made my work easier. I was planning to do the same kind of text analysis project for my higher studies, but I had to drop the idea due to lack of technical support and infrastructure, and lack of technical literacy".

Another scholar, Shenbaga Priya, who recently completed her scholarly research titled "Computational Personality Recognition in the Novels *The Road* and *No Country for Old Men* by Cormec McCarthy", says:

> I have used R to write algorithms. As a researcher, I faced a number of difficulties to complete my project in digital humanities. Lack of technical assistance and technical facility are the major limitations. I struggled to find any reference to approach digital humanities methodologies. Whenever I have doubts regarding algorithms, with no one to guide me technologically, I used internet sources. Finding the appropriate answer for my queries took more time than usual due to a lack of technical knowledge.

As we can see here, there is a notable unawareness about the potential of existing computational methods and tools and lack of digital literacy. However, as mentioned earlier, humanities scholars can utilize open sources to discover new research questions for cultural production. There are numerous digital tools that exist online, and the researcher can select the tools for their particular need. There are many digital humanities organizations, communities, and journals that offer information about digital humanities research, tools and methodology. A Digital Research Tools Directory (DiRT Directory)[9] collects materials about the digital tools for scholarly practice. It categorizes the tools according to the kind of research methodology, such as analyzing data, interpreting data, annotating, modelling data, archiving data, analyzing networks between data, capturing information, organizing data, cleaning up data, preserving data, collaborating, commenting, publishing, communicating, recording audio/video, analyzing the content of data, analyzing relationships between pieces of data, contextualizing data, sharing, analyzing the geographical aspects of data, storing data, crowdsourcing data enrichment/analysis, analyzing the structure of data, designing, analyzing the stylistics of data, finding information, theorizing, disseminating data, transcribing audio, video or manuscripts, adding markup to an object, translating, enriching metadata about an object, visualizing data, collecting information, building a website, and adding identifiers to data and writing. It includes both open source and closed source.

The following is a list of a beginners' Digital Humanities Open Access Tool Box, which will be useful for students in any of the disciplines and sub-disciplines of humanities and social sciences:

Gephi[10] is a free software that offers features to explore data through visualization and network analysis.

Recogito[11] affords a personal workspace where the researcher can upload, collect and organize sources such as texts and images. It helps to collaborate annotation and interpretation of the data.

Textométrie (TXM)[12] is an open source cross-platform Unicode, XML and TEI-based text analysis software.

Weave[13] (Web-based Analysis and Visualization Environment) is a visualization tool designed for visualization of any available data. Weave has the ability to integrate, disseminate and visualize data.

Overview[14] is an open source tool for analysing large sets of documents. In contains a search engine, word clouds, entity detection and topic-based document clustering. If the researcher feels the existing feature is not sufficient, they can use their own plugins through API.

Textpresso[15] is a text-mining tool for scientific literature. It includes two major components: (1) it allows access to full texts, which helps for searching entire articles, and (2) it helps to divide categories of biological concepts and classes.

Lexos[16] is an online free digital tool. It enables the scholar to "scrub" (clean) the text(s), cut a text(s) into various size chunks, and manage chunks and chunk sets. It offers tools for investigating those texts. The analysis can be made as dendrograms, making graphs of averages of word frequencies and visualizations of word frequencies, which includes word clouds and bubble visualizations

Text Analysis Markup System (TAMS) Analyser[17] is a program that works with TAMS to let you assign ethnographic codes to passages of a text just by selecting the relevant text and double-clicking the name of the code on a list. It then allows you to extract, analyze and save coded information.

Time Flow[18] is an open source timeline. It offers a timeline, calendar, list and table to help explore thousands of data points. It is a desktop application.

Search and Retrieval of Indic Texts (SARIT)[19] is a collection of electronic editions of Sanskrit and other Indian-language texts. The scholar can perform a text search, retrieval and analysis of works in SARIT. They can download the text as a PDF and HTML file.

Pliny[20] is a note-taking and annotation tool for research scholars. It is a desktop application and may be used with both digital and non-digital materials, such as web pages, images, PDF files, and digitized analogues.

Bookworm[21] helps to explore lexical trends in repositories of digitized texts.

Voyant Tools[22] is a web-based reading and analysis environment for digital texts.

VisualEyes[23] is web-based interactive tool developed at the University of Virginia to weave images, maps, charts, video, and data into highly interactive and compelling dynamic visualizations.

Some more open source tools, such as **Ngram**[24] and **RAW**,[25] also support digital humanities research.

However, these tools have their own limitations. Humanities scholars must be aware of the constraints and features of the tool before employing it for their specific projects. Also, some mainstream tools are designed with "collaboration in mind" (Brown, p. 55). When compared to other disciplines, collaboration scholarship also lags in the humanities. Susan Brown discusses the sustainable practice of scholarly culture in terms of long-term and short-term collaboration with communities. She also highlights the problems of open source software which humanities scholars should explore before they apply it for their projects. She says, "Scholars who collaborate in humanities research participate in a vast array of activities: entering existing materials to transform it in into 'data'; the more or less manual processes that are variously termed cleaning, munging" (55).

Of the vast array of activities mentioned by Brown, some processes may require a simple selection of text or cut, copy and paste, but other processes may involve modifying or adding codes to the tool in order to enhance it. Even in the DiRT directory, one of the descriptions of the tools mentioned, "If that's not good enough, you can write your own plugins using the API". Additionally, coding is another challenge for the humanities scholar to learn for their project. The jury is still out on the question of whether students in the humanities should acquire skills such as coding, and there are scholars who argue for and against it. For us, it is a moot point – some basic research skills are necessary across disciplines. For example, nobody would today argue that a humanities student does not need to use MS Office because his/her work is about literature from the sixteenth century; clearly he/she will use the computer to make several tasks easier than for a researcher in the seventeenth century. Similarly, knowing some of the ins and outs of programming or AI will become imperative for a humanities scholar, and our curriculum will have to keep pace with the changing technological demands from our current and future students. Therefore, introducing courses on technical literacy for the humanities community is necessary at this point. Though digital humanities practices have been initiated in research projects at research universities, it is important to bring digital humanities hermeneutics to the undergraduate and postgraduate students through digital pedagogy. This ensures that research scholars who trained during their undergraduate studies in some form of digital scholarship not only can critically engage with possibilities of interdisciplinary humanities research but will also be cognizant of new reading and writing practices, even when writing or researching in traditional domains. Some Indian institutions have started interdisciplinary courses, such as Digital Humanities and Cultural Informatics, History and Computer Application and so forth, which is a welcome advancement within the field. Sneha recognizes some of the institutions that are involved in digital humanities practices. In her words,

> The individuals and institutions mentioned here have been engaged with some of these concerns within their respective fields of research and practice. Four institutions – Jadavpur University, Presidency University,[26] Centre for Digital Humanities[27] and Srishti Institute of Art, Design and Technology[28] – have actively adopted the term DH for some of the work they have been

doing, whereas the remaining have been working with digital technologies as part of research, pedagogy, and creative practice.

(12)

Since some institutions have been using "digital technologies as part of research, pedagogy, and creative practice" (Sneha, 12), we wonder whether institutions around the country have incorporated digital scholarship courses in their curriculum. Among the premier Indian Institutes of Technology (IITs), our research group, the Digital Humanities and Publishing Research Group,[29] is the only one that focuses on the intersection between literature, publishing and humanities. Our research group takes a two-pronged approach: (1) we develop digital projects that come out of our research that is firmly based in textual, film and postcolonial studies; and (2) we challenge and critically examine the rhetoric of technodeterminism that informs the digitization era in India. In other words, we perform what is a very traditional humanities mandate – question, examine and understand the changing role of the citizen, the state, the text, the reader and all their intersectionalities. We argue that this role will be undermined if our humanities and social science students at the university level do not have more than a superficial understanding of technology in all our lives. That, in short, constitutes the humanities in digital humanities. Digitizing the humanities is the only way our students and future scholars will be equipped to critically evaluate, caution and in doing so fulfil our obligation to humanize the digital.

In this last section, we will give a short narrative about KSHIP (Knowledge Sharing in Publishing), an open access publishing project that has been launched from IIT Indore. KSHIP is an independent publishing centre that will focus on academic scholarship primarily in areas of humanities and social sciences, but will also host journals in the STEM fields. With an aim to develop a publishing catalogue that is dynamic and diverse, the centre also has an ambition to publish translations of scholarly works in regional languages. As we are based in Madhya Pradesh, Hindi is a natural first choice; eventually, we hope to diversify into other languages. The publishing project will focus on specific areas of research, such as urban studies, globalization, gender, translation studies, contemporary geography and others. As we are based in IIT, we would also consider engineering and science publishing projects on a selective basis; our focus in the engineering and science disciplines would be largely translations that can be used by university students in different parts of the country.

This is a digital humanities publishing project that identifies and fulfils a key gap in our research work across universities around the country: (1) lack of a quality university press that publishes high-quality research across disciplines and in multiple languages of the country, and (2) research inaccessible to a vast number of students across India in languages other than English. We also recognize that apart from inadequate academic publishing, professional scholarly indexing is also a challenge and need. To address this, a major project of the centre will be to develop multilingual databases that will index humanities and social sciences scholarship in different languages. The National Digital Library Project at IIT Kharagpur's data sets will be a model for this project, and we will also explore the possibilities of linking our project with their data sets. This project will further augment and collate the indexing of databases such as Shodhganga, Digital Library of South Asia, by expanding the scope of citations from research in different languages. One such project in literature scholarship is already underway with the Digital Humanities and Publishing Research Group at IIT Indore. Our project will both complement the existing efforts and also further its scope and reach through a digital open access platform and collaborations with international university presses. The centre's catalogue will reflect IIT Indore's motto of *Gyanam Sarvajanahitaya* – access to knowledge and knowledge production made possible through harnessing digital technology in the service of furthering education and research. The long-term goal of the project is to support educational access and research access to students in India across different languages and universities. The emphasis on open access is to ensure that IIT Indore is a non-profit platform that facilitates access to education for students/researchers in all disciplines, but with special emphasis on humanities and social sciences areas.

KSHIP is a partner with Ubiquity Press, UK, a consortium of open university presses that utilize the same digital platform. The consortium network is very useful both for shared resources and shared expertise among them; all of the presses involved are academic non-profit research entities. The consortium includes fledgling presses like the University of Stockholm Press, which, like IIT Indore, have just begun their foray into academic publishing, and experienced long-term players such as the University of California Press. KSHIP will be publishing its first monograph very soon, but as a nascent digital humanities project, we face financial challenges; more importantly, as a consciously multilingual press that is born digital, we are grappling with technological challenges with Indic script. That is a subject for another chapter, but suffice it to say that the learning curve has been steep.

The objectives of KSHIP are at the core of the humanities mandate – access to research, multilingual publishing and collaborative research that includes humanists and technologists to address issues that are at the heart of humanities as a discipline. Projects such as this or national repositories and archives cannot be created without the active participation and involvement of students and scholars in the humanities; they call for scholarly choices and nuanced understanding of the subjects and subject matter so as to ensure that new technologies are developed with an understanding of and reflect the latest research in the field.

We will end with another example: in an article for *Indian Express,* "Digital Native: Face Off", Nishant Shah, Professor of Media Studies, discusses the Google Art and Culture app and critiques the data sets that it depends on for implementation. Shah concludes:

> Even as the world turns digital, this app is a stark reminder of the huge inequalities of data-modernity that map our globe in a new way. It is important to realise that digital India thus, would not mean just producing these apps and techs in the country, but also claiming ownership and stakes in

building diverse global databases that represent us in fairer ways. It also shows why the effort of digitisation is not merely in producing users and building connecting infrastructure; but, in digitising and carefully curating the vast corpus of historical archives – textual and visual – into databases that are going to inform and structure the AI of the future. Google's app will slowly roll out for a global usage, but the problem of racist algorithms is not going to be solved by a tweak. It is going to need structural attention at building databases that are inclusive, diverse, and representative of the multiplicity that our digital futures need.

(Indian Express 2018)

Building databases that are inclusive and diverse, paying attention to digital infrastructures to confront questions of structural inequities appear to us to be the core of postcolonial studies and research. Many of the challenges that we need to address are now manifested in a digital ecosystem that encompasses algorithms, artificial intelligence, machine learning and natural language processing, which makes it imperative that we train tomorrow's humanities researchers in the complexities of this new world order so they can question, critique and challenge its underlying presumptions. Acceptable tools can work for everyone without perpetuating a definitive technodeterminism; on the contrary, demystifying some of the processes of technology development will equip them to investigate the changing modes of ethics, diversity and inclusiveness to ensure that the digital frontiers incorporate these factors at the developmental stage.

Notes

1 For more details on our project, Knowledge Sharing in Publishing (KSHIP), please view https://iitikship.iiti.ac.in/, accessed 26 May 2018.
2 "About Digital India Programme." Digital India, Ministry of Electronics & Information Technology Government of India, www.digitalindia.gov.in/content/about-programme.
3 "About." IITI KSHIP Knowledge Sharing in Publishing, Indian Institute of Technology Indore, iitikship.iiti.ac.in/site/about/.
4 There are many comprehensive digital projects, such as Shodganga and National Digital Library (NDL), which offer a digital ecosystem for researchers.
5 For more information on the Centre for Internet and Society, please see https://cis-india.org/, accessed on 26 May 2018.
6 *Information & Communication Technology*, imprint-india.org/domains/computer-science-ict. *National Digital Library of India*, ndl.iitkgp.ac.in, accessed on 26 May 2018.
7 For more details on the Digital Library project, please see https://ndl.iitkgp.ac.in, accessed on 26 May 2018. As such, the main goals of all these projects are to create tools and software in Indian languages and offer Internet to all villages of India and digitization of cultural heritages.
8 *Shodhganga: A Reservoir of Indian Theses @ INFLIBNET*, http://shodhganga.inflibnet.ac.in, accessed on 26 May 2018.
9 *DiRT Directory*, Andrew W. Mellon Foundation, dirtdirectory.org, accessed on 26 May 2018.
10 Gephi: Makes Graphs Handy, https://gephi.org, accessed on 26 May 2018.
11 Recogito, Pegalios Commons, https://recogito.pelagios.org, accessed on 26 May 2018.
12 Textométrie, http://textometrie.ens-lyon.fr/?lang=en, accessed on 26 May 2018.

13 "Visualize Your Data." *Weave Visual Analytics*, www.iweave.com, accessed on 26 May 2018.
14 "Overview." *Overview – Visualize Your Documents*, www.overviewdocs.com/, accessed on 26 May 2018.
15 "Textpresso." *Textpresso Downloads*, www.textpresso.org/downloads.html, accessed on 26 May 2018.
16 "Lexos {loader} An Integrated Lexomics Workflow." *Lexos*, lexos.wheatoncollege.edu/upload, accessed on 26 May 2018.
17 For more information on TAMS Analyzer, please see tamsys.sourceforge.net/, accessed on 26 May 2018.
18 Timeflow, http://hint.fm/projects/timeflow/, accessed on 26 May 2018.
19 For more information on SARIT, please visit http://sarit.indology.info/, accessed on 26 May 2018.
20 *Pliny: Welcome*, pliny.cch.kcl.ac.uk/, accessed on 26 May 2018.
21 *Bookworm*, bookworm.htrc.illinois.edu/develop/, accessed on 26 May 2018.
22 *Voyant Tools Documentation*, docs.voyant-tools.org/tools/, accessed on 26 May 2018.
23 Shanti Interactive with VisualEyes, www.viseyes.org/, accessed on 26 May 2018.
24 "Google Ngram Viewer." *Google Books*, books.google.com/ngrams, accessed on 26 May 2018.
25 "RAWGraphs." *RAWGraphs*, rawgraphs.io/, accessed on 26 May 2018.
26 Presidency University, www.presiuniv.ac.in/web/department.php.
27 Center for Digital Humanities, www.facebook.com/cdhpune/, accessed on 26 May 2018.
28 Srishti Institute of Art, Design and Technology, http://srishti.ac.in/, accessed on 26 May 2018.
29 "About." Digital Humanities and Publishing Studies Research Group, Indian Institute of Technology Indore, people.iiti.ac.in/~dhiiti/index.php/about/.

References

"Accessibility." *Centre for Internet & Society*, <cis-india.org/accessibility>, accessed on 26 May 2018.
Alawadhi, Neha, and Surabhi Agarwal. "Digital Village: India's Ambitious Free WiFi Project Covering 1,000 Gram Panchayats." *ET Tech*, From the newsroom of the Economic Times, 17 Jan. 2017, <tech.economictimes.indiatimes.com/news/internet/digital-village-indias-ambitious-free-wifi-project-covering-1000-gram-panchayats/56614278>, accessed on 26 May 2018.
Ambati, Vamshi, et al. "The Digital Library of India Project: Process, Policies, and Architecture." International Conference on Digital Library Models, Architecture and Technology, 5–8 Dec., TERI in Partnership with Ministry of Culture, Government of India, New Delhi, <www.serc.iisc.ernet.in/~balki/papers/ICDL2006-Delhi.pdf>, accessed on 26 May 2018.
Andhra *University*, <andhrauniversity.edu.in/webnew/coursesoff.html>, accessed on 26 May 2018.
Bharathiar *University*, <www.b-u.ac.in/Home/UniDepts>, accessed on 26 May 2018.
"Bharathiar University: Coimbatore 641 046 M.A. English Literature Choice Based Credit System." *Bharathiar University*, <www.b-u.ac.in/Home/DeptEnglishSyllabus>, accessed on 26 May 2018.
Borgman, Christine L. "The Digital Future Is Now: A Call to Action for the Humanities." *Digital Humanities Quarterly*, vol. 3, no. 4, 2009, <www.digitalhumanities.org/dhq/vol/3/4/000077/000077.html>, accessed on 26 May 2018.
Brown, Susan. "Towards Best Practice in Collaborative Online Knowledge Production." *Doing Digital Humanities: Practice, Training, Research*, edited by Constance Crompton, Richard J. Lane and Ray Siemens. London: Routledge, 2016.

"Digital Native: Face Off." *The Indian Express*, 11 Feb. 2018, <indianexpress.com/article/technology/social/digital-native-face-off-5058464/>, accessed on 26 May 2018.

Eve, Martin Paul. *Open Access and the Humanities: Contexts, Controversies and the Future*. Cambridge: Cambridge University Press, 2014.

Flowing *Media: Your Data Has Something to Say*, <flowingmedia.com/timeflow.html>, accessed on 26 May, 2018.

Gardiner, Eileen, and Ronald G. Musto. *The Digital Humanities: A Primer for Students and Scholars*. Cambridge: Cambridge University Press, 2015.

Hirsch, Brett D. "</Parentheses>: Digital Humanities and the Place of Pedagogy." *Digital Humanities Pedagogy: Practices, Principles and Politics*, edited by Brett D. Hirsch. Cambridge: Open Book Publishers, 2012.

Jadavpur University, <www.jaduniv.edu.in/>, accessed on 26 May 2018.

Jakacki, Diane, and Katherine Faull. "Doing Dh in Classroom: Transforming Humanities Curriculum Through Digital Engagement." *Doing Digital Humanities: Practice, Training, Research*, edited by Constance Crompton, Richard J. Lane and Ray Siemens. London: Routledge, 2016.

Jawaharlal Nehru University, <www.jnu.ac.in/node#school_center>, accessed on 26 May 2018.

Juola, P. "Killer Applications in Digital Humanities." *Literary and Linguistic Computing*, vol. 23, no. 1, 2007, pp. 73–83, doi:10.1093/llc/fqm042.

Lopez, Andrew, et al. "On Scholarly Communication and the Digital Humanities: An Interview with Kathleen Fitzpatrick." *In the Library with the Lead Pipe: An Open Access*, open peer reviewed journal, 14 Jan. 2015, doi:10.5749/minnesota/9780816677948.003.0002.

Mohan, Kumar. Personal Interview, 26 Jan. 2018.

North *Eastern Hill University*, <http://nehu.ac.in/school>, accessed on 26 May 2018.

"The Open Graph Viz Platform." Graph exploration and manipulation, <gephi.org/>.

Padmanabhan. Personal Interview, 29 Jan. 2018.

Pondichery University, <www.pondiuni.edu.in/programmes>, accessed on 26 May 2018.

Priya, Shenbaga. Personal Interview, 28 Jan. 2018.

Siemens et al. "The Humanities Scholar in the Twenty-first Century: How Research Is Done and What Support Is Needed." Paper presented at ALLC/ACH 2004, Gothenberg: University of Gothenberg.

Sneha, P.P. "Mapping Digital Humanities in India." *The Centre for Internet and Society*, The Centre for Internet and Society, 30 Dec. 2016, <cis-india.org/papers/mapping-digital-humanities-in-india>.

Spiro, Lisa. " 'This Is Why We Fight': Defining the Values of Digital Humanities." *Debates in the Digital Humanities*, edited by Matthew K. Gold. Minneapolis: University of Minnesota Press, 2012, pp. 16–35.

St. Stephen's College, New Delhi, <www.ststephens.edu/courses-offered/>, accessed on 26 May 2018.

Toms, Elaine, and Heather L. O'Brien. "Understanding the Information and Communication Technology Needs of the E-humanist." *Journal of Documentation*, vol. 64, no.1, 2008, pp. 102–130, doi: 10.1108/00220410810844178.

University of Delhi, <www.du.ac.in/du/index.php?page=syllabi>, accessed on 26 May 2018.

University of Kashmir, <www.kashmiruniversity.net/degreeprograms.aspx>, accessed on 26 May 2018.

University of Kerela, <www.keralauniversity.ac.in/courses>, accessed on 26 May 2018.

University of Madras, <www.unom.ac.in/index.php?route=academic/schools>, accessed on 26 May 2018.

8

DIGITAL HUMANITIES, OR WHAT YOU WILL

Bringing DH to Indian classrooms

Souvik Mukherjee

Lady Ada Lovelace, daughter of the poet Lord Byron, is supposed to have pro-tested, "Could you give me poetical philosophy or poetical science instead?" (O'Toole 2010: Ch 1), when her mother discouraged her from writing poetry. Ada was a key influence on Charles Babbage and his analytical engine and is often considered the first person to have written a computer program. The early con-nections of computing and poetry are not fortuitous and Lady Lovelace's comment has been realized in the comparatively recent fields of humanities computing and, now, digital humanities. Nevertheless, despite being such a meeting point of ideas and disciplines, digital humanities (DH) remains a marginal notion in large parts of the world where the divide between the sciences and the arts is seen as funda-mental, and information technology, or IT, is seen as an integral part exclusively of the scientific mind.

Such a scenario is also true of India. In the fuller realization of its IT dream, "Digital India" ("Digital India" 2017) does not count the digital understanding of the arts and culture among the key points of its vision statement. As far as educa-tion is concerned, the government actively promotes digital resources (such as an e-learning portal called Swayam), but the universities and educational centres across the country have not yet caught on to the importance of viewing the digital as a key pathway to understanding culture. Nevertheless, given the recent importance of DH in universities the world over, some Indian educational institutions, both private and government-sponsored, are taking an active interest in DH research. In view of these very new developments, this chapter aims to explore two questions in the main: first, how does DH feature in the pedagogical programme of Indian higher education, and, second, what are the potential challenges in conceptualizing a pedagogy involving DH in higher education humanities departments? Two case studies, taken from rather disparate projects, will be considered as indicative entry points towards answering these questions.

Speaking of the importance of pedagogy in DH the world over, Brett D. Hirsch raises some fundamental questions:

> Do we teach digital humanities? Do we profess it? Do we profess to teach it? Or, do we teach (courses like computer-assisted text analysis and others surveyed in this collection and beyond) so that we might profess (our scholarly understanding of the digital humanities as the intersection of humanities and computing)? However seemingly simple the question "what do we do?" may be, we do a disservice to our field and ourselves if we fail to consider the importance of pedagogy when it comes to answering such questions, no matter how commonsensical they might at first appear.
>
> *(Hirsch 2012: 17)*

Hirsch claims that present-day academia models itself on the nineteenth-century German *wissenschaft* ideal in which professors are not teachers but rather specialists responsible only for the quality of their instruction. The clear distinction between scholarship and teaching that such an idea promotes the image of the professor as the creator of knowledge and the teacher as a conveyor of knowledge. Such categorizations, however, are not supported by current pedagogical research, which views the teacher as a "facilitator of student projects, a co-inquirer, a learner"; as such, Hirsch advocates socially constructed knowledge and activity-centred learning. He notes that DH is particularly suited to this new pedagogical thinking in that instead of being a single discipline, it is a set of shared techniques across disciplines. Replacing the radical individualism of the traditional concept of the humanities, DH invokes what may be compared to the hacker ethic.

A slight clarification might be necessary about the hacker ethic, given the generally pejorative impression of hacking. As opposed to the Protestant work ethic, which, as Max Weber states, involves the realization that "[l]abour must, on the contrary, be performed as if it were an absolute end in itself, a calling" (Weber 2013 [1905]), the hacker ethic is about playfulness and exploration. Pekka Himanen describes the joyful and passionate nature of the hacker ethic by connecting it with some of the big success stories in the world of information technology:

> Hacker activity is also joyful. It often has its roots in playful explorations. Torvalds has described, in messages on the Net, how Linux began to expand from small experiments with the computer he had just acquired. In the same messages, he has explained his motivation for developing Linux by simply stating that "it was/is fun working on it." Tim Berners-Lee, the man behind the Web, also describes how this creation began with experiments in linking what he called "play programs." Wozniak relates how many characteristics of the Apple computer "came from a game, and the fun features that were built in were only to do one pet project, which was to program. . . [a game called] Breakout and show it off at the club." Flannery comments on how her work on the development of encryption technology evolved in the alternation

between library study of theorems and the practice of exploratory programming: "With a particularly interesting theorem . . . I'd write a program to generate examples. . . . Whenever I programmed something I'd end up playing around for hours rather than getting back to plodding my way through the paper."

(Himanen 2010: 5)

The pervasive nature of the Protestant work ethic is also evident in the idea of higher education in humanities contexts, where research and teaching are both solitary activities dependent on and defined by intensive specialization and mutual exclusivity. Hirsch is, of course, quick to disassociate DH from hacker culture especially as embodied by the "console cowboys" or "data jockeys" of cyberpunk literature, who are known for their swashbuckling solo adventures in the world of code. Nevertheless, hacking in as much as it is about making innovative changes to the system is certainly more in the spirit of what Hirsch has in mind for DH education, and it will be necessary to come back to it in the Indian context, in a later section.

Moving on from humanities pedagogy in general, Hirsch addresses the scenario of DH in general and applying the very techniques of making a digital concordance to two definitive texts in the field, ascertains how "research" gets primacy over "teaching" in DH. He takes *The Blackwell Companion to Digital Humanities* (Schreibman et al. 2008) and *The Companion to Digital Literary Studies* (Siemens and Schreibman 2013) as his main objects of enquiry and establishes that the word "research" and its analogues by far exceed the mention of "teaching" and related words (with 504 occurrences of the word "research", as opposed to 66 of "teaching"). The comparison is, of course, meant to be indicative and indeed, there may be far more complex issues involved that are not evident on such a cursory analysis. Nevertheless, the observation does underscore the urgent need for thinking about pedagogy in DH as the field grows ever larger.

In India, as a fledgling discipline, DH can already begin with a dual focus: on research as well as teaching, on equal terms. The recently formed Digital Humanities Alliance of India (DHAI) is a group of researchers from across the country who have teamed up in the hope of steering the diverse DH projects in the country towards a common goal of research and teaching. Judging from the comments on their website, the balance of research and teaching is already being achieved. One of the commentators states, "DH for me is a networked process that [is] always inherently, when not explicitly, pedagogical. It focuses more on the creation rather than memorization of archives, and also compels us to think creatively about literacy and textually in the 21st century" ("DHAI" 2016). Another comment makes the need to link research and teaching in DH quite explicit: "[b]esides theorizing about DH or working on projects, our interest is in looking at how the digital can be useful in helping rethink humanities research and teaching in India, in general" (Ibid.). Both of the two DH programmes running in the country, at Jadavpur University, Kolkata, and Srishti School of Art and Design, Bengaluru, emphasize teaching DH at the postgraduate level – Jadavpur University runs a diploma course and Srishti offers a master's degree. Besides these two courses, Presidency University offers an introductory course for DH as a "gen-ed" offering for undergraduate students; the nature of this "gen-ed" is that the course caters to both students of the humanities and the sciences from across all disciplines except English literary studies.

The master's course at Srishti offers "[an] expertise in hacking, making, coding, interface design, user experience and human-centred design supplemented by a strong knowledge base in humanities scholarship in areas such as public history, multilingual literary studies, human geography and cultural studies",[1] and all of this is expressly connected to a South Asian context with the aim that the students may facilitate the growth of this discipline in India. The coursework involves seminars, workshops and a capstone project (as in American universities), among other things. Students are informed of career opportunities such as "Interactive [Design], Human Computing Interaction, Video Games, Digital Publishing & Online Content, Building resources and digital policies for cultural institutions such as museums, libraries archives and galleries, R&D for consulting and technology companies, Policymaking . . . and Data Journalism".[2] It is intriguing to see that the list does not include traditional humanities teaching as a career option. This last point will connect to the later discussion of the absence of the digital in Indian humanities curricula. It is important to note that the course goes much further than the earlier conception of DH that involved digitizing archives towards DH 2.0 and 3.0, effectively incorporating a strong element of programming, design and cultural studies. The focus on South Asia is also unique to the course in that it is self-aware of its role in shaping the field in the country.

As Padmini Ray Murray and Chris Hand state in their article:

> As the digital humanities grows more visible in South Asia, it is necessary to recognise the ways in which disciplinary practices might diverge in these regions, owing to the exigencies of language, rate of technological growth and obsolescence, and different institutional and cultural histories, all of which combine to create an alternative definition of what the discipline might offer. The contours of the discipline necessarily shift with both geographical and intellectual location, and theoretical practice emerging in the Global South has to adapt to different infrastructures, languages, and technologies.
>
> *(Ray Murray and Hand 2015)*

Ray Murray and Hand are implicitly underscoring the importance of recognizing DH as a global phenomenon as opposed to an exclusively West-centric understanding of it. This gen-ed course is run by me, every alternate semester, and it, in effect, achieves three goals. The first is that it is one of the few undergraduate courses the world over and certainly the only one in India that addresses DH directly. The aim is to introduce an awareness of the impact of the digital in the humanities and culture in general but one that is cognizant of the Western bias in the field and, therefore, able to reshape the pedagogy according to local needs. Ray

Murray herself is the course leader at Srishti, and the South Asian focus is only to be expected.

The School of Cultural Texts and Records (SCTR) and Jadavpur University offers a thorough introduction to traditional DH methods of archiving, digitization and data mining together with software studies and other aspects of digital culture. The course's blog clarifies that the core principles are "the attempt to use digital technology and computational methods to enhance the study of the imaginative variety of cultural expression".[3] The advertised aim of the course is to equip its students "not only for further research at the doctoral level but also for work in publishing, museums, libraries, business and the public service". Again, teaching DH has not been factored in, although doctoral-level research has. Another important message that the course's blog provides is that the students will learn how to tweak existing software to learn to meet the needs of their academic practice. One could infer from this that such tweaking is especially necessary, given that the existing software do not cater to the context of Indian DH practice. This course seems quite heavy on traditional archives and digitization and there is much project-based activity. In such projects, the absence of a reliable Bengali optical-character recognition (OCR) software is deeply felt, and the result is that students have to devise workarounds and tweaks to existing programmes. This course offers a postgraduate diploma and is, consequently, popular among those who already have a master's degree. One of the advantages is that there is a level of maturity and research experience among the participants. Indeed, some of them come to the course with a specific target in mind. The disadvantage is, however, that there is a marked divide between those participants who are familiar with digital tools and those who are not digital natives at all.

The third course that comes to mind is the author's own undergraduate "gen-ed" course that is indeed one of the few undergraduate DH programmes the world over. The principle of "gen-ed" courses at Presidency University is that students from both Arts and Science take them all except those from the home department. So unlike in most other such courses elsewhere, where English studies houses the DH initiative, here the target audience comprises students from other humanities disciplines and those from the sciences. While the course scores on multidisciplinarity and indeed, in being able to introduce the field to a wider section of students, the varying skills in spoken and written English as well as in the use of computers often proves to be a hurdle. Nevertheless, the course continues to be popular and attracts over a hundred students each semester. This adds to an additional problem: unlike DH courses elsewhere in the world, the lack of computers in Indian universities can be quite acute, and DH activities tend to be print-based or, increasingly, compatible with mobile phone software platforms.

In all three cases, there is a clear awareness of a lack of resources and the curricula are consciously involved in a constant tweaking of what is available. In this sense, the pedagogy incorporates a principle similar to the hacking that was mentioned in the earlier section. In the Indian context, this is often referred to as *jugaad*. In their article quoted earlier, Ray Murray and Hand introduce that the concept of "jugaad" is somewhat different from hacking, although there are some similarities:

> The conceptual category of hacking is slightly altered by both linguistic and cultural context: to hack contains within it both the meaning of subverting the authority of proprietary systems through some sort of destructive action as well as to come up with a quick solution, whereas the aim of jugaad is almost always constructive, often unaware of the capitalist systems it undermines and is truly born out of necessity.
>
> *(Ray Murray and Hand 2015)*

Jugaad is almost always positive and arising out of dire economic need and the lack of facilities. It is never entirely innovation for the pure fun of it. There is another aspect to jugaad that Ray Murray and Hand do not mention: it is usually always about the construction of a makeshift solution, and quality is rarely a consideration as long as the end product works. Further, jugaad is a Northern Indian concept more than a pan-Indian one, and although much pride is attached to it and recent management jargon has linked it to business innovation, an important caveat is necessary. As Thomas Birtchnell claims:

> [F]ar from being an example of "disruptive innovation", jugaad in practice is in fact part and parcel of India's systemic risk and should not be separated from this framing. Viewed from this optic, jugaad impacts on society in negative and undesirable ways. Jugaad is a product of widespread poverty and underpins path dependencies stemming from dilapidated infrastructure, unsafe transport practices, and resource constraints. These factors make it wholly unsuitable both as a development tool and as a business asset.
>
> *(Birtchnell 2011)*

What is also very important in the context of teaching DH is that jugaad is considered outside formal pedagogy; there are no schools or books that can teach it. The latter is not entirely true for hacking, these days. If one is to consider teaching DH in India, then concepts such as jugaad need to inform the curriculum. On the other hand, whether the curriculum itself may be said to be about a kind of jugaad is a moot question. First, the pedagogic process across the different courses need to have a kind of uniformity and connect; the often solitary innovation of jugaad does not describe this well. Second, the DH curricula are flexible rather than makeshift. Here, the undermining of the system is one that is quite self-conscious, but all said, if the DH pedagogy in the Indian institutions is about hacking the system, it is cognizant that the "hacking" is of a somewhat different type than what it is understood to be in Western academia.

Another issue that crops up in Srishti's master's programme is that of the representation of South Asia in the academic discourse around digital cultures. As I have said elsewhere (Mukherjee 2015) and as Ray Murray and Hand have also pointed out, digital games such as *Age of Empires: The Asian Dynasties* often misrepresent

Indian history to the large number of gamers who play these games. With the widespread appeal of such media, which often wittingly or unwittingly transmit proimperialistic and colonial messages, it is indeed important to address their problems in the pedagogy that is built around DH in Indian institutions. Also, recent digital cultures phenomena, such as the exponential rise of trolling, the importance of social media in politics, the encroachment of Twitter into governance, and issues such as the impact of the Unique Identification number or Aadhar are topics that are specifically germane in the Indian context and need to be represented both in DH discussions worldwide, as well as closer to home in our DH curricula. Likewise, in the discussions of equality and diversity in digital cultures, caste also needs to figure as an important category in addition to race, ethnicity, and gender.

Large-scale DH projects are extremely effective in shaping DH pedagogy, as Lindsay Thomas and Dana Solomon note in their article:

> [W]e did not necessarily see pedagogical concerns as primary when we began the project. RoSE grew out of the Transliteracies Project, an existing research group on online reading practices, and, as such, we focused in the beginning of the grant period on epistemological concerns related to social computing, networked knowledge, and bibliographic data. However, in the following discussion, we reflect on how this focus shifted throughout the year. We report on the involvement of undergraduate students in the development process and on the importance of this involvement for refining our own understanding of RoSE. Thanks to the feedback we received from the students involved in the project, we began to see RoSE by the end of our development year as a tool for discovery and learning – as a system that, in many ways, has pedagogy at its core. In this way, the value of incorporating undergraduate students into the project development process has been quite obvious for us.
>
> *(Thomas and Solomon 2014)*

They note that many previous commentators, such as Stephen Brier (2012) and Luke Waltzer (2012), have lamented the fact that DH projects do not contribute to pedagogical practice. Thomas and Solomon's experience is rather better connected to the experience of DH in India.

Here, the crucial role of the School of Cultural Texts and Records (SCTR) at Jadavpur University is to be noted. Under the direction of Amlan Dasgupta, the diploma course at Jadavpur University has a slew of projects that can be viewed on the Granth South Asia website (Granth South Asia 2017). With funding from the Indian government, private donors such as the Ratan Tata Foundation and international organisations such as the British Library, the SCTR has more than thirty projects to its credit, and in many of these, the students of the diploma course are participants. For example, the latest project, a digital transcription of the poem *Tilottama Sambhaba* by the Bengali poem Michael Madhusudan Dutta, was carried out by the 2016–2017 batch of the postgraduate diploma course students. Any analysis of DH in India will remain grossly incomplete without mention of the

Bichitra project, which was completed by the SCTR in 2014. Bichitra (2016) is the online variorum edition of the massive oeuvre of the Bengali poet and Nobel Laureate Rabindranath Tagore and consists of "47,520 pages of manuscripts and 91,637 pages of printed books and journals". The Bichitra project, led by Sukanta Chaudhuri, is probably still the largest project of this kind globally. Peter Shillingsburg highlights the enormity of the project's achievement as a DH endeavour:

> Chaudhuri modestly calls it a "mere archive" to explain why the site does not explore the genetic process or explicate the significance of textual variants – except for a small range of examples to show the potentials. He rightly points out what a major project that would be in itself. The site enables genetic study; it does not do it for us. There is nothing "mere" about this archive.
>
> *(Chaudhuri 2016: vi)*

In his description of Bichitra, Chaudhuri writes of his team, "Never let it be forgotten that Bichitra was as much about human management as computer operations; . . . Except for two office staff, they were young scholars with good Master's degrees, nearly always in the humanities but with formal or informal computer training" (Chaudhuri 2016: 4). He also emphasizes how the project was more a result of *bricolage* than adherence to best-practices: "We thought, improvised, sometimes almost wished our way through problems: we could not hope for elaborate support according to the best practice" (Ibid.). Herein, one might observe that jugaad has often been compared to Claude Levi-Strauss's concept of bricolage, but whether they mean the same thing is a moot question. What needs to be stressed on most, however, is that Bichitra was a learning experience for its young team, and it reshaped what they had learnt in university (most of those who worked for the project had studied humanities disciplines in the same university). Quite a lot of what they achieved was learnt on the job, as even the project leader attests through the comparison with the *bricoleur*.

Despite the struggles it faced, Bichitra had nevertheless received a substantial grant and also garnered both national and international support and recognition. It was also more akin to the traditional DH projects based on archiving and digitizing printed texts and manuscripts. As a digital archive, it is not a Web 2.0 product and has very little user feedback built into it; then again, that, perhaps, is not its intention. A Web 2.0 integration has been planned for the website, but that is for the years to come. As far as DH projects in India go, Bichitra certainly set the benchmarks very high; other projects in the region are mostly smaller in scope and involve different constraints and methodologies.

Meanwhile, going by the Digital Humanities Manifesto 2.0, one can safely point out that DH has moved on from its earlier avatar of digitizing and archiving to something quite different:

> Like all media revolutions, the first wave of the digital revolution looked backward as it moved forward. Just as early codices mirrored oratorical

practices, print initially mirrored the practices of high medieval manuscript culture, and film mirrored the techniques of theater, the digital first wave replicated the world of scholarly communications that print gradually codified over the course of five centuries. . . . It harnesses digital toolkits in the service of the Humanities' core methodological strengths: attention to complexity, medium specificity, historical context, analytical depth, critique and interpretation.

(Presner and Schnapp 2009)

This is a more current understanding of DH and one that moves away from earlier DH (described here as "first-wave"), both in terms of project interests and interactivity. This type of DH is more inclusive of the affective and also of digital culture(s) and in the fledgling efforts of the DH team at Presidency University, Kolkata, it was this aspect of DH that was recognized more. The DH initiative at Presidency was started with a view to establishing a centre at a later stage, but although that project did not materialize, it led to the thinking through of a supplementary notion in relation to the other DH projects in India. A conscious Derridean usage is intended here. Jacques Derrida describes the "supplement" as a surplus and an addition but goes on to say "the supplement supplements. It adds only to replace. It intervenes and insinuates in-the-place-of, if it fills, it is as if one fills a void" (Derrida 2001: 3). The supplement both adds to and makes flexible the concept of the "centre"; indeed, it intervenes in and even substitutes the centre. With such a programme in mind, the DH initiative at Presidency University started its digital archive of the colonial cemeteries at Chinsurah and Kareya Road. The aim was to treat the tombstones as a repository of biographical information from which further investigations could be initiated and then a biography of those buried constructed. Further, with the multiple biographies, the related metadata trees, and the recording of data (demographic, geographical, and temporal, among other types), the archive was intended as a means to reconstruct the narrative of these colonial settlements and their mixed communities of Europeans and Indians. Such a narrative would then be of those voices that are usually not reflected in established histories of the British Raj and those of the trading companies in India. Two projects on colonial cemeteries were completed in 2014–2015 and 2015–2017 under my supervision, and with the help of a team of students of both Presidency and Jadavpur Universities. One of these students had already completed the diploma course in DH at Jadavpur University, and the rest were first-timers to any project work whatsoever. They were involved in data collection from online sources such as Google Books, Archive.org, the Digital Library of India, West Bengal State Central Library (digital collection), the Families in British India Society (FiBIS) database, the British Association of Cemeteries in South Asia (BACSA), and online journals, as well as ephemera on family history blogs, social media groups, and genealogy forums. The FindMyPast project had just opened up its digitized collections of ecclesiastical records from Calcutta, and this included transcripts as well as high-resolution scans of the original documents. All project members were given access to a subscription of FindMyPast and could view the burial records, birth registers, wills, and marriage registers, all of which revealed a wealth of information about those who are buried in the cemeteries, their kinsfolk, and indeed the Dutch settlement at Chinsura and the Scottish community serving in East India Company–ruled Calcutta. Other major sources were the *Bengal Obituary* published by Holmes and Co., digitized issues of the *Bengal: Past and Present* (Calcutta Historical Society 1907 onwards), C. R. Wilson's *List of Monuments* (Wilson 1896), and also the Kolkata Scottish Heritage Trust's database, as well as their transcriptions of the Scottish cemetery epitaphs.[4] Besides the digital sources, the project members had to access the archival documents at St. Andrew's Kirk, Kolkata, as well as in the National Library, the Bangiya Sahitya Parishad Library, and the Presidency University Library. A substantial amount of data was also gathered from various sources at the British Library, London. A sample entry from the Scottish Cemetery archive (Figure 8.1) and screenshots of maps and word clouds (Figure 8.2) generated from

FIGURE 8.1 The entry on Doorga Moni Basu in the Scottish Cemetery Archive

Fisher mentions that Dwarkanath was sponsored by a public subscription from the leaders of Calcutta Society while Bindrabati Das Bose and Gopal Chandra Basu had won gold medals in the Medical College Examinations and were sponsored by Dwarko Nath Tagore. Churumohun was sponsored by the Directors themselves. All four enrolled in 1845 and settled in 7 Upper Gowan Place under the direct supervision of Professor Goodeve. Fisher states that Dwarka Nath Bose had challenged English youths to a swimming match at the Hobson Public Baths. He also goes on to say:

The eldest, Dwarkanath Bose, proved least obedient to Goodeve and college discipline, and received the least recognition from them. Goodeve wrote that he "obtained only a certificate in Midwifery: this certainly is not encouraging on his part and I regret to say I am not surprised at his want of success, for though possessing considerable ability he has not the industry of the rest and he is wholly deficient in zeal for the cause in which they are all embarked."

Apparently, to prevent him from deteriorating further, Goodeve sent him back to Calcutta with Dwarkanath's son, Nagendranath Tagore. He subsequently received an appointment as assistant Demonstrator of Anatomy at the Calcutta Medical College at Rs. 250 a month and also started private practice.

Also see this article in the *Patriot* published in London, Sep 2, 1852:

In England, Dwarkanath Bose, Kaist [kayastha], baptized 17th February, 1837, by the Rev. Dr. Charles. After completing his studies at the General Assembly's Institution, he entered the Medical College, and was one of the four natives sent to London by Government to complete their medical education. On his return to his country, he was appointed to the office of Assistant Professor of Anatomy in the Medical College. He is at present attached to the Punjaub Division.

http://www.myheritage.com/research/collection-10025/newspaper-archives?...

It seems that Dwarkanath Bose may have been kidnapped by his relatives after his conversion. He was travelling with Dr Ewart and was attacked and robbed by his relatives. He managed to escape and the case was brought before the magistrate who offered these public protections. (See Neill, p. 380). The *Evangelical Magazine* reports that Bose was excommunicated and disinherited by his father Kristoram Bose of Duali Para.

Bibliography

Evangelical Magazine and Missionary Chronicle, s.n., 1858.
Fisher, Michael H. *Counterflows to Colonialism; Indian Travellers and Settlers in Britain, 1600-1857.* Orient Blackswan, 2006.
Neill, Stephen. *A History of Christianity in India: 1707-1858.* Cambridge University Press, 2002.

Bibliography

Evangelical Magazine and Missionary Chronicle, s.n., 1858.
Fisher, Michael H. *Counterflows to Colonialism; Indian Travellers and Settlers in Britain, 1600-1857.* Orient Blackswan, 2006.
Neill, Stephen. *A History of Christianity in India: 1707-1858.* Cambridge University Press, 2002.

Any reason for importance:
Wife of one of the first F.R.C.S doctors of Indian origin.
Buried by:
W.H. Mackay, Dissenting Minister
WebLink 1:

http://www.myheritage.co.uk/research/collection-10025/newspaper-archives?u...

Photo name/s:

http://www.myheritage.com/research/collection-10025/newspaper-archives?u...

Photo name/s:

Photo 2 close up:

FIGURE 8.1 (Continued)

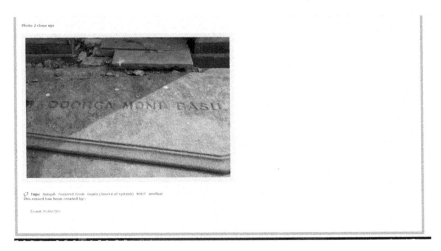

FIGURE 8.1 (Continued)

FIGURE 8.2 Map showing the places to which those buried in the cemetery were connected and also the distribution of their professions, causes of death and
the biblical inscriptions on their tombstones

Common Causes of Death

Word cloud showing the most common causes of death among those buried in the cemetery. Not surprisingly, Cholera and childbirth are the likely complaints.

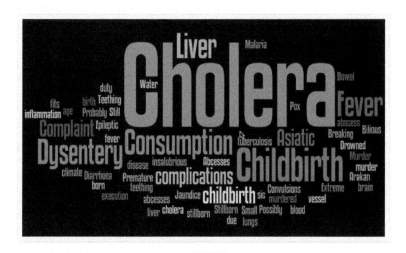

Common Professions

Word chart showing the most common professions among those buried in the cemetery.

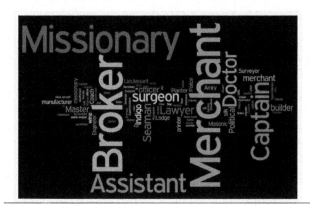

Verses from the Bible

Word cloud showing the most common Biblical references in the epitaphs of those buried in the cemetery. Any guesses why Thessalonians features in the top ten Biblical books from which epitaphs are drawn?

FIGURE 8.2 (Continued)

the information in the database will serve as indicative illustrations of the kind of work the project aimed to do.

The entry for Doorga Moni Das(i) Basu will show the process of recording and research in detail. After establishing the basic mechanism that students were introduced to as first-time researchers, the pedagogical process will be explained. First, however, a short history of Doorga Moni and her husband needs to be outlined.

Doorga Moni Dasi was the wife of one of India's first Indian MRCS surgeons. Dwarka Nath Basu, who returned from England to start practising as an obstetrician at Calcutta Medical College. He seems to have had a colourful life and yet been all but forgotten in the pages of history. Michael H. Fisher mentions Dwarka Nath Basu in his *Counterflows to Colonialism* (Fisher 2004) in connection to Indians who first went to Europe to study medicine. The *Times* newspaper dated 2 May 1845 carries an interesting story about how Dwarka Nath challenged the locals at a Holborn swimming pool to a swimming competition (see Fisher 2004: 370). Dwarka Nath had clearly converted to Christianity in his youth, and his wives (there were two others besides Doorga Moni) are all buried in the Scottish Cemetery on Kareya Road, Kolkata. Doorga Moni and Dwarka Nath's narrative is but just one of the untold stories in the two projects, which include illustrious figures such as the reformer and writer Lal Behari Day and lesser-known ones such as the Dutch *fiscaal* (the Dutch equivalent of an accountant/bursar) Gregorius Herklots, whose daughter, Hannah Mullens, is one of the contenders for having written the first novel in Bengali.

Besides the biography(ies) of the deceased and their relations, each entry provides the location of the tomb, the age, occupation, year of death names of relatives, gender, address, places with which the deceased was connected, the full epitaph, information about the burial and the officiating priest and finally, even the details about any Biblical references in the epitaph. Each team member was assigned a set of names to research and the first steps involved taking high-resolution photos from multiple angles and also recording the exact location using GPS. The tombstones were in various stages of disrepair, and very often Photoshop filters and other software techniques were required to decipher them. Sometimes the students had to make repeated visits to the cemeteries to recheck their GPS readings and retake photos under different lighting conditions. At other times, they had no other option but to rely on plain guesswork in deciphering faded inscriptions or ones that were partly missing on the tombstones. A list of metadata terms was agreed on by the team and attached to each entry as relevant. Once the entry was prepared by a student, a bibliography was then supplied at the end to indicate the sources from which the information was obtained, and then one of the team supervisors checked the entry. Finally, each entry was checked by the project leader. In the case of the Scots Cemetery archive, the PG Diploma students of Jadavpur University were roped in to check the entries, the hyperlinks, and the metadata as part of their semester project. For the Dutch Cemetery project, around twenty-five students of the DH gen-ed class of Presidency University volunteered to help with the Dutch Cemetery archive as part of their end-semester project.

None of this is in any way new in terms of pedagogical practice and the way research is done. Around a century ago, the Jesuit priest Father Henri Hosten was doing the same thing with his students when he transcribed the inscriptions of numerous tombs from across Bengal for the Bengal: Past and Present project. Father Hosten notes the joy that his students felt when working with him in the cemeteries of Serampore: "By this time my youthful coadjutors had become so thoroughly imbued with the spirit of antiquarian research that a picnic to Serampur without plenty of inscriptions to copy would have been the dullest thing imaginable" (Hosten 1921). The students on the DH projects also indicated that it was both an enriching and enjoyable experience. In interviews (Mitra et al. 2015) conducted for the project, Sarbajit Mitra from Jadavpur University highlighted how he had uncovered hitherto unknown details about the role of the Bengali missionaries in building the Indian education system, and Purba Hossain noted how important it was to consider cemeteries as an archive, although traditional history courses kept ignoring them. Sujaan Mukherjee, also from Jadavpur, stressed the importance of the digital aspect of the archive in that the digital tagging made it so much the easier for clustering of data and for future researchers to use the archive to suit their respective interests. Like Hosten's students, those involved with the cemetery-archive projects found them a joyful experience. Especially, since the Indian academic system (at least in humanities disciplines) does not stress project work and research as much as it does written examinations, the opportunity to bring together their research interests and their digital skills proved an enjoyable experience. In terms of the established humanities pedagogy, this was a "hack", and hacking, as mentioned before, often associates itself with a joyful experience. As said earlier, however, if these projects are indeed hacking the established Indian pedagogic norms, then this hacking is of a different kind than how it is understood in the West. One is still unsure, though, whether to call this a process of jugaad in pedagogy, given the distinctive characteristics of the practice as found in Northern India.

The cemetery archiving projects faced many problems both in accessing resources and in procedural matters (especially within an untrained system that still cannot fathom how the humanities can link with the digital). Nevertheless, help came from many unexpected quarters. The university's website officer, Sanjib Chatterjee, played a crucial role in following the project's progress and then brainstorming a way to include JSON data in the archive's framework so that the exact geographical location of the tomb could be recorded. Chatterjee had used his earlier experience from elsewhere in mapping the water bodies within certain zones in the city. It was also a serendipitous discovery that a free Android app called Wolf GIS was able to record the latitude and longitude up to twelve decimal places the accuracy required to be able to separately show the tombs that are very close to each other. In case of the Scots Cemetery project, the company hired to design the website went bust at the last minute, and the WordPress template designed for the Dutch Cemetery project had to be tweaked to fit the requirements of an entirely different archive. Despite all of these issues, the project was never a makeshift affair or a "making do", as is implied by jugaad. These projects were somewhat like a bricolage in the Levi-Straussian sense, just as Bichitra has been described by Chaudhuri, in the sense that much was learnt on the job. Although there was a project plan in place with prior theoretical underpinnings and a pre-formulated technical framework, there were many surprises in store for the project team. Digital filters that did not work on the photographs of badly eroded tombstones, incorrect transcriptions of the available archival materials (especially for Indian name spellings), variable GPS readings (sometimes because of the cloud cover), and more than everything, administrative hurdles are among some of the problems the project faced. Added to this was the fact that there were no prior projects that could be emulated, and also there has been very little research on the colonial cemeteries in terms of their funerary architecture and the construction of the tombs.

Innovative solutions to all of these problems had to be worked out and very often even presented themselves serendipitously. For example, a few days into the project, it was discovered that a Scottish team had come to Kolkata a few years back and had done detailed architectural listings of a few graves; what was even better, they were willing to share their findings and methodology. In another instance, a simple tweak to the WordPress location template was enough to display each grave on Google Maps in a more precise way than before. In none of these cases did the team have to resort to putting together makeshift alternatives to make the projects succeed; rather, there were more instances of tweaking the system and also pooling a diverse range of talents. When viewed as a pedagogical exercise, these two projects were certainly a learning experience that involved hacking the traditional education system in India.

As stated earlier, there are only a very few institutions in India that have consciously engaged in DH projects and in teaching DH courses. Of these, not all are academic institutions, and even when they are, then large sections of such places are unaware of the DH initiatives, unless maybe they are of the scale of Bichitra. Pedagogy, as in other places the world over, still takes a back seat in Indian DH, but given the inflexibility of the traditional higher education in the humanities and the rapid growth of access to digital resources, the popularity of DH in Indian universities might finally take hold. If this happens, then it must be remembered that DH will serve as a "hack" and also as a process of innovation more unique to its Indian context in reorganizing the very foundations of higher education pedagogy in the country. In the process, of course, DH in India can actively intervene in restoring the balance between DH as research and teaching DH that many commentators now claim is skewed in DH programmes the world over. Both the DH teaching programmes in three higher education institutions listed earlier (and more being added to the list) and research projects such as Bichitra and others will contribute to this. The first fledgling steps have been taken, and whether these are enough to start a systemic intervention in Indian humanities teaching is now a moot point. When and how far the digital humanities will also be part of more mainstream programmes, such as Digital India, depends on time and, of course, changing mindsets.

Notes

1 For course details, please visit <http://srishti.ac.in/programs/postgraduate-program-in-digital-humanities-2018-19>, accessed 26 May 2018.
2 Ibid.
3 To consult the blog, please go to <https://sctrdhci.wordpress.com/>, accessed 26 May 2018.
4 These were kindly made available by the KSHT's chairman, Lord Charles Bruce, and were compiled under the direction of Mr Ian Stein.

References

"Bichitra: Online Tagore Variorum." n.p., 2016. 9 Oct. 2017. <http://bichitra.jdvu.ac.in/index.php>. accessed 10 Oct. 2017.

Birtchnell, Thomas. "Jugaad as Systemic Risk and Disruptive Innovation in India." *Contemporary South Asia* 19.4 (2011): 357–372. *Taylor and Francis+NEJM.*

Brier, Stephen. "Where's the Pedagogy? The Role of Teaching and Learning in the Digital Humanities." *Publications and Research* (2012): n. p. <http://academicworks.cuny.edu/gc_pubs/201>. accessed 10 Oct. 2017.

Calcutta Historical Society. "Bengal, Past & Present: Journal of the Calcutta Historical Society." *Bengal, Past and Present* (1907): v.

Chaudhuri, Sukanta, ed. *Bichitra: The Making of an Online Tagore Variorum.* 1st ed. 2015 edition. New York, NY: Springer, 2016.

Derrida, Jacques. *Writing and Difference.* 2 edition. London: Routledge, 2001.

"DHAI." *DHAI Digital Humanities Alliance of India.* n.p., 3 Sept. 2016, 8 Oct. 2017. <https://dhaindia.wordpress.com/>. accessed 10 Oct. 2017.

Fisher, Michael H. *Counterflows to Colonialism: Indian Travellers and Settlers in Britain 1600–1857.* New Delhi: Permanent Black, 2004.

"Granth South Asia." n.p., 2017. Web. 9 Oct. 2017. <http://granthsouthasia.in/>.

Himanen, Pekka. *The Hacker Ethic.* New York: Random House, 2010.

Hirsch, Brett D. *Digital Humanities Pedagogy: Practices, Principles and Politics.* Cambridge, UK: Open Book Publishers, 2012.

Holmes and Co. *The Bengal Obituary: Or, a Record to Perpetuate the Memory of Departed Worth, Being A. . .* Calcutta: W. Thacker & Co., 1851. *Internet Archive.* 10 Oct. 2017. <http://archive.org/details/bengalobituaryo00calgoog>. accessed 10 Oct. 2017.

Hosten, Henri. "Christian Inscriptions from Serampur." *Bengal: Past and Present* 23 (1921): n. pag.

Ministry of Electronics and Information Technology Government of India. "Introduction | Digital India Programme." *Digital India.* n.p., 11 Aug. 2017, 8 Oct. 2017. <http://digitalindia.gov.in/content/introduction>. accessed 10 Oct. 2017.

Mitra, Sarbajit et al. Interviews with Project Members of the UKIERI Scots' Cemetery Project. May 2015. MP3.

Mukherjee, Souvik. "The Playing Fields of Empire: Empire and Spatiality in Video Games." *Journal of Gaming & Virtual Worlds* 7.3 (2015): 299–315. *IngentaConnect.*

Presner, Todd, and Jeffrey Schnapp. "Digital Humanities Manifesto 2.0." 29 May 2009. <http://manifesto.humanities.ucla.edu/2009/05/29/the-digital-humanities-manifesto-20/>. accessed 10 Oct. 2017.

Ray Murray, Padmini, and Chris Hand. "Making Culture: Locating the Digital Humanities in India." *Visible Language* 43.3 (2015). Web. 16 Apr. 2020. <http://visiblelanguagejournal.com/issue/172/article/1222>.

Schreibman, Susan, Ray Siemens, and John Unsworth, eds. *A Companion to Digital Humanities.* Malden, MA: Wiley-Blackwell, 2008.

Siemens, Ray, and Susan Schreibman, eds. *A Companion to Digital Literary Studies*. 1 edition. New York: Wiley-Blackwell, 2013.

Thomas, Lindsay, and Dana Solomon. "Active Users: Project Development and Digital Humanities Pedagogy." *CEA Critic* 76.2 (2014): 211–220. *Project MUSE*.

Toole, Betty Alexandra. *Ada, the Enchantress of Numbers: Poetical Science*. Sausalito, CA: Critical Connection, 2010.

Waltzer, Luke. "Digital Humanities and the 'Ugly Stepchildren' of American Higher Education." *Debates in the Digital Humanities*. Eds. Matthew Gold and Lauren F. Klein. Minneapolis, MN: University of Minnesota Press, 2012. 9 Oct. 2017. <http://dhdebates.gc.cuny.edu/debates/part/6>. accessed 10 Oct. 2017.

Weber, Max. *The Protestant Work Ethic and the Spirit of Capitalism*. New York: Simon and Schuster, 2013.

Wilson, C.R. *List of Inscriptions on Tombs or Monuments in Bengal Possessing Historical or Archaeological Interest*. Calcutta: Public Works Department, 1896.

APPENDIX

Online databases and archives:

The Dutch Cemetery in Chinsurah, http://dutchcemeterybengal.com
The Scottish Cemetery in Bengal: Digitising the Untold Empire, http://scotscemeteryarchivekolkata.com/
Families in British India archives (FIBIS), www.fibis.org
British Association for Cemeteries in South Asia (BACSA), http://bacsa.frontis.co/bin/index.php
Internet Archive, https://archive.org
Find My Past, www.findmypast.co.uk
Hathi Trust, www.hathitrust.org
South Asia Archive, www.southasiaarchive.com
Public Library of India, Internet Archive, https://archive.org/details/digitallibraryindia

9

DECOLONISING DESIGN

Making critically in India

Padmini Ray Murray

Most digital humanities scholars working in institutions in the Global North know the origin story, how they got there – the romantic narrative of archaic humanist scholarship catalysed by computational technology to produce a new alchemy of knowledge – while potent is also now well-rehearsed.[1] But as we begin to establish a cohesive digital humanities community in India, it is intriguing to consider what *our* origin story is, closer to home. Is there one at all? Or is the digital humanities merely a convenient, possibly even cynical, shorthand for work that was already being done in India, but a welcome taxonomic and institutional convenience to anchor it more firmly in the university? In this chapter, I will be exploring the ramifications of transposing digital humanities practice into Indian academic environments, and how some modes, paradigms and methodologies might be more suited to this context than others.

In 2015, as a plenary panelist at a seminal conference entitled Digital Diversity,[2] I created a stir by proclaiming "Your DH is not my DH." But what I hadn't bargained on learning was that "my DH" was a mere distraction from the work that really needed to be done in India. There could be no place for "my DH" without acknowledging that the whole idea of the humanities in India needed to be rehabilitated and resuscitated, due to its colonial, and latterly, Brahmanical underpinnings – and, moreover, that we had very little by way of infrastructural or archival foundations on which to build this idea of the new humanities.

In order to realise this vision to lay the very foundations of new humanities work in India, there needs to be training, infrastructural support, but most importantly an attitudinal shift towards making as a form of knowledge making. Roberto Busa himself left us with this very generous definition of what humanities computing entailed: "Humanities computing is precisely the automation of every possible analysis of human expression (therefore, it is exquisitely a "humanistic" activity), in the widest sense of the word, from music to the theater, from design and painting to phonetics, but whose nucleus remains the discourse of written texts.

Busa's emphasis on the written, however, is the inevitable opinion of someone who is heir to the Christian scriptural tradition, and begs the question whether such an emphasis can be easily transposed to our locally and culturally specific epistemological conditions, which even today are shaped as much by orality, making and embodied knowledges as they are by print and the digital. Working as I do, in an institution that was established to train designers, I see an opportunity to reshape the way we do humanities work drawing on methodologies from outside the traditional field, but keeping the values of epistemological inquiry and critique as still central concerns.

Situating digital humanities

It is instructive to remember that the humanities itself, as an institutional cornerstone of the university, was a consequence of the British policy of aggrandisement instrumentalised through the orchestrated spread of "Western education," as encapsulated by the Macaulay Minute in 1835. The rise of the "modern" university in India, therefore, was necessarily coterminous with the embedding of the humanities in the Indian intellectual ecosystem. This paradigm of modern, Western thought was predicated on, as Sanjay Seth has elegantly demonstrated in his work *Subject Lessons*, the creation of "a knowing subject who is set apart from, even set up against, the objects to be known." Though the digital humanities has often been lauded for its Utopian vision, it is undeniable that the discipline is inevitably with skewed towards this Western mode of knowledge, due to the reinscription of such perspectives on technology. Miriam Posner has highlighted how technologies (often built for contexts other than humanities research) can often be a blunt instrument, demanding data perform in ways which its underlying ideological biases demand, rather than allow space for accounting for lived, embodied experience, or uncertainty and nuance. In this chapter, which will draw on both anecdotal and theoretical insights, I hope to demonstrate why, while there are definitely lessons to be learnt from different paradigms, it is essential to define and locate local practices in order to shape a decolonised notion of the humanities in India.

I am keen to posit our current engagement with the digital humanities in India as a necessary phase, but not one whose outcome further embeds the discipline, rather than its practices, in the academic landscape. Instead, I feel we should be using digital humanities in India as a jumping-off point and tactical mode for enlarging the scope of the humanities in general, in order to prise open institutional resistance to accommodate and legitimise essential research in fields such as Dalit, feminist and indigenous studies. These interrogations of received knowledge must operate on different terrains – primarily, ontologies, epistemologies, praxis, archives, pedagogies, histories and technology[3] itself. Of course, these categories do not operate in isolation, and are necessarily complementary and reciprocal in their scope, but this roadmap, as it were, allows us to think constructively about what is at stake, and hopefully serve as a compass for the work we need to do going forward. These sites of inquiry are necessarily inextricable from one another, and it is essential to remain alert to all of these while we delineate what might account for digital humanities work in India.

A recently updated 2016 edition of a seminal DH text, *A Companion to Digital Humanities* edited by Susan Shriebman, Ray Siemens and John Unsworth, published in 2004, dedicates four separate sections to this meta-conversation, both in the context of interdisciplinarity and the "ever-emergence" of the discipline, inserted alongside several chapters dedicated largely to methods and approaches. This format itself serves as an emblem for DH and its nervousness about asserting itself as a disciplinary category, embodying the tension between the "hack" and the "yack" – terms that were used in their initial context in 2008 to differentiate between making/building and theorising – but where the latter finds itself persistently saddled with a navel-gazing myopia.

These exploratory engagements are not restricted to the US alone, and closer to home, P. P. Sneha's significant and necessary document commissioned by the Centre for Internet and Society in Bangalore as part of their "Papers" series, entitled "Mapping Digital Humanities in India," rehearses this tension yet again:

> While the study began as an attempt to understand the growing interest around the term itself in India, its scope has extended to explore what specific contexts and conditions are in place in India that give it critical purchase. Academic and applied practices focus on building of digital archives, film studies, game studies, textual studies, cultural heritage and critical making to name just a few. While these efforts have managed to create a growing interest in DH, there is still a lack of consensus on what exactly constitutes the field in India. Thus, questions around definition, ontology, and method remain pertinent, as does the need for recognition by the national academic bureaucracy.

These considerations, as Sneha points out, also act as a corrective to the notion that conceptions of digital humanities as a discipline are universal – the originary narrative underpinning its emergence in Anglo-American academic discourse necessarily diverges in India and other countries in the Global South, due to differences in access, language, sociocultural mores and infrastructure. She also gestures towards the need for caution when "applying" DH to the Indian landscape: "The mapping did not begin with an assumption of a field called DH as being extant in India, and therefore as an examination of its challenges and possibilities, but rather to understand how DH-like practices have evolved and converged at the moment under what appears to be like a place-holder term, and the implications of this for research and learning."

My own context for these considerations is my implementation of the first master's degree course in the digital humanities in India, uniquely located in a design school rather than in a humanities department. This recontextualisation has required a reconceptualisation, or at least a shifting of emphasis from the more traditional approach of digital humanities courses that have a logocentric focus, to one that privileges "modes of making" as tools of enquiry, in keeping with the philosophy of Srishti, my home institution. This shift has allowed me to look at other methodologies, such as critical making, that are still relatively less visible in digital humanities scholarship, but are more appropriate for, as I will argue, my context of working at a design school as well as in India.

These decisions were by no means formed in a vacuum: the trend of digital humanities scholarship being considered chiefly useful for textual analysis of large corpora has palpably shifted; and this shift is markedly evident from the 2016 edition of *Debates in the Digital Humanities*, edited by Lauren Klein and Matthew Gold and the newest volume in the series, *Making Things and Drawing Boundaries*, edited by Jentery Sayers. In their introduction, Klein and Gold propose that the digital humanities could be considered as an expanded field, which "is constructed by the relationships among key concepts, rather than by a single umbrella term." This is a conscious move away from, as Klein and Gold point out, the idea of the "Big Tent" which shaped digital humanities discourse to a notable extent, though largely in the American academy – a metaphor intended to signal the capaciousness of digital humanities practice. Despite the well-intentioned nature of the "Big Tent" ideal – the discipline's annual conference, which was established in 1989, demonstrated a "growing conference, growing research team sizes" but "poor gender diversity, poor (but recently improving) regional diversity, and some shifts in topical focus of presentations" (Weingart and Eichmann-Kalwara). Representation from India has been sporadic (the data shows a ten-year gap between the first presentation by an Indian contingent in 2004), which might be for a number of reasons: prohibitive costs of travel and registration, no doubt a significant factor. However, this might also be symptomatic of the belatedness of the use of "digital humanities" in India to describe a cluster of practices that were undertaken "albeit in specific pockets of the country, and it would be safe to say that it has been approached in markedly different ways by several institutions" (Sneha). Such work has been undertaken in the formal university space, such as the School of Cultural Texts and Records at Jadavpur University, and more recently at the Centre for Digital Humanities, Pune and at IIT Indore, as well as research institutions such as the Centre for Internet and Society that works towards "digital accessibility for persons with disabilities, access to knowledge, intellectual property rights, openness . . . internet governance, telecommunication reform, digital privacy, and cyber-security." Sarai in Delhi (established 2000) brought together critical analysis and artistic interventions to contemplate media, urban space, and the public domain and was unique in locating itself outside mainstream academic practice, while producing intellectually rigorous work. However, the digital humanities programme at Srishti is first of its kind to dedicate itself to a sustained use of making as a methodological praxis, a potential made possible by its location in a design school.

Historicising design and technology: the colonial impulse

In 1881, as the freedom struggle was gaining momentum, the headmaster of Poona High School, M. M. Kunte, was invited to contribute to the Vasant Vyakhyanmala, a lecture series which still runs today. Kunte used the opportunity to proselytise "the art of mechanization" – exhorting his listeners to travel from village to village, district to district and "start the activities of blacksmithy with frantic haste and zeal." He said:

> For eradicating the undesirable and establishing the desirable in society, there is no option but to follow and spread widely the art of mechanization. If you want to eat, be a machinist. If you want to live as luxuriously as our rulers, you have to run the machines. If you want this country to progress like that of England all of you have to become blacksmiths.
>
> *(1)*

Kunte appears to be collapsing blacksmithing with that of being a "machinist" – simply put, to evolve from a rural economy to the industrial, one must know one's craft intimately enough to make and run a machine that can emulate it. What makes this occasion even more notable is that his audience was not naturally given to blacksmithing, or any sort of technical craft as they were dominant caste Hindus, and were unlikely to have ever worked with their hands. Rather, they were intellectuals and scholars in keeping with their Brahmanical identity, but Kunte's theory was that to counter such dire consequences, the educated, dominant castes also had to enlist themselves in the "making" industry. In his remarkable work *The Technological Indian*, Ross Bassett uses this anecdote to illustrate the circumstances that fostered the rise of the Indian IT professional and, in particular, the role that MIT played in this rise, as the destination of Indian engineers from as early as 1882 onwards, and thus shaping the "technological imaginations" of many. What Bassett's account, as well as Dhruv Raina and Irfan Habib's work on the emergence of modern scientific discourse in India reveals that rather than "the transfer of scientific knowledge as a passive process of diffusion . . . the recipient culture subverts, contaminates and reorganises the ideology of science," which is viewed as a Western cultural import, with a view to challenging the colonial status quo.

Gurminder Bhambra similarly addresses the Eurocentrism of the narrative of modernity, describing it as characterised by "rupture and difference" which "silences historical and transcultural entanglements" which "sets Europe at the global centre from where modernity begins" (2). Instead, she argues, that "modernity itself developed out of colonial encounters, encounters which are hardly captured by the idea of "diffusion." The figure of Kunte's Brahamanical blacksmith, who could have embodied a configuration of another, alternative, contextual and culturally specific modernity but was thwarted by the agenda of imperialism, holds some significant implications for the way we think about technology and knowledge making in India today. Raina and Habib carefully point out that the institutionalisation of scientific study was that ignores the "*doers* of science" (such as artisans, manual workers and technicians) in favour of the "*carriers* of science" suffers from a Western enlightenment bias that privileges the individual, rational thinker. Instead, they write, if "science is as much social as cultural activity where tacit knowledge is as important in the trades as in the sciences, then the history of techniques, technical education and technology . . . are equally important for the history of science as they are for the history of ideas."

These techniques are part of what constitute design practice, though this approach has been largely neglected in postcolonial and subaltern studies. Arindam Dutta's fine essay entitled "Design: On the Global (Re)uses of the Word," however, is informed by this approach and draws on his detailed study of the archives of the Department of Science and Art, a British nineteenth-century institution which lay the foundations of what we have now come to understand as design. Dutta traces the shifts in register of the word itself: *disegno*, used by Vasari in his *Lives of the Artists* to describe the tension between the object of art and its depiction, was used more in the sense of draughtsmanship, drawing – but the modern conception of the word came to be "distinctly invoked as a displacement from the classical problems of mimesis: its key deployment is to intervene in the unruly vicissitudes of the marketplace" (170). Design was used to create the illusion of choice in world of mass-produced identical objects, and that was to be achieved by optimising a balance between, as William Dyce put it, "artisanal imitation" and "practical geometry" (DSA 1854, qtd. in Dutta 170) – which Dyce argued required a very specific skill that the DSA would impart.

However, as Dutta puts it, the "ontological indeterminacy of design renders its value fraught in the calculus of trade" (173) and ornamentists, or designers, as they were coming to be known, realised that the value lay in the proprietary nature of their designs, elevating the "merit of the idea" (Tennent 1841 qtd. in Dutta, 174) rather than the object itself. This anxiety demanded a reinforcement of intellectual property rights, and the mind behind the DSA, Henry Cole hastened to reform patent laws on the eve of the Great Exhibition of 1851, so as to punish any form of counterfeit. The Indian gallery was second only to the British in scale at the Grand Exhibition, and the "orientalist" designs of the Indian craftsperson were in such demand that they were immediately imitated by British and European designers, who then hastily copyrighted them under their own names. As to those Indian makers – they were attributed to some sort of noble savage like disposition, which implied that there was no skill in what they achieved: "every ornament arises naturally and quietly from the object decorated, inspired by some true feeling" – similarly, Thomas Webster confidently declared: "In fact, we should not imagine that the Orientals, in the period when they constructed the buildings, had a well-defined theory on which to base their richly varied intention. The Arabs made use of geometry without any understanding of the science of geometry" (qtd. in Dutta 181).

But what of our Brahmanical blacksmith? Dutta recounts two separate incidents which perfectly capture what might have been the fate of Kunte's would-be acolytes: in 1851 and 1882 respectively there were two separate claims made by local Indian mechanics to file patents on improvements made to the mechanism of the sugar mill. Both were rejected on the grounds that the machinery existed from "time immemorial" in India and did not demonstrate sufficient "novelty."

What then, does this fraught history mean for a discipline that increasingly deploys making and remediation as a mode of inquiry? Radically different technological and infrastructural conditions as well as historical mean that this narrative diverges from those which underpin established histories of digital humanities in the Global North, and this difference necessitates alternative methodological approaches in order to reconstruct alternative histories. The work of Jentery Sayers and others at the Maker Lab at the University of Victoria on their cultural kits for history, for example, while emphatically not exercises in replication but more of remediation, and foregrounding "how the past is interpreted through present conditions, exhibiting history as a collection of refreshed traces, with both loss and gain" ("Kits") often relies on historical material culture such as patent documents, illustrations, artefacts in order to inform their creation, much of which is conserved and made available by Victorian values of empire-building and taxonomic collection. In contrast, the history of indigenous technologies in India is patchy and often obscured by more visible archival material that asserted colonial structures of oppression, complicating the use of a mode of inquiry such as Sayers et al.'s cultural kits for digital humanities work in India.

To demonstrate the contextual circumstances of practising digital humanities in India, it is necessary to ask a range of questions regarding the particular conditions that shape the digital locally, in order to both understand and differentiate local formations from those of the global. Irani et al. posit "postcolonial computing as an analytical orientation" in order to address these differences of: "technological cultures, digital divides, multiple stakeholders, economic disparities . . . a discourse centred on the questions of power, authority, legitimacy, participation, and intelligibility in the contexts of cultural encounter, particularly in the context of contemporary globalisation."

The postcolonial turn, while now hyper-visible in the humanities and social sciences, has only recently begun to make its presence felt in design research and practice. When Irani et al. bring this sensibility to human–computing interaction, it is an acknowledgement that "all design research and practice is culturally located and power laden." Acknowledgement of these conditions means noting that while we are working in resource-poor contexts, any intervention needs must be sustainable and co-designed with community engagement or otherwise be destined to be a "top-down" experiment without any lasting impact, a luxury those of us working in developing countries cannot afford. The manufacturing of digital devices reaffirms the colonial logic of material and labour exploitation by using resources in these developing countries to undergird the creation of the mobile economy.

Making critical making in India

The Srishti Institute of Art, Design and Technology is the first institution in the country to offer a masters level qualification in digital humanities, and the degree's location in a design school offers a unique foundation given the institution's already existing emphasis on the importance of making. The decision to establish this programme in digital humanities has been a risky one – digital humanities as a discipline is yet to gain "brand recognition" in India, and in a world mediated by search algorithms, students might not even know to look for such a qualification when deciding where to apply and what to apply for. But much of the conviction behind this decision was fostered by the recognition that it was no longer possible to envision a future for the humanities without acknowledging the role interface, system design, human-computing interaction played in our understanding and dissemination of humanities knowledge. Furthermore, the logocentrism that had shaped (and indeed nurtured) digital humanities in English departments in Anglo-American institutions, with its legacies from the world of print, created a very different ecosystem from what current contentions and concerns were in India. The notion of the humanities itself, as enshrined at most universities in India, was largely a colonial construct, unsurprisingly given that most of the country's modern education system was shaped by a diktat given by the British in the shape of Macaulay's minute. The immediate context, therefore, was informed by an awareness that the Indian design (as well as the humanities) curriculum had to be decolonised, especially given the circumstances of its origins – the founding document of the National Institute of Design was written by American designers Charles and Ray Eames in 1958, shaped by a strong Bauhaus sensibility (Ray Murray and Hand).

The design classroom encourages exploratory modes that might not be commonplace in humanities education – but the approach at Srishti has been to reconcile design and the humanities as a way of extending the potential and relevance of both. The institutional approach has been embedded in a cluster of what has come to be known as "new humanities and design" that "position[s] the Humanities as a practice – not only a field" (Dwibedy). The decision to introduce research-intensive postgraduate degrees at Srishti has encouraged practitioners and researchers to consider what the future of design research can look like, and these ideations reconcile thinking and making and valorises embodied knowledge, as John Dunnigan states: "The very process itself opens up new possibilities for deep expansive thinking and the serious enquiry that stimulates discovery" (qtd. in Lambert and Speed 105). This reconciliation of "head and hand" gives way to two modes of making: "hylomorphic and morphogenetic," as Tim Ingold describes it. The hylomorphic is goal-based, taking the framework of a project with a premeditated outcome in mind which is achieved once its form is realised. Humanities scholarship often follows a similar model – the traditional journal article, or monograph will predicate itself on a central argument which presents itself as original and/or game-changing and enact this originality by drawing on the work of peers to either affirm or refute the argument, which is often in conversation with a primary source such as a text or artefact.

Design practitioners too are not immune from focusing too much on a final outcome – the undertaking of professional client projects often inspire a "solutioning" approach which often fails to take into account larger contexts and contingencies (Osmond and Tovey 50). The apogee of this issue is the role that design plays in Silicon Valley: often products are over-designed and under-conceived in order to "solve" just one problem, without any consideration given to sustainability or a utilising a systems perspective. While the design thinking movement spearheaded by David Kelley and Tim Brown at IDEO encourages designers to undertake a "human-centred approach," the motivation at its core is to meet "the requirements for business success." Maker culture is emblematic of this non-sustainable, apolitical mode, as parodied by Garnet Hertz's sticker *Make: Technology on Affluent Leisure Time* (Sayers, *Making*, 128) that gestures at the irony of the maker movement in the West, which is "frankly, a luxurious pastime of wealthy people who rightly recognize that their lives are less full because they are alienated from material culture" (Csikzentimihalyi, qtd. in Ray Murray and Hand).

Ingold prefers "morphogenetic" making, which prioritises process over outcome, and materiality over form, and "making is inextricable from the resulting artifact" (qtd. in Lambert and Speed 106). Matt Ratto, in his formulation of critical making, has transposed the morphogenetic process into the context of the digital humanities to encourage "explicit practice of concept elaboration within the social study of technology" (252). Critical making activates different modes of thinking about technology differently, and consequently challenges students and scholars to also rethink design, and how it is inextricably implicated in the mediation of human-centred technology.

Making critical making work

A collaboration with a colleague, Dr Naveen Bagalkot, who works in human-centred design, demonstrates how a design school can a conducive context for digital humanities work. In a course entitled "Disrupting Self-Quantification," we encouraged students to challenge and disrupt the market-driven ideal of the quantified self, and how these are understood in the light of different cultural understandings of the self. Students were encouraged to deploy speculative design to demonstrate the limits of these technologies. Bagalkot extended these explorations to the field, looking at how health tracking can be usefully deployed in rural communities where access to medical service is somewhat limited. He and his project team worked together with a not-for-profit organisation called Maya Healthcare, which trains talented, driven and ambitious young women as health navigators: who not only care for their communities, but also aim to earn income through offering allied care focusing on preventive care and management of chronic conditions such as diabetes and high blood pressure. The HNs are keen to train up others like themselves, and the task of the project team was to create an open source "design scaffolding kit" to facilitate the HNs in implementing design thinking in their work. The only technological intervention given to the HNs is a tablet, and some of the project focused on enquiring what would be the most useful and appropriate application for use in the HN's every day work. This was arrived at by staging enactments of typical client-HN interactions, during which the other participants had to literally raise a red flag when they felt the enactment had reached

a crucial tension point, which in turn was then used as a prompt for rapid prototyping. Most of the HN's felt that a diet chart that helped plan and track food
consumption, and a recording app for blood pressure, blood sugar numbers would
be the most beneficial for their clients, and thus created paper prototypes that could
feed into the design process for the apps.

Bagalkot's exercise was a conscious move away from institutionalised design practice that anticipates a model of consumption and instead anticipated and encouraged co-creation. Digital humanities methodologies can disrupt this mode by with
its legacy of interpretation that discourages a one-size-fits-all response – thus moving us closer more usefully towards processes of participatory and co-designing.

In a country like India, where literacy is still at a premium, design and making
privileges the value of other forms of knowledge found in communities, such as
crafts or indigenous traditions. This collaborative codesigning is instructive for us
as go forward in teaching digital humanities in the design space – creating a useful methodology to turn the lens of scrutiny upon digital artefacts and activities
as well as being observant of different materialities and modalities of knowledge
production in order to both historicise and limit the overdetermined nature of the
digital. It is too early to assert whether these design scaffolding kits might embed
themselves sufficiently to be hacked for use in other contexts, but they are a step
towards sustainable innovation, a necessity often underestimated in a regime that
values making as a "hobby," or churns out vapourware. By adopting these ways of
working, we also stand to reclaim the local, which in turn can help inflect and create new understandings of digital humanities only made possible by its geographical
particularities.

A commitment to this way of working demands a pedagogical intervention
that can facilitate other teachers to institute these ways of working with their own
students, and my work over the last year or so has focused on how to introduce
critical making into the design classroom over a range of contexts and scenarios.
The case study that I will be discussing here is drawn from my experience of working with four students who are already trained professionals, but pursuing a Professional Practice and Design in Education diploma at Srishti focused on pedagogical
practice. My two-week workshop on critical making attempted to challenge their
assumptions about the design process (two of the students trained at the National
Institute of Design) and to demonstrate how morphogenetic making coupled with
a humanities sensibility of asking critical questions can be used in their classrooms,
at university as well as school level. It is important to note that these students all
had a layperson's knowledge of digital technologies, with varying degrees of understanding and competence.

The students were, by their own admission, challenged by "mov[ing] away from
the outcome/solution based approach" (Arvind) but also found it freeing:

> The core idea of Critical Making; which is that, functionality or the evoc-
> ativeness of the product/outcome is secondary to the process of making,
> expressing and critique; is a very liberating idea. It allows for the design

process and thinking to take on directions which it may otherwise have not pursued at all . . . directions which could be purely speculative, completely dysfunctional and disruptive, not remedial in nature; or a satirical commentary raising questions without attempting to "solve" any issues or "design."

(Arvind)

I introduced the idea of Garnet Hertz's Critical Making Process Cards in the classroom, which were, in Hertz's words,

> built as an aid for technology designers to sketch and prototype new designs that are culturally relevant, socially engaged and challenging of current biases in commercial design. They bring together critically-engaged design methods and concepts like critical making (Ratto), critical technical practice (Agre), reflective design (Sengers), near futures (Bleecker), critical design (Dunne & Raby), values in design (Nissenbaum), tactical media (Lovink) and adversarial design (DiSalvo) into a practical brainstorming tool suitable for university classroom or commercial studio use.

While the cards themselves were not available to us to work with, it inspired us to consider what we might need to take into account if these cards were made for the Indian classroom, and for students who were not already involved with designing technology. My main goal as the instructor was to ensure that students could distinguish between the traditional design process and critical making, and understand how the latter privileges humanities values of criticality and epistemological frameworks. Class discussions culminated in deciding major categories that the cards could be divided into – depending on context, the decks of cards that could be used were: technologies, concepts, time, space, materials, techniques and elements. Two of the students working together responded by creating "The Tinkerer's Toolkit," which they described as "A toolkit for educators and students to understand the concept of critical making by immersing in a card based gameplay" (Arvind and Sinha). These cards could be envisioned as a stepping stone to Hertz's cards that facilitate prototyping but assume knowledge of critical making as a practice. The gameplay encouraged users to "reconfigure–reiterate–remake" using materials immediately and "share–critique–reflect," moving them towards a collaborative mode of meaning-making and away from the design process of "problem to opportunity identification to implementation across contexts." Yoking the making process to foster critique demonstrates how critical making emphasises "the inability to unmoor materials from how we interpret materials" (Sayers, *Making*, 4).

One of the other students, Riya Banik, volunteers in an environment that is lacking in resources – that of a government school – and works with a younger age group (five to eight year olds). He experimented with creating a "makerspace" environment to encourage students to think creatively and productively. While her classroom lacked in the high-end resources that usually characterise such environments – laser cutters or 3D printers, for example – what Riya attempted to do was to bring the *ethos* of such spaces into her classroom. An excerpt from Riya's reflective report reads:

> By the third day, we wanted to introduce playful activities around making with hands. So we bought colourful stationery to class. The day was to use their stories as a draft to create something for their classmate [*sic*] whom they had interviewed. Again there was minimum instruction but the children were more receptive. . . . While the students were thrilled to see the bright colours and stationery, they were equally hesitant to use it. Upon noticing the hesitation, the instructor clarified there were no "failures" only positive outcomes and all outcomes were welcome. . . . There were discussions about the kind of material, the weight, size of objects. As there were limited Fevicol, each found creative ways to compensate for the absence of it. Some used threads or a piece of cloth to tie things other joined cut outs by making gaps between the cardboard.

Despite a number of limitations (lack of equipment, inflexible curricula, shortage of teaching staff, and a preference for rote learning over other forms), Riya found that the activity to be effective because, as she put it, "the students from in a government school live in an environment of 'jugaad' on a daily basis – they may lack in the understanding of their actions or complete 'knowledge' in terms of piecing information together but they are good with their hands and need slight nudge towards experimentation." This recalls the tacit knowledge possessed by those Raina and Habib alluded to in their description of "*doers* of science," and privileges imagination and creativity, even when working with technology. These qualities are of particular value that set students apart in the current educational landscape, when open courseware and MOOCs allow anyone to upgrade their skillsets at their own pace and often for free, but inventiveness and curiosity cannot be learnt, but only encouraged.

All of these case studies demonstrate how an engagement with the materiality of technologies can be a useful starting point to start challenging the hegemonic, proprietary nature of our digital devices and begin to imagine alternative models by which to configure future iterations of knowledge universes. My experiences of working at a design school teaching digital humanities has persuaded me that a more culturally honest and appropriate response to these difficult histories are processes of critical and speculative making – but one that, rather than looking to the future, attempts to imagine and build what might have existed, and restore some agency and legitimacy to the many whose work and creativity was devastated by the violence of empire. This mode, like critical making, also allows for more fluid responses to making, mirroring subaltern practices such as *jugaad*, rather than reinscribing imperial authority by using documents such as patents as a primary source. Hannah Perner-Wilson writes, with reference to the exploded view common to technological diagrams, "These parts have been optimized for speed, efficiency, and repeatability of assembly." They are creativity in a box: "prescribed workflows and prefabbed systems disseminated for uniform use" (Sayers, *Making* 5). This "uniform use" is the homogeneity of empire, of colonial and cultural authority, the black box guarded by the patent. As Roger Whitson has said, and I have written elsewhere, alternative speculative universes can either be fascist or liberatory in its allegiances, but as we embark on this quest for our origin story, I believe that these methodologies can help us stay on the right side of history.

Notes

1 The catalyst for the encounter between humanities scholarship and these emergent technologies was the seemingly unlikely figure of Father Roberto Busa, a Jesuit priest, who was on a quest to simplify the task he had undertaken – to compile an index of all the utterances in the works of St Thomas Aquinas and his associates, which amounted to a mammoth eleven million Latin words. In 1949, Busa correctly intuited that computational assistance might ease his task, and thus approached Thomas J. Watson at IBM to see if the new mega machines would be up to the challenge. As it turned out, they were, and thus the first massive "humanities computing" project got under way, over a duration of forty years, concluding only in 1992 with the publication of a CD-ROM.
2 Digital Diversity, University of Edmonton, 2015.
3 I am grateful to Trevor Munoz for pointing out the addition of "technology" to this list on the occasion of my delivering this as a keynote at the Global Digital Humanities conference at Michigan State University in March 2017. This chapter features excerpts from that presentation.

References

Arvind, Kavita. *Assignment 1, Critical Making, PPDE Module*, 2017. Unpublished Coursework.
Arvind, Kavita and Tulip Sinha. "The Tinkerer's Toolkit." Applied Learning Conference: Perspectives, Pedagogy, Practice, Singapore, 2018. Conference Presentation.
Banik, Riya. *Assignment 3, Critical Making, PPDE Module*, 2017. Unpublished Coursework.
Bassett, Ross. *The Technological Indian.* Cambridge, MA: Harvard University Press, 2016.
Bhambra, G. K. *Rethinking Modernity: Postcolonialism and the Sociological Imagination.* Basingstoke: Palgrave Macmillan, 2007.
Busa, Roberto A. "Foreword: Perspectives on the Digital Humanities." *A Companion to Digital Humanities*, edited by Susan Schriebman, Ray Siemens, and John Unsworth. Oxford: Blackwell, 2004. Web.
Dutta, Arindam. "Design: On the Global (R)Uses of a Word." *Design and Culture*, 1.2 (2009) pp. 164–186.
Dwibedy, Biswamit. *Content for the School of New Humanities and Design Webpage*, 2018, unpublished.
Habib, S. Irfan and Dhruv Raina. *Domesticating Modern Science: A Social History of Science and Culture in Colonial India.* New Delhi: Tulika Books, 2004.
Hertz, Garnet. *Critical Making Process Cards*, 2015, http://conceptlab.com/cards/.
Kelley, David and Tim Brown. "Design Thinking." *IDEOU*, www.ideou.com/pages/design-thinking.
Klein, Lauren and Matt Gold. *Debates in the Digital Humanities.* Minneapolis, MN: University of Minnesota Press, 2016. Web, http://dhdebates.gc.cuny.edu/debates/2.
Lambert, Ian and Chris Speed. "Making as Growth: Narratives in Materials and Process." *Design Issues*, 33.3 (Summer 2017), pp. 104–109.

Osmond, Michael J. and Jane Tovey. "The Threshold of Uncertainty in Teaching Design." *Design and Technology Education: An International Journal*, 20.2 (2015), pp. 50–57.

Ray Murray, Padmini and Hand, Chris. "Making Culture: Locating Digital Humanities in India." *Visible Language*, 49.3, http://visiblelanguagejournal.com/issue/172/article/1222.

Sayers, Jentery. "Kits for Cultural History." *Hyperrhiz 13 Special Issue: Kits, Plans, Schematics*, edited by Helen J. Burgess and David M. Rieder, Fall 2015. http://hyperrhiz.io/hyperrhiz13/workshops-kits/early-wearables.html.

Sayers, Jentery. "I Don't Know All the Circuitry." *Making Things and Drawing Boundaries: Experiments in the Digital Humanities*. Minnesota, MN: University of Minnesota Press, 2017.

Seth, Sanjay. *Subject Lessons: The Western Education of Colonial India*. Durham, NC: Duke University Press, 2007.

Shriebman, Susan, Ray Siemens and John Unsworth. *A Companion to Digital Humanities*. Oxford: Blackwell, 2016.

Sneha, P. P. "Mapping Digital Humanities in India." Centre for Internet and Society, 2015, https://cis-india.org/raw/digital-humanities-in-india.

Weingart, Scott B. and Nickoal Eichmann-Kalwara. "What's Under the Big Tent? A Study of ADHO Conference Abstracts." *Digital Studies/Le champ numérique*, 7.1, p. 6, http://doi.org/10.16995/dscn.284.

PART III

Subaltern digital humanities

10

ETHICS AND FEMINIST ARCHIVING IN THE DIGITAL AGE

An interview with C. S. Lakshmi

Nidhi Kalra and Manasi Nene

The Sound and Picture Archives for Research on Women or SPARROW was started in Mumbai in 1988 by Dr C. S. Lakshmi, along with Dr Neera Desai and Dr Maithreyi Krishna Raj, who, along with Dr Veena Mazumdar, are considered grandmothers of women's studies. This archive, by an NGO meant for the public, is a unique effort in capturing herstories of women's lives and work through the Freedom Movement, Left and other Progressive Movements, the Feminist Movement, the Ambedkar Movement, experiences of Dalit women, the Environmental Movement, Pioneering Science Studies, tribal life and struggles, traditional systems of medicine, traditional healers and practitioners, women who lived through communalism, violence and human rights violations, literature, and women from the fields of art and culture and education. SPARROW has holdings in multiple media, as their name suggests; it produces films based on their research, does multilingual publishing, and organizes workshops for students.

In an article written for the magazine Humanscape *(February 2004, pp. 24–25), C. S. Lakshmi has written in great detail about the challenges involved in setting up a women's archives in the context of development. In it, she says, everything concerning empowerment of women was seen only in terms of giving sewing machines to widows and kitchen gardens to women. The entire article, entitled 'Archiving in Days of Development', detailed how SPARROW was conceived and established. An excerpt from the article would provide the right background for the present interview, which focusses on SPARROW, thirty years after:*

> *The idea of setting up SPARROW took root in 1988. Before that, those who are now trustees of SPARROW had met several times and discussed the possibilities of setting up a Women's Archive with a difference. The need for such specialised Archives had emerged from their own work in Women's Studies. The idea was not to set up a Women's Archives as just a collection centre but to create an Archives which would be more vibrant and more communicative. This Women's Archives was conceived as an organisation which would bring people together; an Archives which would be an*

agent of conscientisation. It is a fact that many women do not record the history of their life and work in ink. Beginning with the mythical grandmother who gathers her grandchildren around her, sits on the parapet outside the house under the stars and tells them ostensibly the story of her life (which in reality becomes the story of many other people) and many other experiences, the stories of women emerge mostly in spoken words. SPARROW wanted to collect these stories, which contain the politics of everyday life, and make them a part of history. The idea was not to look for 'achievers' or 'victims' and create an archive of anecdotal history. We planned to go much further than that and make oral history a valid way of rewriting history. Oral history combined with images of life, work, action, media images, music, folklores, films extending into video documentation, workshops with students, film festivals, photographic exhibitions culminating in a Power Museum based on all these materials was how the Sound & Picture Archives for Research on Women (SPARROW) was conceived.

Several important photographic and other collections were made in the first four years with the help of donations from friends and supporters of SPARROW. Along with these activities, there was also the work of sending letters to various funding agencies requesting financial support. Almost all the funding agencies responded with enthusiasm and wished us the best of luck in our ventures, but felt that what we had planned did not quite fall within their funding design. Third World countries were supposed to worry about slums, environment, legal aid for women, health care, rural development and so on. Setting up a Women's Archives did not figure anywhere in anybody's plans either in India or abroad. We visited many government officials. One wanted to know what oral history was and when we explained to him, he exclaimed, 'You mean you want to call chit-chat of women, history?'

Along with pedestrian comments such as these, there were academicians who felt that archiving was really just glorified library work. The real researcher with a keen mind would be dealing with concepts and theorising, not looking at history this way. That archiving itself – the process of generating, collecting and archiving material for research – entailed research activity was not something that was accepted. Despite being perceived as attempting non-scholarly work SPARROW continued to generate alternate material for research for it strongly believed that the kind of material that is used for research can alter perception, methods and language.

Another pattern that SPARROW wanted to break was the notion of the national and the regional. There was a general belief that everything national had to be set up in Delhi and anything that emerged from elsewhere was regional. Setting up SPARROW in Mumbai as an archiving centre that would archive the history of women and the nation was our way of decentering activities that concerned the nation.

This interview was taken after a talk delivered by C. S. Lakshmi at FLAME University for students of Literary and Cultural Studies. She spoke on Tamil women's poetry and the concerns of the female body as it integrates with representations of nature in their works. Here, she goes back to the inception of SPARROW, her opinions on open access archives via digitization, and the ethical dilemmas they throw open.

Q. You have been doing archiving for over thirty years, and from that standpoint, what is your opinion regarding digitizing of archives?

A. One or two things I'd like to make clear about archiving, digitization, and what they call open archiving. What happens is the demand for fully open archiving comes from the West. I'm not for fully-open archiving. I'll tell you why. For example, let me say I have interviewed an Indian woman worker who tells me all about her life: her personal life, her sexual life, everything. It's available with the archives. We have also digitized it in a way that people can read it on their computer; it's possible. I can give excerpts of it, for example, but we can't make the whole thing available online because I feel that when you put it on the web, millions of people can read it for no purpose. And there is always a curiosity about a woman's life, so I don't want to make her life openly available and make it a consumable product. I feel I don't have a right to do it either, because for all these women, we take permission from them to use the material for research.

When I put it online completely – whatever she has said – it can be used for research in purposeful ways, but it can also be used for sensational purposes or for vicarious purposes or, you know, to give those UN type of images – children with running nose, and tears in their eyes – that kind of image of women. I don't want to produce that, and I don't want to be party to it. So, we are digitizing, and to a large extent, we put excerpts of the interview on the web. We want to open a blog where we can put excerpts, but they won't be downloadable. People can read it, but only those people who can sign in, register and tell us why they want to read it.

Another reason why I don't want to put in online is that research is taken as something that can be made so easy and nobody needs to visit libraries or archives. Everything is available on the web, and very often it's not even cross-checked. Somebody else has done the research for it and you merely use it in your research.

This has also happened because in India UGC has laid down this rule of lecturers and others having to publish. So, if you're publishing in regional language you get some twenty points, and in Indian English magazines you get twenty-five. If you publish in international magazines, you get fifty. So, those marks are available for promotion, which I personally think is ridiculous. So, I don't want my archives to be used for such purposes.

Another thing is, mostly those who write to us to come and consult the archives . . . suppose you tell me your subject, like 'we are working on working-class women' or 'we are working on Urdu writers' or whatever. You tell us beforehand – whatever material we have . . . interviews of women . . . or whatever, we keep them aside, so you can come and consult it. But it's a matter of coming and consulting. Even that you want to skip.

Whenever we show interviews, we show the entire interview. But to be taken and photocopied, we give only 25 per cent – which is the rule of all archives. Even Nehru Memorial Museum doesn't give you the entire thing.

Though we give 25 per cent, they have to read 100 per cent – they want to skip that entire process. We have received requests, where they tell me to choose the 25 per cent myself, so I have to do to research for them and decide how much is required.

Sometimes bigger and well-established organizations from abroad ask for images to be posted on their blog or websites and they say it is meant for better outreach, that they won't be downloadable and that we can withdraw from the contract anytime. Such offers come from friends who have become in charge of such programmes.

But I ask, tell me who is going to use it? I would like to know, who's going to use the photographs because when we interview women, normally we ask them for their photographs from their family albums. And we request permission to copy the photographs. They give us the photographs, and they give us details. But we know how to use them. We have rules of how to use these photographs or how to give them for dissertations, publications or for other purposes. We have certain rules, and they – the women we have interviewed – don't mind we if we use them. But there are certain kinds of photographs I don't like to give. For example, photographs taken to show it to grooms' party or something like that . . . they'll give it to me – it's historical reference – but they may not want me to use it because they also tell me 'you use your discretion'. Now I am allowed to use my discretion; after my lifetime, the archives may not know how to use it so we have made some rules for that.

Q. Do you have other guidelines or rules on your archival practice?

A. Yes, we have all guidelines, and we also have an oral history manual as to how to do interviews, which normally when people intern with us, or want to use, we give them a manual to read to say how to do interviews, to teach them. And then we also give them forms, as to how to take permissions. And there is . . . suppose in an interview with a writer, she talks about marital rape. She talks to me openly about it, but she says that 'when you use my interview, I would appreciate if you don't mention marital rape'.

So when I use the interview I will avoid mentioning the marital rape incident as per her request. It is because the concerned writer's husband, even if she may have left him, may still be alive and it creates unnecessary problems in her life. And so, there are ways in which we protect the privacy of women. Not only because it's ethical, but because as a woman you can't expose another woman.

Q. Right, absolutely. When you think of archives, it's a cold objective place. Is it true for your women's archives, which would incorporate intimate or private aspects of their lives?

A. Yes, I feel that women's archives should not think like that. When we started the archives, we had all these questions about 'how will we do it?', 'how will we take permissions?', 'how will we use it; who will use it?', and so on.

Suppose you start a digital archives, and we enter into an agreement of sharing material – that's a very different thing because we will share it according to our rules only. Maybe we have interviewed Maharastrian women and you would like to keep some of those, that is a totally different thing. But one has to enter into an agreement and also decide on how it will be shared and utilized and I feel that all archives must be utilized and we can't be keeping closed archives. Our archives are open – anybody can come and use it. So, I would like to train more and more people to start digital archives. I have no problem with it.

But I would train them with all this – that the younger generation must not forget that the older generation – or whoever we are archiving, because we do interview younger people – have a life that they have lived. We have to respect that life, we can't take it for granted. Another thing is that SPARROW conducts workshops on women in Indian history and culture – we have done it in a few universities. That is also a way of sharing the archives.

Q. When SPARROW began, how did you imagine the archiving practice and how has that exactly changed with developments in digitizing?

A. You see, I did this book called *Face Behind the Mask*, where I interviewed women writers and I went through several documents. So, whichever state archives I would go to, I would look under 'w' – there will be nothing called women; there's no category, no library category. But, if I look under 'education', there will be something on female education. They will also not have anything under 'widow', but they will have it under social reform.

So, I realised it will be very necessary to create archives of our own. You know that in research there is something called primary sources and secondary sources. All books are considered secondary sources; primary documents are government documents and official papers and other things. So when I did research on women writers, my resource will be books, what they've written. But many researchers told me how can books be a primary source? I said, but I'm writing about women writers, so what they write will be a primary resource – this is ridiculous, the way they were looking at the whole thing. So, at that time, I had not recorded the interviews. I did not have the facility for a tape recorder because this was 1974, and the fellowship I got was for a small amount, a thousand rupees per month. So, I didn't have money enough to buy a tape recorder, so I was merely taking down notes and other things instead of recording them.

But I had collected a lot of photographs and other things. Then I did collect material for a project called 'Illustrated Social History of Women in Tamil Nadu'. It was to be illustrated with photographs, oral history, interviews, stories, and then public speeches, diary entries, letters, and all those things. So, when I collected those materials, I interviewed women and I recorded the interviews. And I have a very close friend, Dr Geraldine Forbes, who is doing similar work on India from the US. I met her in 1972, in fact. So we started thinking how should we keep these materials, where should we keep such materials? We realized that oral history was very important; how are we going to do it? The only way we can do it is to start an archive, a women's archive.

There is no women's archives in India. As I have mentioned elsewhere, there was a general feeling, that anything national – because we didn't want to collect only from Maharashtra, but from all over India – should be in Delhi. But we wanted to do a little decentring, and bring it out [of Delhi]. Why should everything be in Delhi? [chuckles]

So we decided that it was going to be in Bombay, and then there was Prof Neera Desai, who was head of the Women's Studies Department in SNDT [Shreemati Nathibai Damodar Thackersay Women's University in Mumbai] and I approached her and asked her, 'Would you be interested?' I was an independent scholar. I asked them if they'd be interested in joining me, and if the archives could be started as an extension of women's studies – whether they would host the archives, which I would design.

Till then, women's studies departments were basically doing surveys and other things. She was interested in the idea, so she told me to go and meet the Vice Chancellor.

The meeting with the Vice Chancellor did not quite work out. Before that we were running a small group called 'Reaching Out', and we used to bring out feminist calendars and diaries. I had gone from office to office, and collected money for the calendars. There was some five thousand rupees left, so I told Neeraben, let's form a trust with her, me, and another women's studies person who is an extremely good scholar, Dr Maithreyi Krishnaraj – her husband was the editor of EPW in which I used to write. She said okay, so with the five thousand rupees we created the trust, and we printed the letterheads. I had a blueprint as to how it will be done, and I had done a course on archiving and conservation offered by the Wellcome Institute, London – well-known archivist, Tony Bish, came and conducted it in Chennai.

We started it, and the initial documents which had already been collected with a women's archives in mind were in my bedroom, in two cupboards. And slowly, we started increasing the material and I have a very small house, so my husband said it looks like we are going to sleep outside our house very soon so we have to do something.

So in 1992, we held a painting exhibition and we raised some money and we took a small room on rent, and there we were for one year. And then we were in a closed garage for one year, then we got a ten years' grant from HIVOS, a Dutch agency. It's a humanist agency. Why I accepted the grant was that they don't interfere in your work – they never tell you this is what we want. I never take up grants which come with strings attached. So, it was a very open grant. And it was a wonderful ten years with the support of HIVOS. In fact, at the end of it, they also supported us to buy a place of our own to house the archives.

The major problem or why archiving is difficult is that archiving is not part of development. Developmental policies are something totally different. I had written an article on 'Archiving in Days of Development', on how difficult it was to conceive of archiving when everybody is talking in terms of quantification. And, the work we are doing is qualitative work, it's not work of quantification. As I always explain, quantification in development is when you have given one hundred sewing machines to one hundred widows, that is quantifiable, but the work we do in archiving, it's not quantifiable. But I think archiving is very much a part of development, I think it's because we don't see it like this that our educational policies are not going on the right track. We don't have a uniform system of education.

Q. Let's talk more on archiving and development. Between the inception of SPAR-ROW in 1988 and now, how has the role of the archive changed?

A. The role of the archive hasn't changed at all. So, there are these CSR [Corporate Social Responsibility] funds; of this not a single funding has come to us. CSR do actual developmental field work – water conservation, energy conservation, environment. They do nothing imaginative, or interpretive. Then, computer classes for women, that kind of thing or classes for underprivileged. We would like to open a library for the underprivileged, but it doesn't fall within these things. So, lots of things like that, and they have very rigid developmental policies and these policies also give way to lot of corruption.

So, in so many ways I have to teach my team as to what to accept, what not to accept and what is something that falls within our guiding principles. So whenever I write a letter accepting or rejecting a grant, it's marked to all my senior persons in my team, nothing is secret – everything is transparent. They may be as young as you, however, they should know how the archives function because all power must not rest with just one person and they can also take their decision and make mistakes, and correct. A lot of things like that are possible.

I think unless you run an archive democratically, which is not controlled by just one person, it cannot run. Like, my senior librarian is a Maharastrian, and she speaks better Marathi than English so some of the colleges, she goes and does the workshops because those students understand Marathi better and so she goes and does that job.

Q. I wonder how the storage [is done]; archives require a lot of space and different kinds of technologies and in terms of those tangibles, what has shifted since the inception?

A. One thing we do is – you know in the women's studies department, there are all theoretical books in women's studies on women. We don't buy theoretical books, because why must you duplicate? What we do is, we concentrate on autobiographies, biographies, case studies, fictional works and we like to buy books on art since we are a sound and picture archives. Then, we get magazines, journal articles, we collect material in some eight languages and then we also collect photographs. We scan the photographs, but we keep the originals, if they are given to us otherwise we return it to them. So photographs are scanned and when sufficient photographs are collected, we put them in a hard-disk and we keep it in our archival vault. All our audio recordings are turned into sound files so it's easier to keep. We keep them in originals also, if we have them; otherwise we keep them in CDs.

So I feel that by restricting the range of collections, so that you don't duplicate what others are doing we can utilize space properly. Like, for example, there may be one library where they collect only on labour – we won't repeat it. We may interview some workers, that's fine, but we won't repeat what the other library collects, because there's no point. They'll also collect it, and we'll also collect it but there can be difference in perspectives. So, we sometimes interview the same persons, like we have interviewed Captain Lakshmi Sehgal, but she's written her autobiography and others also have interviewed her. So we may do interviews like that for different perspectives, but certain things we will avoid doing.

We have also done oral history documentaries, almost two hours long.

Q. When you do oral history projects, how do you choose whose oral histories you are representing?

A. We have a list of who all we should interview. We try to interview surviving freedom fighters, then we try to interview women activists, women in the left movement, Gandhian women, women writers, women artists, also feminists who may not belong to any organization, but are feminists. We don't like to keep a very narrow view of feminism at all.

I'll give you one example. Once, a family approached us and said their grandmother, during the Second World War, she had walked from Burma and she would like to record that aspect of her life and would we like to record it because she is very old. We said yes; we went and recorded it.

So, some of my feminist friends asked me, what is so feminist about walking from Burma to India? I said walking from Burma to India is not feminist, but wanting to record it is feminist. So I said your idea of feminism is a very narrow one, but I think feminism is about leading a non-degraded life and many women who may not even know what feminism is – like I feel my mother is a feminist because she helped me to get educated, and I know so many other mothers like that – may be taking many feminist decisions. I feel that all these women are feminists, and we should also have a broader perspective of everything and not just the contextual perspective of today. Personally, I feel this kind of archives has broadened my vision in such a way, it also made me very humble about how little we know about how women have functioned in history and how women have managed the politics of everyday life.

Q. In the thirty years or running SPARROW, have you seen a shift in how women have talked about themselves and their lives – anything traceable in the archives about how we see womanhood?

A. Yes, it has certainly changed because feminist organizations have been very active. They came on the road and protested and all that, but it has also created a backlash because I feel in the eighties how much we went on the roads and did so many things. Now everything is being done on the social media, and it has created a terrible cleavage as to what can be seen as feminist or not . . . what has happened is the current days require a lot of self-projection, where a person would not only like to be a feminist, she would like to be rewarded for it in this period itself. So those days – when I talk of sisterhood and all that we had in the seventies and eighties – I don't think they exist anymore.

I know that when the Gujarat incident took place, we all gathered in front of Flora Fountain in Mumbai to protest. Some people wanted to go on a hunger fast demonstration, but the police surrounded us which has never happened before. The police used to march along with us, because we used to take permission before that. So they said, you can go on hunger strike but you cannot say what you are doing the fast for, which was okay. We were all there – whoever was there in the early eighties – not a single young person was there because all the young people had been absorbed into the corporate world. And there was our part of the group, that was still struggling to establish things. That was very sad and many of us came home that day and cried because we were looking into each other's eyes and we have been there for ages and there was not a single young person, even daughters of my friends were not there. They were studying abroad or they had been absorbed into the corporate world and these kinds of things didn't have any meaning for them, and even in terms of university and college, people do it for the sake of a PhD or something. And, also I realized that where the students themselves were concerned they were getting heavily politicized by political parties – forming very strict groups with very strict notions.

Q. How do you think the archives can be a political tool?

A. I think my archives is going to be political in the way that it's going to accept all women that have been active, and we clearly lay out what their politics is. There are many women who have functioned outside this politics. We have recorded them also. We have recorded women in the left movement, and we have allowed them to speak what they want. We're not going to ask them, why are you saying this? At a certain point, this is what they've felt . . . and we have recorded this, and that should be done.

We want to do a larger project on women and religion. Why we want to do it is because in the initial phases of feminism, many people felt that feminists should be atheists. Now, the trouble with this is that many women find a lot of solace in religion, and I feel that so long as they don't impose it on others and they're not hurting others and they're not asking you to do rituals which you don't want to do, it's okay. So, how women think of religion and look at religion, that has not come out at all, because there is a general guilt for a woman to say that, yes, I do puja, or in the evening I light a lamp, or something like that. They make her feel guilty – if you're a feminist, you won't be that.

So, I feel to restrict feminism to that is problematic. So we have started to do a series of articles in our newsletter. The first one we have done is on a poet-saint from Punjab called Peeru. Then we want to do on Akka Mahadevi and Andal, who are part of the Bhakti movement, and then we would like to do on women of all religions. We also want to interview women who are called saints, like Mata Amritanandamayi and then maybe very senior nuns from convents, and Jain women who take sanyaas. We want to interview all of them and see what their attitude towards religion is – women across the spectrum.

Q. What is the affinity of SPARROW to transgender people?

A. It's good you asked that question. SPARROW has collected a lot of material on transgenders. We have made a two-hour film called 'Degham', which means body, on five transgender women. We feel that the issue of transgender and LGBT is very, very important. I've done a long conversation with a lesbian musician, and we have a one hour interview with her. We feel that LGBT issues and all issues of sexuality are very, very important. I don't think that we would even ignore questions of homosexuality, but we are concentrating on transgenders because I feel that if you take up the whole issue then it becomes difficult. There are other organizations that are planning to set up archives on them, like the Sangama in Bangalore, and they have collected a lot on homosexuals.

Q. You talk about the inside space and the outside space, and how as women we are walking this inside/outside/public/privateness – this conflicting duality. I was wondering how you address this complicated dimension of women's lived lives in interviews you conduct for SPARROW? Do you like to focus more on the public aspects, or the private? Do you like to focus on one, do you take it interview by interview?

A. That's a very important question because that's one of the first things I thought of – because I don't believe in the public and private worlds. These are two worlds that run into each other – public and private is a current dichotomy we have created, and many refer to the women coming in the freedom movement as coming out of the house – that's why they ask them to go back, you see. But, when I interview women I will not ask the question from my perspective, which theoretically they may not be able to answer, but I will ask, 'When you wanted to go and see Gandhiji in Sabarmati Ashram, what was the reaction of your family?' There have been women who went to the Sabarmati Ashram. Gandhiji had this notion that you should take permission from your family, and there have been instances where the family was not very keen and women have gone on hunger strike, a satyagraha, and they have gone to Sabarmati ashram. Women have gone to jails. Women marched on the roads. They burnt silk cloth and foreign cloth on the road – they didn't think of it as coming out very often. But, some women in their stories have written about it as 'think of the nation as your home', so they also have that notion of public and private. But there are also many women who never thought there was any kind of clear division between the home and the outside world.

And also, when you say that women were inside and men were outside, women were going on so many religious journeys; they were going on yatra and all that – so that was the outside world only, so how did they go? And women worked on farms and lands and all that; was that outside their house or inside? So you are thinking only of particular kinds of women when you say men were outside, in the public sphere. You're not considering women who worked in factories. So they're all outside their home, isn't it? I feel that these narrow divisions, historians can put for the sake for fitting things into frameworks, but my whole idea is to break out of frameworks and let the lives speak for themselves.

Let us not theorize before interviewing somebody – let her life teach me something else, that's my way of learning and I feel I have learned a lot from these interviews of women. We don't have much to say, these women would say and then tell us so much.

You know, there's a very interesting thing an American researcher wrote – she was interviewing women in the labour movement, you know, and she had a questionnaire. I don't believe in the questionnaire system by the way. So her questions were of the variety: 'how many times did you attend a trade union meeting?' She wrote that – and she went and asked a woman this question, and the woman said I didn't attend any because of some reason. The researcher said, so you didn't attend and would note this down. She realized later that what the woman was trying to tell her was: I didn't attend because I was taking care of the children, or I was taking care of the home and my husband was in the union so he went and attended. The researcher said, 'I didn't take that into consideration because it didn't fit into my dissertation or research paper that I was doing. For me, I only wanted to know how many women attended trade union meetings.'

The other aspect, the emotional aspect, the feelings, and other things she was not interested in. Same thing when Urmila Pawar wrote 'We Also Made History'; she wanted to interview Dalit women who were in the Ambedkar movement, so when she started looking for these women, many of the Dalit men told her, 'What are you talking about? Or who? Which women attended the meetings?' They were not a part of the movement. But she identified women, and when she asked them, 'Did you attend meetings?', they would say, 'We didn't attend meetings because we would have to work in the fields.' But they contributed in the Ambedkar movement in many different ways, and she has pointed it out. There are distinct women who have talked directly to Ambedkar; they could talk to him and he would listen to them, and in every meeting Ambedkar would say, 'Bring your wives.' And one of the women said that when people came to call them to come for some meeting or something, the husband if he's not part of the movement, they would start sarcastically saying, 'Go, go on, your lovers have come to take you.' A woman who goes out is always thought to have bad character, so women had to face all that.

Q. If I understand correctly, I think the way you are talking about the public and private as being linked, is also something similar to how SPARROW and your own work blend into each other. And I wonder how you see that; is that a conscious decision?

A. Yes, it is, and I feel that that kind of approach should never fail. It should be there, be there in how we look at things. I will never ask a writer, how did you run home and also write, unless she wants to say or unless it is relevant in a particular case. I will ask her, 'What are the times you chose to write, and how did you do it?' Or, if I interview a man, ask him also, 'How did you manage to write with your family?', and sometimes the woman herself would say. Like Urmila Pawar, she used to write in the nights, and nobody wanted lights on, so she would write in the dark with a torch or in candlelight. She herself would say how I wrote and all that, that marriage makes a lot of difference in your writing.

I have a beautiful photo of a Tamil writer, Anuthama, sitting in the courtyard and writing. Earlier, in Tamil magazines, you'll have photographs of male writers sitting at a table and posing like writers. There's not a single photograph of a woman writer. Where was that taken? [laughs sardonically] Even I don't have a table to write, I keep a plank and I like to sit down and write although there is a table at home. I first handwrite and then I feed it into the computer, so now last birthday my family presented me with one of those foldable tables, which you can keep down – like a Muneemji table, now I use that. But I never found that a problem. I find it difficult to sit at a table. But sitting down and writing is very good, I do it even now.

Q. So, how do the SPARROW archives help you as a writer of fiction?

A. Whatever we have collected in terms of oral history, I never bring it into my writing because it's not ethical to write about a woman's life even if I fictionalize it – and I don't do that. Most of the characters I have written are from my own personal experience of meeting people because if I write about a specific woman from SPARROW's archives, I feel that it is not proper because we have told them that we will use their interviews only for research purposes.

I have consciously dealt with women's lives in general in my fiction, like if you read my story 'Squirrel', I talk about many women who were in the public field and information of which I have learned from my research, where women have taken part in certain events – that I can write, but what I'm saying is I won't take the life of one person. There is a lot of information, which is in the public sphere – I use that.

Q. Are there any collaborations across other organizations – which are prominent and important that you want to talk about as they stand out?

A. So far, we have not collaborated with anybody, but we have collaborated in projects, like for example, the University of Michigan had a project called 'Global Feminisms', and we have been a part of it. We made ten films of ten women of our choice, but when we started negotiating the project they said the budget will be this much, and I asked for a bit more and they agreed. Then, I said that but I have certain conditions and they asked what are the conditions, because the films are going to be made in four countries – the US, China, Poland, and India and the funding was coming from Michigan University, which was going to take the American part of it. After some hard negotiation, they said okay.

Then later on, when we made the ten films our films were accepted as the best.

Q. Where do you see the future of SPARROW, especially considering all of the changes in terms of funding, technology?

A. In terms of technology, I'm not worried because digitization is something we'd love to do. We'd like to start SPARROW digital archives which can go online in ways in which I understand. Like we can have excerpts of interviews, we can have images which can't be downloaded, we can have articles on specific subjects which people can sign in and read. Those articles belong to the public sphere in any case. We can stream our films, which again can't be downloadable. The Conversations series that we have – six or seven conversations are on You-Tube. So there are things which we have already digitized and we would like to put it up. Technology doesn't scare me at all.

What really scares me is funding because we are not part of a larger institution, and I am happy we are not part of a larger institution because I couldn't have run the archives the way I wanted if we had been part of a larger institution. This has given me much larger freedom, but what I am very keen on doing is collecting a corpus, so that from the interest SPARROW can run, apart from getting projects. Last year I turned seventy-three, and I would like to collect a corpus before I am seventy-five.

I go to the archives every day and we do teamwork on projects and other things; we also have an associate director and others, but I would like to train one more person because the associate director will take my place. I would like a younger person to take her place who believes in certain kind of commitment and I would like to train them in the ways I have worked. That is all that I have to do in the next two to three years, I feel. So the funding is the most difficult thing.

I have approached so many private universities, but it's very tough to get funding. And the corporates' aid is even more critical – we have to write every year. We have gone to NGO expos and all that, but they'll come and say we are doing good work but they're not willing to fund us. What has happened is that big corporates have come. They have their own NGOs so they put money in their NGOs, they won't give us. That's very tough. Earlier I had a large staff when HIVOS was funding, then it got reduced. Also, it depends on the way others see us – because Dorabji Tata Trust also supported us for three years.

There is also a great fear that people have about feminists. I remember, once we held this exhibition and we wanted a small amount from a trust, and I went to get the cheque. The director himself came to give me the cheque and then he told me, 'I hope you're not one of those feminists.' I said, 'Why?', and I had taken the cheque already. He said, 'Because feminists break families.' I said 'Really?', and I just walked out because I had the cheque, in any case. So we have to deal with all these insults.

But what I do is we also approach women's groups for support. Women's groups which come and tell us in March – come and show us some film on the 8th of March. The film will be of their choice. For screening a film, we charge a thousand rupees and they'll give us. Then we tell them, see for Navratri, you spend so much money – each one of you buys clothes and so many things. I tell them, every Navaratri, you've got eighty members, so each one of you put a thousand rupees and you give it to SPARROW. We don't say this to everybody, though. Every person in my family, when she or he gets a job and gets the first salary, I go and ask, 'Make a donation to SPARROW.' They all run away from me! I'll not spare anybody. But some of my friends are very nice. When they have a wedding anniversary, they'll send ten thousand rupees to SPARROW – friends support us like that.

11

DESIGNING LGBT ARCHIVE FRAMEWORKS

Niruj Mohan Ramanujam

Specificities of the LGBT[1] universe and *Koushal v. Naz*[2]

The last couple of decades has seen impressive success in integrating the struggle for rights of Lesbian, Gay, Bisexual, and Transgender (LGBT) people into the wider human rights paradigm in India, like in many other countries. Concurrently, the specificities of this struggle have also been analysed and talked about in great detail. In particular, these specificities have assumed enormous importance while strategising around legal interventions, for example repealing of section 377, National Legal Services Authority (NALSA) case for transgender rights, and the recent campaign for a broad anti-discrimination law.

One of the main issues that had to be dealt with in these legal interventions was the question of how can one effectively make a case about denial of rights to a community when a large part of that community is (1) unable to openly declare that they belong to that community and (2) unwilling or unable to articulate their oppression to the state? That the existence of these two problems are themselves indicative of said denial was indeed argued in the Supreme Court (SC)[3] but was unfortunately not seen as convincing by the bench.

Many of the arguments laid out in front of the Supreme Court in *Koushal* in favour of decriminalisation relied on evidence that had to be either testimonial (by members of the LGBT community and their families) or academic (by professionals in mental health, education, etc.). The court rejected almost all of this evidence and ruled in favour of reinstating Sec 377. For example, it was argued that the term "order of nature" was archaic and based on religious dogma, and that the proscribed sexual acts are indeed natural. The evidence was primarily from the medical and mental health profession and repeal of anti-sodomy laws in other countries. Next, the link was made that this law has been used primarily against LGBT people, leading to disproportionate impact and hence inequality under law. It was also shown that 377 was used in this fashion as a threat rather than actual prosecution.

This was evidenced by testimonies by LGBT people and human rights reports by various organisations. Next, it was argued that LGBT people deserve full citizenship and that struggle to attain equality was not possible as long as 377 remained, based on arguments of right to life, especially in the context of HIV/AIDS as well as equality. This was evidenced both by testimonies as well as examples and judgements from abroad. However, these links were not seen by the bench as tenable. In addition, the bench did not consider LGBT people as a class or a community that can be identified, counted and separable from the others.

Contrast this with the arguments presented by historians in the Supreme Court of the United States of America for *Lawrence* vs *Texas*.[4] Here, as pointed out by Hurewitz, the lawyers for the LGBT community successfully argued that anti-sodomy laws did not target homosexuals, which implied that the legal validity of earlier anti-sodomy laws did not impact the need to allow homosexuals their full sexual rights, thus illustrating the contrary use the same evidentiary claims can be used for (205). This was partly motivated by the earlier *Bowers v. Hardwick*[5] judgement upholding the anti-sodomy law, where, in an uncanny similarity to *Koushal*, Justice White concluded that it was "evident that none of the rights announced in those cases bears any resemblance to the claimed constitutional right of homosexuals to engage in acts of sodomy", prompting Lynne Henderson,[6] in her critique of Bowers, to state that "more personalized and vivid storytelling about the lives of gay people might have changed the outcome of that case".

We now need to ask ourselves what kind of evidence in the Indian context would further advance the arguments that were not accepted easily by the Supreme Court. We also need to ask, similarly, what are the impediments in the thinking of society at large that lie in the way of acceptance of a diversity in sexuality and gender. This is not to argue that once we marshal enough logical evidence, people will automatically be convinced.[7] However, attempts at creating LGBT archives need to be guided by these considerations. There have many instances where a social science perspective on traditional evidence gathering has helped strategise for legal battles against discrimination and harassment.[8]

In this chapter, we will describe how queer archiving can serve this need, and what is the nature of queer archiving practice that is necessary to achieve these objectives. Much of the available material, especially over the last few years which have seen many pride marches as well as public protests, is of a digital kind. The more experiential material, that seeks to elicit, preserve, and evoke memory, may not be very amenable to digitisation. However, we will, towards the end, explore some initial attempts to do precisely this. Much of the formulations in this chapter were inspired by the material presented at the workshop on "Queer Archiving in India", organised in Bengaluru in August 2013.

Nature and process of archiving

Archiving as an ongoing non-passive community activity can serve many purposes. First, archives primarily collect oral and written evidence of denial of rights, and these can be used in courts (Sheikh, 2013, 104). Second, they can also help people to affirm their existence as LGBT individuals as well as belonging to a larger community by providing a wider picture, allowing self-reflection, and actively foregrounding the marginalised within the LGBT world. As Hughes and Roman state in their essay "O Solo Homo", "queer memoir operates as a form of collective witness". Historical archival research, in the words of Stone and Cantrell, "has always involved serendipity and creativity, exploring silences and unearthing a hidden past". Third, archives can, and should be used as a tool for advocacy and activism, whose motto is "Queer Archiving = Queer Activism".[9]

These are lofty aims. Can such an archive be thought of, and if so, what form would it take? It has to be decentralised, crowd-sourced, extremely flexible, evolving, have many avatars, replicable, and be more than the sum of its contents. In addition, given the nature of LGBT experiences, privacy, and confidentiality are of tremendous importance. Such an archive would also have to stand up to criticisms about objectivity, and be able to assert the truth value of its contents within its own context. When, for example, the judges in *Koushal* do not take seriously the overwhelming evidence presented about the emotional and psychological effect of section 377 on the lives of LGBT people, how can an *archive of feelings*, as envisaged by Ann Cvetkovich, make a case for itself? Can the archiving process reveal and synthesise the diverse LGBT subjectivities that can challenge the presumed universality of the section of the law, as demanded by Ambasta? The question is, therefore, what kind of archival material and archiving processes enable the production of evidence, the preservation of memory, and promotion of advocacy and solidarity, apart from the obvious oral testimonies and written affidavits? Can an archive bear witness to discrimination and humiliation, pain and suffering, in short, trauma both personal and collective?

Trauma, according to Ann Cvetkovich in her book *Archive of Feelings*,

> puts pressure on conventional forms of documentation, representation, and commemoration, giving rise to new genres of expression, such as testimony, and new forms of monuments, rituals, and performances that can call into being collective witnesses and publics. It thus demands an unusual archive, whose materials, in pointing to trauma's ephemerality, are themselves frequently ephemeral. . . . The memory of trauma is embedded not just in narrative but in material artifacts, which can range from photographs to objects whose relation to trauma might seem arbitrary but for the fact that they are invested with emotional, and even sentimental, value.
>
> *(7–8)*

When the courts ask why LGBT people form a class, or why is a facially neutral 377 seen to apply almost exclusively to LGBT people, or how many LGBT people are there and why is this number not known, or how is repealing 377 going to help prevention of HIV/AIDS, can an archive, functioning as community memory and community conscience, answer these questions? Outside of courts, can an archive help LGBT people to come to terms with who they are, understand the shared struggles of the past, and build on them to create new solidarities? In addition, can it serve, by its very presence, to constantly remind the nation-state that it has always hosted and continues to host a diversity of sexualities and genders? We must remember that one of the first libraries that were publicly burnt by the Nazis for being "un-German" was that of Magnus Hirschfeld's Institute for Sex Research, which was the first substantial documentation and research centres on LGBT lives.

The very process of archiving has to be devised in such a way that it is simultaneously a tool for community building and advocacy as well. The archiving framework should enable us to realise new forms of experience and evidence, and not pre-judge its nature. Lastly, the format of the archive must be able to capture emotions, experiences and moods, of individuals and of the community at large, in addition to just "facts at issue". To quote Ann Cvetkovich again, "Sometimes the archive contains tears and anger, and sometimes it includes the dull silence of numbness. Its feelings can belong to one nation or many, and they are both intimate and public. They can make one feel totally alone, but in being made public, they are revealed to be part of a shared experience of the social" (286). How do we devise ways of archiving that capture this? Can such an archive also sensitively and faithfully capture the arguments and disagreements within the LGBT community?

Another issue that we need to grapple with is the fact that the nature of LGBT lives is changing drastically over the last couple of decades, mediated partly by technology and partly by the increasing number of people willing to talk in public about their experiences. Given this, there is an urgent need to document the lives and practices of older generations of LGBT people. This also raises the issue of formulating legal and other formal ways by which individuals can safely leave their papers, letters and other memorabilia to an archive that can house them with appropriate privacy constraints.

Ways of archiving: some recent examples

Having raised some of these questions, let us now look at concrete examples of new archiving methods that, hopefully, try to address some of these issues. The last couple of years has seen many new small LGBT archiving projects that aim to go beyond the usual documenting. These, inspired by projects like SPARROW[10] and pad.ma,[11] hope to address some of the questions raised earlier. Three of these are summarised here.

The Archive of Gender and Sexuality Minorities Experiences in India (ArGaS-MEI) is a project that is coded by Amrita Chanda of Bengaluru. This is a software written in Django and can include diverse collections of objects. Each collection, based on some digital artifact, is made of similar objects, and is key-worded under categories and is searchable. Its strength is in the diversity of possible collections and the flexible nature of the categories themselves. This is now being used by a few LGBT groups – for example, Digital Archive for LGBTIQ Information and Learning (DALIL) by Sappho for Equality in Kolkata – for internal documentation, and aims to become a public nation-wide platform soon.

A second archive that blossomed from originally being an information website is orinam.net.[12] It is a Tamil-English bilingual website that has now grown into a one-stop national resource centre for information on events, mental and physical health, legal issues, psycho-social support, family narratives, religion, support in educational and employment spaces, and media kits. We would like to highlight two particular aspects of Orinam that are unique among LGBT archives in India. First, starting a week before the Koushal judgement was to be announced, all relevant documentation on the case against 377 was actively solicited and put online,[13] and this continued well into the months of protests, the review, and the curative petitions. This was used extensively by the media as well as the LGBT community for information and updates. In addition, the very availability of all this information in one place, in easy accessible formats itself led to further mobilisation of the community and awareness building in the months following the verdict (for example, support groups in many places organising sessions using the material available on the website, and widespread real-time publicity of protests in the process of being organised in many cities adding to the resolve to organise one in other cities). The second point is that Orinam, following an event or a crisis somewhere in India or the articulation of a new idea,[14] actively solicits opinions and write-ups from various stakeholders in the community, asking for particular perspectives, and also makes this available in translation when possible. This then turns the practice of archiving into an ideological process of advocacy and activism. As the transgender activist and curator of the Sexual Minorities Archives in Northampton Massachusetts says, "We LGBTQ people have a right to our own history books, literature, music, art – our own lives. This is archival justice". An example is the campaign to send personal letters to the CJ of the Supreme Court why decriminalisation matters to oneself. This campaign (ideated by one of the lawyers involved in the case) was initiated and supported by orinam.net, with copies of every letter published online.[15] Thus the archiving process was made a part of the advocacy process itself.

Sunil Mohan and Rumi Harish from Bengaluru had undertaken an oral history project where they interviewed LGBTI people, both on and off-camera, to provide an opportunity for them to talk about their identities, their experiences, and reflect on their lives. By doing so, Rumi and Sunil elicit a diversity of thought and expression, both of imagining one's own gender and sexuality, as well as of ways in which one's lives are seen as linked to so many other issues of caste, class, gender, and so forth. These interviews have been catalogued in a blog[16] and the annotated footage is also online at pad.ma.[17] Following this, they worked with the Marapachi theatre group in Chennai to convert some of the material in these interviews into plays. The process of working with the theatre people, of converting the lived experiences of the interviewees into a story that could be enacted, and the enactment itself were seen as a part of the project of archiving, activism and self-reflection.

Analysis of archives

There have been many archival projects where a lot of sensitivity and thought has gone into collection of material from the community. However, in this digital age, it becomes even more imperative that equal amount of sensitivity and thought be put in the design of the archive itself, since that determines both what fits within and what does not, and also what is accessible from outside and what is not. As Danbolt says, "[a]rchives are constituted by exclusion" (90). Strict adherence to confidentiality timelines by SPARROW, or the design of annotations and hyper-texting by pad.ma are good examples. As mentioned earlier, the conscious decision to make the categorisation of artifacts dependent on the collection in ArGaSMEI is another such.

A good design for an archive must (1) not exclude entire kinds of material for reasons of non-digitisability; (2) allow for decentralisation; (3) allow for differential privacy settings; (4) not pigeon-hole identities and issues into pre-determined lists; (5) allow for analysis of bias of the archiver and of the archive itself and self-reflection in the activist community.

We will now describe a few initiatives in digital archiving, some ongoing and some yet to start, that are being designed with these issues in mind. Digitisation and data analysis cannot substitute for the necessarily subjective and ideological thinking needed to create archives, and it would indeed be dangerous to claim so. However, we believe that certain tools can be made use of, to further these aims. We illustrate this with a few examples.

A new archival project that is being set up in Bengaluru is Queer Archive for Memory, Reflection and Activism (QAMRA). This aims to "chronicle the genesis and growth of the struggle for the rights of sexuality and gender minorities in India". Founded by T. Jayashree, a documentary filmmaker, QAMRA is, crucially, a physical archive as well as a digital library. Starting with her personal collection of two decades of video footage of protests, parades, interviews, and so forth, the archive aims to be a "living archive", which can be used for activism, solidarity building, as well as legal battles.[18] QAMRA is also collecting documentation, newspaper clippings, reports, and so on from the past two decades, and is in the process of devising ways of meaningfully annotating and storing them in a way that would make it a tool for advocacy. It is also soliciting physical material from individuals on both the LGBT movement as well as their personal lives.[19] Having a safe physical space that can store and use material that many individuals have locked up in cupboards at home is essential, as is evidenced by many similar archives in the west, and QAMRA is a step in this direction. Designing the physical and digital space in a way that activists, students, and individuals can access and explore is the challenge that it faces.

ArGaSMEI, as mentioned before, is a software tool that can ingest diverse collections of objects. For each collection, we define categories under which each object is keyworded by people. These categories can be different for different collections and these collections can be, for example, scanned newspaper articles, links to online pages, LGBT themes movies, protest flyers, and so on. These can then be searched through category-keyword combinations. The first collection put into ArGaSMEI was 650 scanned newspaper articles on LBT issues collected by Sangama (a Bengaluru based NGO working on sexuality and gender) over twelve years. A total of 203 unique keywords were used to describe this collection. If this collection is taken as truly representative of all the issues faced by LGBT people that were and could be covered by the media, then can we identify what the major issues were and how they were linked to each other? Can this information, coupled with a political analysis of the same by the community itself, guide future advocacy efforts?

We can go a bit further than just documenting and keywording these documents. We can apply fairly simple statistical techniques to ask, for example, what are the key issues that define most of the collection? We can go further and ask which issues seem to be grouped together, and how these different groups of issues are connected to each other. When applied to the collection in ArGaSMEI, the answers our algorithms give us seem to match well with common sense.

What, however, is the use of these analyses when it seems to anyway conform to common sense? First, common sense is itself ideological and depends on the locus of the person and it is interesting to compare keywording exercises by different people from different backgrounds and identities with what the data throws up. Second, such analyses provide an independent view of the data and help in identifying strengths and gaps in the collection. Third, as our collections become bigger, such analysis will tell us a lot more about the material than we already knew. These results can be used to strategise and plan for future advocacy.

The third example is that of an "events database" that is being developed. ArGaSMEI suffers from a logistics limitation of being able to store only digitisable physical material. We wanted to develop a database that is more generic and can store events of a general nature, events that could be localised in time or space or in groups of people or even represented as ideas. "The archive", according to Judith Jack Halberstam, "is not simply a repository; it is also a theory of cultural relevance, a construction of collective memory, and a complex record of queer activity" (313). Such an "event" can then be tagged in these domains, allowing for ambiguity, as well as associated with documents of any form. The new features in this exercise are that we can then ask for information in terms of viewpoints defined over the entire database – for example, the timeline of issued associated with a place, spatial maps of kinds of events, and even connections between different ideas. In addition, it can help illustrate links and relationships between elements that had hitherto gone unnoticed. "Archives", say Alexander and Rhodes,

> suggest how a narrative of emerging – and changing – queer experience might be constructed over time. They point to the contestations about that past as well, particularly as many queers seek to locate their experiences (of oppression, but also of community building and the formation of productive counterpublics) in particular socio-historical circumstances.

The events database is being designed with this motivation. Implementing this project is a huge task, but is dwarfed by the task of intelligently populating it and we think that crowdsourcing is one way to do this.

The last example, again not yet implemented, is to try to answer the question of whether societal thinking and public morality have changed over the last decades.

All of us have anecdotal as well as empirical notions of how much of a positive change has happened and, more importantly, how this change is dependent on the issue, identity, location, and so on. The optimal way would have been to conduct periodic surveys in the country, like the ones by some magazines.[20] Another possible way is to glean this information from the written response of the public to news relating to LGBT people, via comments on Internet articles and letters to the editor. The former is of course notoriously unreliable, with a large fraction of comments being purposeful trolling from vested interests. Nevertheless, it would be interesting to see if long term trends were indeed apparent. Not only would such information be useful for strategising advocacy efforts, it could also be used as evidence of sorts towards changing societal notions. These days, motivated by the needs of targeted online marketing, sentiment analysis algorithms have become fairly sophisticated in gauging the overall mood of sentences, and we can apply these techniques to our data as well.

All of these examples tell us that we need to design our archives carefully in order to make them truly inclusive and democratic. In addition, once designed and populated, it would be useful to use the power of digitisation, and hence quantifiability, to better inform our understanding of the material, and ultimately help us in our advocacy and activism.

Caveats

Lastly, I will end with a few caveats on fetishing archives of the marginalised. An immediate danger lies in making ourselves transparent to the state. For example, police have in the past made use of activists' personal documentation of events as evidence in court (Danbold, 101). Issues of privacy and confidentiality are paramount in the LGBT context.

A point made by Fajer in "Can two real men eat quiche together" is that there are advantages and pitfalls in choosing how to use archives of stories and experiences. Does one highlight the similarities with the mainstream or emphasise the differences? A perhaps stronger critique is by Joan Scott:

> The evidence of experience then becomes evidence for the fact of difference, rather than a way of exploring how difference is established, how it operates, how and in what ways it constitutes subjects who see and act in the world. . . . [A way out] entails focusing on processes of identity production, insisting on the discursive nature of "experience" and on the politics of its construction.
>
> (22)

Summary

Koushal made it apparent to us that we need to (1) enlarge our documentation on the oppression faced by LGBT people in India as well as (2) find creative ways by which the lived experiences and emotions of LGBT people can find their way to the courts in a form that is legally acceptable. One way to approach this issue is by queering not just the archive, but the process of archiving itself, such that it allows us to capture what is usually neglected as ephemera. We saw a few examples of active LGBT archives that attempt to do so. In addition, we also talked about some examples of digital archiving that use the power of data analysis to aid the process of understanding the archive itself, to help advocacy and activism. Alexander and Rhodes state that "the queer archive can show us a set of rhetorical strategies . . . online archives offer us a space in which to enact queer movement".

In an age when technology, and attendant scientific analysis techniques, are ever present, it is imperative that we think of innovative ways, not for believing in the supremacy of technical solutions, but rather, of adapting technology to our political needs.

The question before us is to find ways of creatively using not just the archive but also the process of archiving as a tool for formulating and creating evidence that can be produced not just in courts of law, but also for society at large and, importantly, for the use of the community itself.

This chapter is based on the presentation that was made by the author at the Law and Social Sciences Research Network (LASSNet) conference Thinking with Evidence: Seeking Certainty, Making Truth, 2016, New Delhi.

Notes

1 We employ the overused and inadequate term "LGBT" in this chapter to indicate sexuality and gender minorities, since the former is more familiar to the general reader.
2 *Suresh Kumar Koushal v. Naz Foundation*, hereafter *Koushal*, was decided by the Supreme Court of India in 2013 in favour of Koushal, who had asked for the setting aside of the earlier judgement by the Delhi High Court in 2009. The Delhi HC had read down Sec 377 as unconstitutional, decriminalising consensual sexual acts between adults. The SC struck down this decision, recriminalising them.
3 See, e.g., page 57 of the transcripts of the proceedings in the Supreme Court, <http://orinam.net/377/wp-content/uploads/2013/12/SC_Transcripts_Hearings.pdf>.
4 *Lawrence v. Texas* was the decision by the US Supreme Court in 2003 that struck down the anti-sodomy law in Texas and, by extension, in all states in the country.
5 *Bowers v. Hardwick* was a judgement by the US Supreme Court in 1986 that upheld the constitutionality of Georgia's anti-sodomy law, later overturned by *Lawrence v. Texas*.
6 Lynne Henderson, "Legality and Empathy", 85 *Michigan Law Review*, 1987, 1574, 1638.
7 See, for example, T. H. Campbell and J. P. Friesen, "Why People 'Fly from Facts'", *Scientific American*, March 3, 2015, and "The Science of Why We Don't Believe Science", Mooney, Mother Jones, May–June 2011.
8 See, e.g., "The Sexual Harassment of Men: Evidence for a Broader Theory of Sexual Harassment and Sex Discrimination", Stockdale, Visio, Batra in Psychology, Public Policy and Law, 1999, vol 5(3), 630; "Emotional Distress among LGBT Youth: The Influence of Perceived Discrimination Based on Sexual Orientation", Almeida et al., Journal of Youth and Adolescence, 2009, 38, 7, 1001; "Subtle, Pervasive, Harmful: Racist and Sexist Remarks in Public as Hate Speech", Nielson, Journal of Social Issues, 2002, 58, 2, 265.
9 Quote is from Queer Archiving in India workshop, 2013, Bengaluru. Also see Rumi Harish for the Sexual Minorities Archives in Northampton, Massachusetts.

10 "Sound and Picture Archives for Research on Women" (SPARROW), <www.sparrow-online.org/>, accessed 28 May 2018.
11 <http://pad.ma>, accessed 28 May 2018.
12 <www.orinam.net>, accessed 28 May 2018. "Orinam" in Tamil means "one community".
13 <http://377.orinam.net>, accessed 28 May 2018.
14 See, e.g., <http://orinam.net/orientation-difference-saathi-iit-bombay/> on campus resources, <http://orinam.net/drraju-ips/> on mental health, or <http://orinam.net/caste-sexuality-akhil-kang/> on caste.
15 See <http://377letters.orinam.net/>, accessed on 28 May 2018.
16 For more information, visit <http://expressionsofsupressedvoices.blogspot.in/>, accessed 28 May 2018.
17 To see this project, visit <https://pad.ma/grid/title/sunil_mohan&source==Sunil_Mohan_and_Sumathi_Murthy&topic==interview&project==Queer_Self-Reflections>, accessed 28 May 2018.
18 For more information, see <www.tarshi.net/inplainspeak/queer-archiving-memory-law-sexuality/>, accessed 28 May 2018.
19 For details, email qamraarchive@gmail.com.
20 For example the annual surveys on Indian sexual mores by *India Today*, see <http://indiatoday.intoday.in/story/india-today-sex-survey-2016-urban-indians-enjoying-sex-like-never-before/1/583321.html for 2016>.

References

Alexander, Jonathan and Jackie Rhodes. "Queer Rhetoric and the Pleasures of the Archive", *Enculturation*, 2012, <http://enculturation.net/queer-rhetoric-and-the-pleasures-of-the-archive> Accessed 28 May 2018.

Ambastra, Kunal. "Inter-Subjectivity in Comparative Law: A Tale of Two Cases", *Journal of Competition Law*, 8(1), 2013.

Cvetkovich, Ann. *An Archive of Feelings: Trauma, Sexuality, and Lesbian Public Cultures*, Durham, NC: Duke University Press, 2003.

Danbolt, Mathias. "We're Here! We're Queer? Activist Archives and Archival Activism", *Lambda Nordica*, [S.l.], 15(3–4), 90–118, 2010, <www.lambdanordica.org/index.php/lambdanordica/article/view/293>. Accessed 28 May 2018.

Fajer, M.A. "Can Two Real Men Eat Quiche Together? Storytelling, Gender-Role Stereotypes, and Legal Protection for Lesbian and Gay Men", *University of Miami Law Review*, 46, 511–651, 1992.

Halberstam, Jack. "What's That Smell? Queer Temporalities and Subcultural Lives", *International Journal of Cultural Studies*, 6(3), 313–333, 2003.

Hughes, Holly and David Roman. *O Solo Homo, the New Queer Performance*, New York: Grove Press, 1998.

Hurewitz, D. "Sexual Scholarship as a Foundation for Change: Lawrence v. Texas and the Impact of the Historians' Brief", *Health and Human Rights*, 7(2), 205–216, 2004.

Scott, Joan. "Experience", in Judith Butler and Joan Scott (Eds.), *Feminists Theorize the Political*, New York: Routledge, 1992.

Sheikh, D. "The Road to Decriminalization: Litigating India's Anti-Sodomy Law", *Yale Human Rights & Development Law*, LJ, 16, 2013.

Stone, Amy L. and Jaime Cantrell (Eds.), *Out of the Closets, Into the Archives: Researching Sexual Histories*, Albany: State University of New York Press, 2015.

12

FIELDWORK WITH THE DIGITAL

Surajit Sarkar

[Samuel] Beckett supplies a direction: "What matter who's speaking, someone said, what matter who's speaking". In an indifference such as this we must recognise one of the fundamental ethical principles of contemporary writing.

– Foucault (116)

We must find ways to narrow the gap. The differences have worsened the condition much more. The low status and the agony so long sustained will only render a vast section of the people as low, degraded and down trodden.

Man must remove by himself his feelings of inferiority, the feeling that he is lesser born than other beings, and attain self-confidence and self-respect.

– Periyar E V R (324)

On October 29, 1969, the first communication test between two computer systems (at UCLA and SRI, California) took place, when a login to the SRI machine was attempted, but only the first two letters could be transmitted. The SRI machine crashed upon reception of the "g" character. A few minutes later, the bug was fixed and the first online login attempt was successfully completed via the Advanced Research Projects Agency Network (ARPANET). In Werner Herzog's film *Lo and Behold: Reveries of the Connected World* (2016), this incident takes on a multilayered meaning. As team leader Leonard Kleinrock recounts, "So, the message was 'Lo' as in 'Lo and behold'; we couldn't have a better, more succinct first message".

Technology, orality and knowledge diversity

How technology affects orality has been a central question for more than a few decades. Important insights have come from studies of orality and popular culture as technological changes have re-opened questions about definition, interpretation and research methodology. As a whole, we see a shift from attention to differences between orality and literacy (a major debate up to the 1970s) to the effects of interaction between orality, literacy and new electronic media. The attempt to answer the question of how technology affects orality has led to divergent interpretations of innovation within oral genres and oral communication through literacy and new media (Merolla). The growth of the higher education system in India, especially over the last few decades, has seen several challenges, of access, diversity and quality among others, which have also informed the development of humanities in a certain way (Sneha 2).

Today institutions in India are struggling to survive the overwhelming impact of digital media technology on learning environments, which has made it not only imaginable and possible, but also desirable, to teach and learn in a classroom without walls. Institutions have tried to manage their situation in order to salvage the old, established notions of certified knowledge, authority and ethical integrity by incorporating digital media technology into knowledge production and dissemination. Only a few have realised that the logic of the digital can and does assert and force educational institutions to change the way things are done. This draws our attention to Ashish Rajadhyaksha's argument that the last-mile problem is more of a conceptual or cultural problem than merely a technological one.

"Discourses, whatever their status, form or value, and regardless of our manner of handling them, would unfold in a pervasive anonymity" (Foucault, 138). Foucault goes on to point at some questions, from circulation and control, to subjects and their place, to the author and the mode of practice. The perception by individuals or a collective, that power is being exercised at the expense of the people, lies behind their speaking and acting for themselves, and at the moments when there is support for a new representativity to the false representativity of power.

In today's world, digital media allow multiple discourse and local narratives, among others, to move out of the narrow temporal confines of orality as ephemera. The discursive practices, in themselves embodied in technical processes, institutions, form and pedagogy; maintain the search for the meaningful order[1] to arrive at a just order of the world.

Drawing upon multiple oral genres and practices that address and give form to underlying questions and the acquisitions of individuals and societies alike, the digital recording allows us to think more about what we do with the interviews once they are made. The evidence of the growing emphasis on voice and the post-interview is found in many places – both in the locality and the online archive. In the process, it also draws attention to the diverse ways by which people remember and narrate their lives – that they will, over time, also change the way we think about memory and personal narrative, about telling and collecting life stories, and about sharing memories and making histories.

For example, the experience at the Centre for Community Knowledge, Ambedkar University Delhi, has led us to believe that finite, project like explorations of places and their aspects – like *Roti, Kapda, Makaan, Jal, Jangal, Zameen* – from different parts of the city work as a way to learn about the human diversity in it. Looking at places in the real world as a collection of huge but finite number of niches, distinct in some ways, yet similar in others, allows researchers to develop questions and conversations along these themes. Explorations of place make good beginnings, especially as it is too large to be carried out by scholars alone, therefore requiring a partnership between scholars and local groups or collectives.

Research, orality, digital – an epistemology of knowledge acquisition

> The arts [humanities], it has been said, cannot change the world, but they may change human beings who might change the world.
>
> – Maxine Greene

An exercise, common and widely used the world over in different ways, involves a digital tool based continuing initiative to gather local histories and knowledge with residents and locals on both sides of the recording device. Here we refer to a project called *Piparia ka Virasat* – a museum of memory of the town of Piparia in Madhya Pradesh, its memory remembered by residents and going back to its settling as commercial centre a little over a century ago. This initiative to record memories and experiences digitally covered two decades of local youth – the 2015s and the 2005s, which corresponds with the decade of Internet and digital penetration in the small agri-commercial town of Piparia in Central India.

C, a first-generation town-bred young man from a farming family, aware of the need for economic diversification and supported from home, met the local digital documentation initiative while looking for a challenging way to engage themselves at work. There during an active and crowded year, he built friends and networks, and in the process his inquisitive mind discovered a knowledge and skill-building opportunity.

Back one evening from a documentation exercise of his working aunt in the village, he was finding it difficult to learn that one sharp farming tool had more than one name, recording one among more than a few farming tools had multiple names, use and action. The forgotten names of the tool and its work were one of many lesser-known work practices, in the diverse range of lived histories, work experiences and narratives of the everyday, that were being recorded as part of recording local oral histories.[2]

This discovery of the unexpected in the "familiar", while documenting the knowledge effects of social and physical location led to thoughtful discussion on themes and knowledge diversity and brought out a consensus of the need for including the human diversity in the storytelling. This continued for a few months and led to periodic revaluation of documentation objectives on the basis of the growing knowledge base. Further themes for interviews and work process record-ings explored *personal-as-political* themes ranging from opportunity and hindrance, challenge and resolution, to perceptions of equity, marginalisation and power. In a conversation a decade later, he recollected how his self-discoveries of the work practices and knowledge in his larger family in their village, partly led to his decision to do an Open University course in mass communication while staying back in Piparia, rather than going to college in the state capital, Bhopal.

During the next decade in the mid-2010s, the exhilaration of discovery of "a world out there" had A, a similarly aged young man, look towards the learning of English as his engagement of choice. Digital tools had proliferated in the smart phone generation, and this semi-rural young man used a range of tools, from printed books, to YouTube and the teaching-learning websites on the Internet. From a similar background as C, in the digital decade, the world that had been brought closer was from many geographies and distances. Yet, a marginal acquaintance with the recording initiatives as an adolescent was remembered fondly at a conversation, where it emerged that this budding computing science engineer wanted to shift career to the social sciences.

Digital documentation practices let the young to enhance their understanding of the local and build "local" knowledge-gathering capacity. The engaged learn a lot more about neighbours, and consequently themselves, by learning to listen. It is evident then that the development of critical orality, as distinct from operational orality, can be an "essential intellectual tool for better understanding representation, fields of patrimony and counter-patrimonies", but even more saliently: "crucial for developing new genres for understanding orality, rearticulating knowledge systems and oral stories or narratives for public dissemination, reimagining structures, and repurposing digital research" (Turin 145).

Digital humanities in the field – an experience and its opportunities

Balmiki Jayanti, 2017: the location, Ayanagar, a large working-class colony on the southern fringes of Delhi, which grew organically as an "unauthorised" residential colony on what was once village commons, farmland and ravines. Despite or maybe because of an unclear legal status, the colony, with its permanent constructions, growing urban infrastructure and services, albeit slowly, has attracted many new residents. In comparison to the costs and prices of acquisition or rentals in the neighbouring corporate cyber city of Gurgaon, the new colony provides affordable land and cheap rentals for the service staff of these offices. Its location on the Delhi Metro line has even attracted middle-class residents, who can get a large plot otherwise unaffordable in most of the city.

Among the newest places to be occupied are the marginal spaces, like the ravines and the stone hillocks that characterise the landscape at the edge of the rocky Aravali hills. Unlike earlier residents, who in their own words "developed the colony" while buying the more accessible land, the houses on the hill were one of the last areas to be built up. Its poor location and difficult access made it affordable home for the labouring wage earners and domestic workers. And in the centre of these, almost at the highest point, is a Kali Mata Mandir.

There in the evening, a musical "*karyakram*" was organised, in the typical way that working people do, where together with family and friends, and *daphli*s, their aim was an evening of collective music making, in many languages and dialects from Bihar to Haryana, that were not the usual bhajans and kirtans, but songs of praise emerging from their lands of origin. The diverse repertoire found an attentive audience and enthusiasm of the groups that followed each other was an indication of this.

At midnight, there was a lull in the proceedings, while some of the audience left I heard someone say, "I enjoyed it, but I wish was it our voices that were heard, the loudspeaker seemed to subdue that. Anyway, there were few tunes based on film music, I really liked that. It was all original, from our lands and homes".

At two in the morning, after the groups had left, this last statement was forgotten. The temple organisers, who were at one level proud of having provided a space for a *Balmiki Jayanti* celebration at their *mandir*, had been uncomfortable at the devotional music that did not have the commercially available film–tune–based repertoire of devotional songs which they usually played. Consequently, after everyone left, these could be heard for an hour until the loudspeakers fell silent.

As this account suggests, the political arrival of the Balmiki Jayanti has its limits, and state recognition does not guarantee recognition by neighbours, co-religionists or larger society. For a field researcher in the humanities in today's digital age, such observations are not unusual. As we see here, the right to the musical space in the Kali Mata Mandir remains contested, though there is no obvious confrontation. So as a humanities field researcher, the question is, how did the singers understand the evening?

The ability to overhear, discover who said what, and follow up on what was heard does not depend on digital tools. Yashwant Zagade, in discussing the work of Suryakant Waghmore, mentions something very important for research on marginalised communities. He says,

> scholars from marginalised communities consider the acknowledgement of "self" and the personal element of the researcher essential in conducting research. Doing research is also a politics since the researcher holds the power to choose the subject for his/her/their research. Hence, a researcher's location has to be clear, so that his/her/their biases are evident, and the readers can better understand and interpret the field and the author.

Applying digital humanities in the field makes it possible to use available tools to expand the opportunity to learn about the event, its genesis, afterlife and the multiple meanings it generates. As an outsider, asking participants about the musical evening, its repertoire and the double ending, led many to recognise what was heard, forgotten or ignored. Suggestions arose to use the ubiquitous smartphone audio recorders to record comments and memories of the event and its conclusion, from residents of the *mohalla* on the hill, and parts of the adjoining colony. Such practices make it possible to bring into the moment, the epistemic privilege that insiders possess, enabling access to information that is sometimes not disclosed to outsiders, and also allows the "insider" field researcher to reflect on their position.

Fundamental questions concerning cultural behaviour we are in no position to ask or to answer intelligently until we explicitly look for and emphasise the cultural discontinuities and unconformities, the fault lines of history and of current cultural organisation and social interaction. As Laurinston suggests, for a more honest understanding of the realities of culture, we should lay less stress on a search for traditional and passive continuities and instead seek out differences, dissonances, conflicts within actual behaviour clusters bound by time or space, and not bound by our imposed, locality-dominated conceptions of "a tradition" and "a culture".

Engaged digital humanities as methodology

One of the major transformations in the humanities in the twenty-first century is the shift from analogue to digital source material. Yet, even as digital technologies are lauded as promising tools for visibility, mobilisation, and liberation, we live in a time of erasure of diversities. Consequently, as researchers in a digitised and interconnected world – where the boundaries between contexts are blurred and where our understanding of humanity is mediated through digital artefacts and tools – some questions require immediate engagement:

- Can one recover the oral, the direct, and the analogue in the digital age? Who can be known across the digital spaces? How?
- Can researchers ever know what communities want, desire, or need? How do we ask them to present this to us, and in what ways in which these can be (re)presented?
- What are the responsibilities in representing communities at the margins, in articulating their desires, their struggles, their suffering, their resistance?

A locally engaged digital humanities programme, located at the intersection of digital practice and human diversity, can also interrogate the abilities and constraints of methodological tools. Exploration into digital technologies recognises that new digital tools for creation, distribution and consumption are not diffused evenly across human societies. Additionally, indications exist that there are significant differences in the way certain populations use these.

As social scientists working with the digital, our research needs to produce a higher grade of knowledge about the social and cultural implications of diversity within the increasingly complex digital landscape, and to generate new thinking about how technology can be used to address human challenges across diverse populations. Rich, compelling and diverse digital tools and resources are making it possible now to challenge accepted definitions of humanities, of how it is seen and what it is. Engaging with human diversity around us allows us to re-cast learning methods as a method of critical observations on the world encountered every day, its people, their experiences and observations.

So what does engaged digital humanities in a university setting mean? Digital humanities is not only about using the computers to write or read humanities-based texts; rather, a digital humanities scholar could use digital devices to

- perform critical and theoretical observations that are not possible with traditional pencil or typewriter-aided analysis; and
- investigate the kinds of questions that are traditional to the humanities.

Going back to the Balmiki Jayanti, the questions that emerge from this public "karyakram" include the idea of cultural power, hegemony, perceptions of the mainstream and an acceptance of language loss among the urban diasporas. Each can become themes on which student learners need to get a background before going to the field. There, they learn to observe, ask questions and listen to answers. This required them to interact with human beings, as well as their readings, in a pretty substantial way before a discussion in class. That makes scholarly explorations much stronger and subsequently learners could include this kind of research into their writing assignments as well.

Both socio-economic and ethno-cultural scholarship builds on the recognition that technological innovation has human consequences. These can be fully understood through the methodologies of humanities research, including a study of the past, a critical theorisation of the present and creative vision for the future. The scale of study can be as small as the family itself, where locating family narratives as a source of oral knowledge and practice lends itself to teaching the art of interviewing.

Digital tools create multiple ways of seeing, knowing and communicating, in the process contributing to new modes of distributing resources, ideas and information, and new interfaces for interaction among diverse human communities. Projects in which off-the-shelf and easily available and widely distributed tools are brought to bear, allow insiders to bring a diversity of perspectives into a public, social, collective occasion, which shared and discussed collectively in turn enables moments of reflection, rather than the instantaneous reaction of the networked digital tool.

Data provided by the digital humanities field tools allow student learners to go beyond individual learning, by collaboratively creating a project that describes the process and outcomes of digital field engagement. Incorporating humanities research methods can help this process by bringing in reflection, that investigates in the Balmiki Jayanti, human self-respect, desire and yearning for a place in the world.

As an engaged researcher, the aspect of returning knowledge to its sources is a critical part of the research process. For the community, it adds in an element of transparency to the researcher's work with them and adds local credibility to the academic initiative. Additionally, for the researcher, providing an occasion to give feedback and comments on what has been shared allows for greater engagement and invites a multiplicity of voices from the community. Everyday digital tools, involving projection and a basic sound system, can convert a public session meant to collectively and publicly give thanks to the community for their support, can become a valuable feedback session that can bring in reticent and missing voices, and fill in gaps that the researcher may not even be aware of. In addition, by making the local community aware that their sharing will also culminate in a local public exhibition additionally fosters the formulation of a response with dignity, one that visualises and (re)presents themselves, and their lives and memories at the margins of the city.

Conclusion

The Zooniverse project, which began in 2009, engages a million registered volunteers as citizen science researchers, requiring their active participation in the process of discovery. It allows members of the public to do hard-core, but not particularly hard, scientific research across a diversity of disciplines. Recognising that humans are better at pattern recognition than computers, the project designs a framework to bring amateur and professional scientists together over the web. Crowd-sourcing data analysis from interested amateurs in straightforward problems – in activities like annotation, filtering, shape recognition, pattern matching, classifying, ranking – has led to over one hundred research papers in science from the ground up.

As this chapter indicates, digital tools and humanities research techniques can make it possible to design and deploy projects analogous to citizen science for the humanities. Awareness of the two aspects of digital humanities, the computational and qualitative intangible approximates of human life, allows us to design and engage with human diversity in an open and transparent way. The increasing prevalence of digital methods and spaces gives a newfound interest to the outcomes of the digital, which in turn brings new cultural power to the citizen. Designing for diversity in digital fieldwork can multiply the opportunities and make the collection of voices an accessible exercise to many. It recognises the fact that the widespread ability to record digitally brings many comments about the world, expands the reach of recording, giving another meaning to the saying "Everyone in this world is seven handshakes away from anyone else".

Learning by doing through an immersive encounter, and learning by traveling in a spatially demarcated field, marks fieldwork as method. Digital culture, its methods and tools, transform the practice of fieldwork by introducing new immersive and expressive forms of practice and pedagogy. Re-examining places, spaces, communities and individuals for multiple and alternative narratives forces field work to retain an emphasis on process as a necessary part of learning. By understanding technologies as "skilled practices", in need of situatedness and contextualisation,[3] is reflective of a turn in fieldwork in the digital era, a move in which digital fieldwork is reshaping the collaborations that exist in all field work. Fieldwork in the digital humanities is a turn toward the process of knowledge production; an engagement with open, collaborative research; and a rethinking of site-specific inquiry.

Notes

1 Nomos – from Peter L. Berger's *The Social Reality of Religion*.
2 For more information, see <www.jatantrust.org/museum>, accessed 28 May 2018.
3 From Donna Haraway in "Situated Knowledges: The Science Question in Feminism and the Privilege of Partial Perspective".

References

Berger, Peter L. *The Social Reality of Religion*. England: Penguin University Books, 1973.
Foucault, Michel. *Language, Counter-Memory, Practice*, edited with an introduction by D. F. Bouchard, Oxford, Basil Blackwell, 1977.
Haraway, Donna. "Situated Knowledges: The Science Question in Feminism and the Privilege of Partial Perspective", *Feminist Studies*, vol. 14, no. 3, 1988, pp. 575–600. *ProQuest*, <http://proxy.lib.sfu.ca/login?url=http://search.proquest.com.proxy.lib.sfu.ca/docview/1295968804?accountid=13800>, accessed 28 May 2018.
Lo and Behold: Reveries of the Connected World. Directed by Wener Herzog, 2016.
Merolla, Daniela. "Reflections on the Project African Oral Literatures, New Media, and Technologies: Challenges for Research and Documentation", *The Global South*, vol. 5, no. 2, Special Issue: Indigenous Knowledges and Intellectual Property Rights in the Age of Globalization (Fall 2011), pp. 154–162, Indiana University Press.
Periyar, E. V. Ramaswamy in *Collected Works of Periyar E V R*, compiled by K Veeramani, 7th edition, 2016, PSRPI, Chennai.
Rajadhyaksha, Ashish. *The Last Cultural Mile: An Inquiry into Technology and Governance in India*. Bangalore: CIS-RAW, 2011.
Sharp, Lauriston. "Cultural Continuities and Discontinuities in Southeast Asia", *The Journal of Asian Studies*, vol. 22, no. 1, Nov. 1962, pp. 3–11.
Sneha, P. P. *Mapping Digital Humanities in India*, 2016, CIS Papers. <https://cis-india.org/papers/mapping-digital-humanities-in-india>, accessed 28 May 2018.
Turin, Mark. "Afterword: Sharing Located." In *Searching for Sharing: Heritage and Multimedia in Africa*, edited by Turin Mark and Merolla Daniela, 143–150. Cambridge: Open Book Publishers, 2017. <www.jstor.org/stable/j.ctt1sq5v1h.11>, accessed 28 May 2018.
Waghmore, Suryakant. *Civility against Caste: Dalit Politics and Citizenship in Western India*. New Delhi: Sage Publications, 2013.
Zagade, Yashwant. "Why Should Dalit-Bahujans and Adivasis Do Research?" *Round Table Talk: For an Informed Ambedkar Age*, 25 Sept. 2017, <http://roundtableindia.co.in/index.php?option=com_content&view=article&id=9198:why-should-dalit-bahujans-and-adivasis-do-research-doing-research-and-self-reflexivity&catid=119:feature-&Itemid=132>, accessed on 28 May 2018.

PART IV

Digital practices

13

DIGITAL HUMANITIES PRACTICES AND CULTURAL HERITAGE

Indian video games[1]

Xenia Zeiler

Introduction

Digital humanities as an academic discipline first and foremost studies and develops digital methods for researching humanities material. But, in a wider understanding of digital humanities, the field also entails the study of digital media and their impact and influence on society. In times of the so-called deep mediatization (Hepp 2016), media are inseparable from all aspects of social life, and actors obtain their information and ideas from many sources (Couldry and Hepp 2016). This information can come from various media, among which video games rank increasingly high. Even though video games are one of the most influential media genres today, especially for those in the younger generation, and are an important factor in social and cultural education, their importance has often been overlooked.

Yet video games actively contribute to constructing perceptions of norms, values, identities, and society in general. They are woven into our everyday lives and influence patterns of social interaction, communication, and shared meanings. Games are increasingly complex, interactive virtual worlds in which, among other things, history, art, cultural heritage, and other aspects of culture and society are constructed by game designers. It is thus obvious that game narratives affect meaning making and society building. In fact, games are so influential and distinctive that some academics have begun to consider games as part of cultural heritage itself (Barwick, Dearnley and Muir 2011).

Game development and production is often a complex and highly reflected process. It is grounded, among other things such as business interests, in the understanding of game developers and influential actors in society that game narratives may mold and transform society. On a global scale, we find two divergent trends in recent game development. On the one hand, most blockbusters – that is, mainstream games and especially the so-called highly popular triple A games – are being developed in a few countries (primarily the United States, some European countries, as well as in Japan and Korea) for global audiences (Zeiler 2015). On the other hand, arguably smaller, so-called indie – that is, independent – gaming companies world-wide are developing games for both international and regional audiences; these games may and in fact are every so often based on regional cultural specifics, such as on cultural heritage (Zeiler 2016).

Given this situation, it is highly relevant to study video game narratives, aesthetics, rule systems, and so on, both world-wide and in India. This chapter specifically introduces and discusses examples of Indian video games which make use of cultural heritage from Indian contexts. How is cultural heritage implemented, interpreted, and constructed in these games? And how are specific aspects such as history, art, and architecture depicted?

Video games made in India

India is not a country with a long history of game development. In contrast to other Asian nations, especially to the video game development giants Japan and South Korea, India entered the game production market relatively late. Nevertheless, elaborative games have been developed in India since about 2008. But, less than a decade ago, whenever notice was given to games made in India by the international gaming community and/or the news media at all, they were often criticized for their low quality. The most prominent example might be the first video game for the console which was developed entirely in India and based on Hindu mythology, *Hanuman: Boy Warrior* (Aurona Technologies Hyderabad for Sony Computer Entertainment Europe, 2009). This console game produced by Sony for PlayStation 2 in 2009 triggered a media debate on aspects of its content – namely, the appropriateness of including Hindu deities in video game environments, a move opposed by some groups (Zeiler 2014). But what was arguably more striking was the widespread criticism of the game's quality overall, which was consistently voiced on both international and Indian levels. In an exemplary way, the reviewer Desai (2009) stated:

> I've tried really hard to look for something positive in this game, but it just isn't there. . . . This is, without a doubt, the worst console game I've ever played, and I'm pretty sure the worst game ever to be published by Sony Computer Entertainment. . . . It just makes you wonder if they have different quality standards for India and the West. . . . Studios need to realize that Indians will not settle for garbage just because they're new to gaming.

But video games made in India have come a long way since then. Around 2012, market studies predicted intensive growth rates of over 30 per cent for the Indian gaming industry for the years 2012 to 2014, and were expected to reach 560 million US dollars in 2014 (exchange4media News Service 2012). It was about this time that large gaming conventions and gaming conferences began to take place in India. Not surprisingly, even as early as 2012, this development was clearly visible in the sheer number of game development studios: "There used to be 15 studios in India, probably three or three-and-a-half years back. Today there are now more than 500 studios" (Rajat Ojha from Version 2 Games, quoted in Handrahan 2012). And certainly, this has not been the end of the story. On the contrary, the game development scene in India has continued to change intensively, especially in the past five years or so. As NODWIN Gaming (2017) puts it:

> For a long time, our country's games have been associated with terrible Bollywood adaptations and whatever the hell Agni was. However, in recent times, game development in India has become so much more. Though the mobile space still has a strong amount of Bollywood and Cricket games, there have been a few new, fun concepts gaining steam thanks to the hard work of Indian developers. These range from puzzle shooting games like Lovely Planet to in-depth RPGs like Unrest, where decisions can impact the entirety of your journey. It has not been an easy road for many of these creators but the results are steadily highlighting India as a strong well for quality games.

Today, video games produced in India reach millions of players. By far, most of these are for mobile telephones. When it comes to content, card and casino games are the most popular. Examples are the very successful *Teen Patti* games, such as *Teen Patti Gold* (since 2014), produced at the Bengaluru studio Moonfrog Labs. Since the whole concept of such card games has proved highly successful, it is not surprising that other studios have tried to emulate the model, and today, numerous versions of *Teen Patti* games are flooding the market. Another highly popular genre of mobile games (and in this case, also of PC and console games) in India is sports-related, with soccer and cricket games dominating the genre.

Currently, what is probably one of the country's most rapidly changing mobile game genres is film related. Increasingly often, every time there is a new large film production, a game is produced and released simultaneously. This development began slowly around 2005, when "Indian companies which have acquired the franchisee rights of international stars like Pat Cash and Charlie Chaplin for their mobile games and are now turning towards Bollywood for the rights of screen icons like Amitabh Bachchan and Shahrukh Khan" (Bose 2006, 112). While Bollywood is still the dominant force in this trend, regional cinemas, such as Tamil or Bengali cinema, are starting to catch up. Today, it is more or less standard procedure that when a film intended to be a blockbuster is released, a game is released along with it. An example is *Sultan: The Game* (2016). Attempts to syndicate Bollywood blockbusters and non-mobile games – that is, console and/or PC games – have so far failed. One of the earliest attempts was *Ra.One: The Game* (2011), which was released as a console game for PlayStation 2 and 3, and flopped.

Indian video games and cultural heritage

Since approximately 2015, a highly interesting development in the larger video game boom in India is a wave of new games that make extensive use of Indian cultural settings. I refer to these cultural settings as heritage, although currently there is no clear definition of what precisely constitutes cultural heritage in academic research. The Indian games I am referring to here include cultural heritage components, such as historical and religious references, and heritage artistic features in a broader sense, including music, dance, architecture, dress styles, and more. But how exactly are forms of Indian cultural heritage represented and constructed in Indian video games, and how does this contribute to craft narratives of India's past and present?

Not surprisingly, the richness of Hindu mythology figures prominently in some of the games produced in India. In fact, some of the earliest are directly based on Hindu mythology from which their storylines and aesthetics evolve (especially in the case of mythological textual narratives from the Epics and Puranas). A case in point is the previously mentioned *Hanuman: Boy Warrior* (2009). Other games have been released since then, which base their narrative on simple versions of Hindu mythology, but all of these remained simple in their execution and did not attract large audiences. At other times, games have revolved around the names of mythological figures without necessarily making direct references to mythology in the storyline, as, for example, in more recent games related to the very popular *Chhota Bheem* TV animation serial and movie franchise. There are also games that allude to Indian cultural heritage forms in a less dominant and/or less explicit way. Such games make use of terminologies such as the names of classical texts, figures, or art styles, or they draw on elements inspired by, but not directly based on, existing heritage – all without making such elements the major theme of the game. For example, the name *Sky Sutra* (forthcoming) clearly refers to the classical Indian genre of text, the Sutras. Moreover, the optics this game implements are inspired by Indian architectural aesthetics.

Raji: An Ancient Epic

Of course, there are also games based on both Hindu mythology in detail and on Indian cultural heritage forms in general. A recent, complex example (the game has not been released yet) which in both its narrative and its aesthetics invoke these themes is *Raji: An Ancient Epic* (forthcoming):

> Raji: An Ancient Epic is a video game set in ancient India. Chaos unfolds as demons invade to conquer the human realm with ambitions to overthrow the mighty gods themselves. Amidst this chaos, a girl is chosen, her destiny to face the demon lord Mahabalasura. The demon lord plans to sacrifice Raji's very own younger brother, which will complete a ritual granting him relentless powers. Blessed by the gods, Raji set's on her journey to rescue her

younger brother, and to face the treacherous Mahabalasura. An adventure awaits.

(Raji: An Ancient Epic 2017)

Apart from storylines that draw heavily on Hindu mythology, game trailers reveal, even at first glance, that many artistic elements of cultural heritage have been incorporated – see, for example, *Raji: An Ancient Epic – Game Teaser* (2017). The music of this game uses tablas and other instruments characteristic of classical Indian music styles. The main character's ankle bells jingle as she walks, and she is clearly dressed in a way that evokes Indian dress styles. The colours and architectural optics are visibly based on Indian cultural heritage forms. All of these aspects are consciously meant to rather accurately depict Indian cultural heritage forms, as the game developers state: "We are an Indie game development company situated in Pune, India. We are working on the game we always wanted to make, a game which reflects lore, myths and stories from our motherland" (NoddingHeadsGames 2017).

Antariksha Sanchar

There are also very creative examples that highlight other aspects of cultural heritage. For example, *Antariksha Sanchar* (forthcoming) is described as "a speculative adventure inspired by the vibrant cultures of South India"; a more detail description reads, "A point and click adventure inspired by the dream theorems of prodigious mathematician Srinivasa Ramanujan, and originating from an opera by the classical dancer Jayalakshmi Eshwar" (Antariksha 2017). The game blends the historically verifiable life story of the South Indian mathematician Srinivasa Ramanujan with elements of science fiction and steampunk to create a story set in South India.

On many levels, this game is based on Indian culture heritage forms, and these are implemented in many ways. It makes reference to classical South Indian music and dance styles, to South Indian cinema traditions, to South Indian architectural heritage, and more. One of the things highlighted is Carnatic music, which plays an important role as background music in the game. "The game features a memorable Indian classical soundtrack of Carnatic musicians and instrumentalists, including samples from the dance repertoire of Bharatanatyam dancer Jayalakshmi Eshwar, and contributions from electronic musicians from India" (Antariksha 2017). Along with these elements, Bharatanatyam dance is integrated into the game; in fact, a Bharatanatyam performance was the starting point for the idea of the game, as the main developer Avinash Kumar explains (cited in Anonym 2016):

> The starting point of the project was a dance production of the same name by my mother and Bharatanatyam dancer Jayalakshmi Eshwar. In this spectacle, she traces the idea of flight from small plants to insects to birds and finally to mythological concepts like Hanuman, the Pushpaka Vimana and the Vaimanika Shastra, an early 20th century Sanskrit text on aerospace technology.

With adequate technical equipment, such as the so-called motion sensor technique, which makes it possible to transfer an actor's, or as in this case, a dancer's movement into the game, very life-like gameplay becomes possible.

Asura *(2017)*

References to mythology and Indian heritage elements may also take forms that move beyond direct approaches. Increasingly, game developers are reflecting on their own cultural backgrounds in refined ways. For instance, the celebrated *Asura* (2017) "is an indie, top-down, Hack 'n' Slash game set in a fantasy world inspired by the richness of Indian mythology. It features heavy rogue-like elements and a unique procedural skill tree which changes on every play-through" (Asurathegame 2017). It is one of the games that take a more complex approach to mythology and Indian heritage, as its creator and the founder of the producing Ogre Head Studio Zainuddin Fahad (quoted in NODWIN Gaming 2017) explains:

> The problem in our opinion is that Indian mythology has been adopted in a not-so-appealing fashion in the past. You cannot literally take mythology from a history book and shove it into a piece of art or entertainment. Instead, what we did – or what we do – is use it as an inspiration to create our own epic world of Rakshasa, Deva and other amazing races.

A unique aspect of *Asura* is that it is the first larger game from India which implies specifics of Indian mythological components not only in the narrative and aesthetics. The developers have thoroughly reflected on Indian mythology and its specific application to video games in a multifaceted way. In other words, mythological elements are not limited to having an influence only on the game's narrative and/or aesthetics, but also affect its rule system: "Rogue-likes have permadeath so every time you die, you will start with a new skill tree. We then came up with the idea to make the protagonist a demon. Because, when demons die they don't stay dead, they reincarnate. Hence, Asura was born." Future games are sure to continue this trend.

Overall, the video game development scene in India is currently undergoing profound transformations. And it is the indie game developers who arguably show the greatest potential in creativity, reflexivity, and enthusiasm. Many of them feel that the game industry in India still needs to clear many hurdles and that, even with its ongoing progress, the industry remains in its infancy. For example, Zainuddin Fahad (quoted in NODWIN Gaming 2017) notes:

> The game industry over here is riddled with sub-par cricket and Bollywood games. It seems that no one cares about design except for the business side of things. We as an industry need to take more risks, be bold and let our passion lead the way. We need to have original IPs in order to truly bring a change in the industry and that is exactly what we are trying to do. We need to be

artists and designers instead of just being a slave and providing services to the western countries.

Despite these challenges, video games made in India have come a long way. Today, there are high-quality games on numerous themes. Some of them deal with educational subjects, actively contributing to shaping our understanding of society: "Now more than ever, game developers have realized that they can use the gaming environment to shine light on important real world issues" (Missing 2017). An example is the prize-winning game *Missing* (2016), winner of Nasscom Indie Game of the Year award in 2016. The players take the role of a missing girl who is the victim of human trafficking and try to find their way to freedom.

I want to emphasize yet again that video games are becoming one of today's most important media genres. Games, including so-called educational games, but also all other game genres as well, will be a major source of information in the future. Globally, game developers are continuously experimenting with this potential. India has charted a highly interesting and, in some ways, distinctive path in this experimentation. One of the exceptional developments is grounded in the highly creative and conscious reflection and practical implementing of elements based on cultural heritage from Indian contexts, which has resulted in some unique games. In this sense, India is an exemplary case for the international study of video games. Video games made in India are likely to hit the global gaming market in the near future for many reasons. As one game developer (Antariksha 2017) put it: "Indian culture is a dynamic, free flowing, encompassing expression of the Universe and its unsolvable magic. Our project connects these ancient expressions to our imminent digital culture, retaining them for future generations in an innocent and inspirational form."

Note

1 This chapter is based on a previously published essay (Zeiler 2017), which was slightly reworked to fit the scope of this volume.

References

Agni, 2008. [video game] (PC) FXLabs Studios.

Anonym, 2016. Watch: A speculative sci-fi video game inspired by Srinivasa Ramanujan and set in 1920s India. *Scroll.in* [blog] 2016. Available at https://video.scroll.in/810125/watch-a-speculative-sci-fi-video-game-inspired-by-srinivasa-ramanujan-and-set-in-1920s-india, accessed 15 April 2018.

Antariksha, 2017. *Antariksha Sanchar | Transmissions in Space.* Available at www.antariksha.in/, accessed 15 April 2018.

Antariksha Sanchar, forthcoming. [video game] (PC, Mac) Quicksand GamesLab in collaboration with Jayalakshmi Eshwar, UnBox Festival and BLOT!.

Asura, 2017, [video game] (PC) Ogre Head Studio, Ogre Head Studio.

Asurathegame, 2017. *Asura Official Game Site – Ogre Head Studio.* Available at www.asurathegame.com/, accessed 15 April 2018.

Barwick, J., Dearnley, J. and Muir, A., 2011. Playing games with cultural heritage: A comparative case study analysis of the current status of digital game preservation. *Games and Culture*, 6 (4), 373–390.

Bose, D., 2006. *Brand Bollywood: A New Global Entertainment Order*. New Delhi: Sage Publications.

Chhota Bheem, 2008–present. [TV animation serial and movie franchise] Pogo TV, Green Gold Animation.

Couldry, N. and Hepp, A., 2016. *The Mediated Construction of Reality*. Cambridge: Polity Press.

Desai, S., 2009. Review: Hanuman: Boy warrior. *Indian Video gamer* [online] 13 April. Available at www.indianvideo gamer.com/reviews/review-hanuman-boy-warrior/, accessed 15 April 2018.

exchange4media News Service, 2012. Indian gaming industry to reach Rs. 3,100 cr. by 2014. *Exchange4media.com* [online] 16 January. Available at www.exchange4media.com/44996_indian-gaming-industry-to-reach-rs-3100-cr-by-2014.html, accessed 15 April 2018.

Handrahan, M., 2012. Emerging markets: India. *Gamesindustry International* [online] 5 March. Available at www.gamesindustry.biz/articles/2012-03-05-emerging-markets-india, accessed 15 April 2018.

Hanuman: Boy Warrior, 2009. [video game] (PlayStation 2) Aurona Technologies Hyderabad, Sony Computer Entertainment Europe.

Hepp, A., 2016. Pioneer communities: Collective actors in deep mediatisation. *Media Culture Society*, 38(6), 918–933.

Lovely Planet, 2014. [video game] (2014 Steam/GOG, PC/Mac/Linux; 2016 Xbox One, PSN, WiiU). tinyBuild, QUICKTEQUILA.

Missing, 2016. [video game] (Android) Flying Robot Studios.

Missing, 2017. *Game for a Cause*. Available at www.savemissinggirls.com/missing-game-for-a-cause/, accessed 15 April 2018.

NoddingHeadsGames, 2017. summary, *indie db* [online] 26 January. Available at www.indiedb.com/members/rajigame, accessed 15 April 2018.

NODWIN Gaming, 2017. *A Peek into the Indian Game Development Scene*. Available at www.redbull.com/in-en/a-peek-into-the-indian-game-development-scene, accessed 15 April 2018.

Raji: An Ancient Epic, 2017. summary, *indie db* [online] 5 June. Available at www.indiedb.com/games/raji-an-ancient-epic, accessed 15 April 2018.

Raji: An Ancient Epic – Game Teaser, 2017. [YouTube video] 25 January 2017. Available at www.youtube.com/watch?v=kVTKwaCaiLA, accessed 15 April 2018.

Ra.One: The Game, 2011. [video game] (PlayStation 2 and PlayStation 3) Trine Games Mumbai, Sony Computer Entertainment Europe.

Sky Sutra, forthcoming. [video game] (PC and Mac, possibly PlayStation 4) Yellow Monkey Studios Pvt. Ltd., Yellow Monkey Studios Pvt. Ltd.

Sultan: The Game, 2016. [video game] (Android, iOS) 99Games Online Pvt. Ltd.

Teen Patti Gold, 2014 and regularly updated. [video game] (iOS, Windows Phones) Moonfrog Labs Pvt. Ltd., Moonfrog Labs Pvt. Ltd.

Unrest, 2014. [video game] (Microsoft Windows, OS X, Linux) Pyrodactyl Games, Kiss LTD.

Zeiler, X., 2017. *Indian Video Games and Cultural Heritage*. Available at http://hdl.handle.net/10138/228559, 85–94, accessed 15 April 2018.

Zeiler, X., 2016. The Indian Indie game development scene: History and cultural heritage as game themes. *Gamevironments*, 5, 257–263. Available at http://nbn-resolving.de/urn:nbn:de:gbv:46-00105664-14, accessed 15 April 2018.

Zeiler, X., 2015. Current key perspectives in video gaming and religion: Theses by Xenia Zeiler. *Gamevironments*, 3, 53–60. Available at http://nbn-resolving.de/urn:nbn:de:gbv:46-00104926-17, accessed 15 April 2018.

Zeiler, X., 2014. Representation versus simulation: The global mediatization of Hinduism in Hanuman: Boy warrior. In: Campbell, Heidi A. and Grieve, Gregory P., eds. *Playing with Religion in Digital Games*. Bloomington: Indiana University Press, 66–87.

14

NOTES FROM A NEWSROOM

Interrogating the transformation of *Hindustan Times* in a "digital" space

Dhrubo Jyoti and Vidya Subramanian

Introduction

My first day at *Hindustan Times* [*HT*] was a puddle of confusion and intimidation. I had been to the building before, many years ago, and remembered being awed by the big foyer and the gleaming staircase. But now, as an employee in my first job, I found it hard to string two sentences together in front of the many important people who swung in and out of the first floor offices of the newspaper.

HT and its Hindi-language cousin *Hindustan* shared a floor dotted with a maze of wood-panelled cubicles. The main reception was beside this and separated the senior editors from the main desk.

Teams would sit in big enclosures closed off by wooden planks infested with rodents and insects. It was not unusual for a rat to be sighted during peak production time, thereby delaying the edition by a precious few minutes as people shuffled in their seats. Food was ordered, shared and eaten liberally on the floor, sometimes even in the form of shared lunches or potlucks. A trek to the printer or the loo was finding your way through a maze.

On the other side of the floor sat the senior editors in what was known as the power corridor – gleaming cabins where the sunlight streamed in, and few could enter. We only heard them at the sleepy 10.30am conference call and two meetings, the last of which was at 5.30pm.

Soon after we joined, we started hearing of a new strategy of "Digital First" – few had any idea of what it was, but we had heard of a bunch of changes that seemed improbable at that point – a meeting at 9.30am, to prioritise the website (which at that point was a poor cousin of print where reporters would seldom give their stories to, or file quickly in case of a development) and finally, a brand new newsroom after pulling apart the one we sat in. Needless to say, very few of us believed everything we heard.

Which is why when we walked into the brand new news floor a couple of years later, we were in awe. Gone were the old wooden partitions, the mouldy sofas and the rats. Instead, the entire floor was open, with pristine white furniture and touch-sensitive lighting. Most of all, the dozens of cabins were gone, instead replaced by just three and the grumbles of many senior editors who would now have to sit with their teams.

Staff were given sermons on how to keep the newsroom clean, repeatedly – verbally and through email. And the most distressing point: no food was allowed in the new newsroom, and guards would often unceremoniously walk up and ask you to stop eating. The CCTVs across the newsroom appeared to have been installed to monitor eating practices.

– Anonymous, 2014–2017

The past decade has seen newsrooms across India transform themselves both in function and intent. Older structures have been torn down, newer practices established, deadlines pushed, new content management systems introduced and new forms of journalism pioneered. The change has propelled legacy newsrooms into the twenty-first century, after the footsteps of their contemporaries in Western countries (Boczkowski, 2004; Deuze, 2004; Domingo and Paterson, 2011; Parasie and Dagiral, 2012). And, yet, the journey has been far from similar, or predictably on the lines of the popular newsrooms in the West. Newsrooms are grappling with readers proficient in multiple languages, fewer resources to devote to long-form and investigative journalism in the face of twenty-four-hour digital news cycles that feed off social media and television.

Moreover, something has fundamentally shifted in what a reader calls news – changing nomenclatures of "content", "producers", "social engagement" – and in what and who we call journalists. Moreover, the radical transformation begs to ask the question: Why digital? Why embrace a mode of publication where revenue models, especially in India, are dodgy and not time tested against print, which still brings in steady revenues and shores up bottom lines? The answer cannot just be "digital is the future". What does this future look like? More importantly, what is this future imagined to be? We focus on *Hindustan Times*, India's second-largest newspaper, that has changed its ninety-old-year processes into a Digital First strategy over the past five years.

This change of strategy brought about a raft of changes – in perception, strategy, morale and everyday processes. For example, *HT* pushed senior editors to come in early in the day, especially before the first meeting at 9.30am, online became the focus of the newsroom, and more stress was given to aggressive curation or matching stories that other newspapers carried.

This led to two changes: first, reporters and editors began to pay close attention not just to stories carried on the website but also to how those stories were doing on the web, and why they weren't performing well if they weren't. This meant simultaneous attention to analytics, social media and other platforms – even though some argued that this took away time and focus from both the print edition and quality stories.

The second change was how the Digital First strategy was marketed aggressively, in both getting more advertisements for the website, and how editorial teams and resources were deployed to maximise impact for the website. People came in primarily for online, stories were edited and put up first on the web, and teams were evaluated based on how many stories they had to offer for the "morning cycle", and how well they did.

This chapter attempts to engage and interrogate, if not answer, some of the questions surrounding the process of newsrooms going digital and its subsequent impact on news and readers. We try to understand digital journalism systems under three broad axes – namely content, processes and focus – through an ethnography conducted within the *Hindustan Times* newsroom in the year 2017.

A brief history

Rajesh Mahapatra, who has been at *HT* for a decade, as Executive Editor, Chief Content Officer and currently Editor-at-Large, and is one of the architects of the newspaper's "Digital First" strategy, says that he realised in 2012 that his teenage son was not reading the daily newspapers that would be in the house every day. As a journalist father, he would fret about this, and even lecture his son about the importance of reading newspapers to learn about new things and to generally be aware of important goings on in the country and the world. But the lectures, he admits, were half-hearted, because he soon realised that it wasn't that his son was not aware of what was happening in the world. It was just that he wasn't getting his news from the daily newspapers like his parents. That, Mahapatra says, was the time when he realised that if the newspaper industry did not change its ways, it (and he, along with it) would soon become entirely irrelevant to his son's generation.

To be sure, there is little data to show how young people are consuming news in India. The latest Indian Readership Survey 2017,[1] which has come out after a gap of three years, paints a rosy picture for the Indian print readership, which is up by 40 per cent compared to the last time the survey was conducted. Most of this rise has come from rural demographics, which is good news for the industry because it means there is still a lot of room to grow. More importantly in this context, newspaper readership in the sixteen to nineteen age group was the highest at 50 per cent, followed by 42 per cent in the twelve to fifteen and the twenty to twenty-nine age group.

Does this mean younger people are reading newspapers in numbers far higher than what is thought of popularly? Unfortunately, this is not clear.

For example, if we don't take the "total readership" (number of people who read a newspaper in the past month) into account, and instead compare the average readership (number of people who read a newspaper the day before), the substantial growth all but disappears to less than a percentage point.

So, then are younger readers moving on? Or is this digital boom a blinkered view of the mostly upper-caste, upper-middle-class urban India? What effect has the WhatsApp-isation of news (fake and real) had on the youth that mostly uses this medium?

The answer, honestly, is that we don't know – except for the fact that Indian digital news consumption habits are very different from the West (think WhatsApp, political party propaganda, reach of regional papers) and that studies done in the West might not provide a valid estimate.

Between 2004 and 2010, the news industry was in an economic boom. Television news had come into its now-familiar twenty-four-hour cycle, newspaper circulation rates were up, companies were still spending large amounts of money on advertisements, and it seemed like the economic slowdown after 2008 was a minor dip. In 2011, newspaper employees in companies such as *HT* got excellent bonuses and pay hikes, says Mahapatra. After two years of no hikes, 2011 was an upbeat year, in which most people thought that the worst was over. It was not until deep into 2012 that it dawned on the professionals within the industry that the slowdown was not just a minor blip and those massive bonuses were now a thing of the past.

It was around this time that at an annual retreat, while discussing how to move forward in a time of economic slowdown, the leadership at *HT* realised that in the past few years it had grown well, but in an unwieldy manner. "It was as though a very large house had been built in bits and pieces . . . sometimes to get from one room to another, you had to walk through too many bathrooms, because nobody had really given any thought to planning", says Mahapatra. *HT* had twenty-three editions, and each one had different page constructs, its own business heads, teams worked in silos, and each edition made its own distinct newspaper. The leadership felt that there was no link between the editorial strategy and the business strategy. To solve these problems, a national edition of the paper was envisioned – a sort of "mother template" that could be used for many smaller editions around the country.

For the national edition, a section of the old newsroom was hived off and a new open floor plan was created – a mini version of the newsroom that was to open for all in the next two years. The visage was brightly coloured, and there was more room for experimentation.

But this also meant that the desks for all these regional editions moved to Delhi, arguably making some of these papers lose some of their regional character. After all, a person living in south Delhi was making a paper for someone living in Ranchi.

This, in many ways, can be considered the beginning of the "digital" story of the *HT*. This was the first time that the ninety-year-old newspaper felt the need to put in place a content management system (CMS).[2] Until then, reporters would simply email stories to editors, and once edited, the desk would put the text on to the page using software called Quark Xpress (this software eventually made way for InDesign, but the filing system stayed the same). It was hoped that the CMS would make filing stories easier and more adaptable to the web-based interface of HindustanTimes.com.

However, some questions remained. Did, as part of the digital story, *HT* move more towards homogenisation, and is that the danger of the online space – that when the audience is thought of as global, it is also thought of as general, and specific nuances and flavours are lost? Second, the increased emphasis on content management and coordination continued to face significant hurdles in the everyday operation of the newspaper. Does this, then, signal that digital processes focus on the wrong things, and maybe smoother integration might be not as important as good content?

Digital? Really?

What is it that makes news "digital"? To put it in the words of Anup Gupta, Managing Editor (Integration) at *HT*, "Digital is different from electronic. It isn't the presence of computers in creating news that makes it digital. For a layperson, 'digital' signifies the possibility of two-way communication. Perhaps 'digital news' is news to which you can respond in real time, and expect those who put out the news to react to your reaction". In many ways, digital news is more immediate in a way that print cannot be.

In 2011, *HT* already had a digital presence: www.HindustanTimes.com existed, but consisted of stories that were already in print – very different from the repository of breaking news, rich content and in-depth analysis that it is today. The website would pick up copies from agencies, use stories from the print editions, and upload them to the web throughout the day.

It was hoped that by bringing in a CMS, there could be more accountability, efficiency and transparency in the news management cycle to minimise duplication of resources across editions, and to improve the quality of news and analysis that was published. The new national edition became a pilot to try out the new CMS and to test out a new model for a template. This edition was launched with eight people (to much success, says Mahapatra) in 2012. So much so that the later metro edition often fell short on the quality that the national edition could carry in terms of headlines and story content.

But can that be seen as the hard line when news becomes "digital"? Alternatively, was news already "digital" when the first desktop publishing tool became integral to the process of making pages? Reporters who filed stories by emailing them to the desk and to their editors were already working in a digital environment. Then what is it about a CMS that makes news "digital" in a way that Quark Xpress and InDesign do not?

"Digital" news cannot merely be news that is produced with digital aids. Digital news and content only become digital when the other end of the chain is digital too – when the consumer of news consumes it in a digital format – not merely as e-papers of the day, in which the print pages are merely replicated as a digital carbon copy; but as individual stories of news and analysis that can be read, shared, commented upon, and – to use that overarching term for all of those – consumed.

This revolution of "consumption" is one that has not been pioneered by newspapers but by what is now known as "content-generation websites" that treat mainstream media outlets as mere inspiration for their content.

Many of these websites take content from newspapers and television, repackage it and generate far more traffic than the parent source. The danger, then, for a newspaper is in trying to copy that model, because on most occasions, questions of propriety or brand will restrain them from using language or spin that makes these websites tick. What is not known is what such behaviour and trend does to newspaper readership, labour and revenue models and what a mainstream website can do to attract new and loyal readers.

Soumya Bhattacharya, Managing Editor at *HT*, believes that "digital" means "to be able to serve our journalism to people who do not have access to the content that a newspaper in print provides in one particular city". He believes that the diaspora is a critical part of the audience for a web presence of a newspaper such as *HT*.

He is making an important point. For him, it appears, digital doesn't mean a new beast, or something for which journalism and newsrooms need to rediscover themselves (or fundamentally change the way they operate, and what they create), but that digital adds to the current model of newspaper journalism. This difference, we shall see, is the fundamental question before *HT* as it goes digital.

The digital process

It was in 2013 that the company officially recognised that the print behemoth that *HT* had thus far been would move towards a "Digital First" policy. To this end, an integrated copydesk was set up to facilitate the process of editing copies for the national edition and online as well. This brought about a change in the manner in which stories would be filed and published.

Until the establishment of the integrated copydesk, in the hierarchy of things, the print version was still the superior prize to aim for, and the website upload was seen as a lowly poor cousin. Reporters who had filed stories for print thought of it merely as a matter of record that their copies would be put up on the website as well. This attitude was slowly changed after the integrated desk was set up; because editors who were filing stories for online were the same as those editing for print; and it became less cumbersome to ask reporters for copies for online.

The digital space was coming into its own and had shed the skin of "poor cousin" to the prestige of print. Analytics soon became the core of the online functions. Until then, only the top bosses had access to analytics – which were seen as a secret that only senior people in marketing and so forth should have access to in order to be able to negotiate ad prices for the website. Once analytics became available to everyone, it became possible to understand the ebbs and flows in the manner in which online content was consumed.

This was an important shift in hierarchy in the newsroom, albeit one that might have had more symbolic significance than any tangible change. Everyone could now see how stories were performing, make decisions about whether something could be done, and how decisions made were having an impact, or not – it allowed more people to break into the circle of "digital experts". Alternatively, it added no new skill sets for many and ended up stretching people beyond their core functions – for example, a desk person was also now manning headlines and looking at how much of the traffic came from which source.

With increasing analytics available including who was reading what, in what format, and for how long, it became possible to give readers what they wanted to read, analyse trends for topics that audiences were reading, and ushered in a time when online went from strength to strength. A video team was set up to provide more video content that was being consumed online, and make web stories richer. A social media team was set up to ensure far and wide dissemination. A data journalism team was hired to provide more interactive stories for the rich medium that "digital" was turning out to be.

It is a testament to how the website grew in that time that the growth in page views in one year was 48 per cent. In April 2013 the number of Twitter followers for the @httweets handle was 170,000, and the number of followers on Facebook was about 700,000. By April 2014, the number of Twitter followers was 2.2 million, and the number of Facebook likes for the official *HT* page was 3.5 million.

Project Butterfly

It was this exponential growth that finally translated into what is now known as Project Butterfly. A new CMS was needed that could integrate the print behemoth with the fast growing digital platform that *HT* had become. Eidos Méthode was that process change that would bring *HT* to a "Digital First/Better Print" cycle. That and the open-plan newsroom that we currently inhabit.

Eidos Methode is a medium and layout agnostic platform. What this essentially means is that it can handle publishing on both the web and the print mediums for newsrooms such as those of the *Wall Street Journal*, the *Washington Post*, the *Boston Globe* and the *Financial Times*. *HT* – and its sister publication *Mint* – both adopted Eidos Méthode as their CMS to facilitate the process of integration.

This was Project Butterfly. There were four strands to it. The first was to be able to leverage technology: a choice of CMS had to be made, and it would have to be one that would have to serve the *HT* aspirations of "Digital First/Better Print". In the market, then, most CMSes were historically print CMSes. And for online uploads, a web CMS would be placed above the print in an unwieldy manner to provide both print and online experiences. But this was not what *HT* had envisioned. *HT* wanted a CMS that would allow a seamless integration of print and web content that would allow the historic strength of the *HT* brand newspaper to flourish, while adding a successful digital layer to operations. Eidos Méthode was seen as the solution to this problem.

One of the criticisms of adopting this software has been that it is quite a cumbersome software that requires a large amount of RAM and tends to slow down things on normal systems considerably. The other criticism has been that it has done nothing to help the person at the desk. While it may be a very effective managerial tool, the ease of use for the journalist filing the story and for the editor on the desk has not improved. This criticism is not a singularly *HT* problem.

When James Grimaldi quit the *Washington Post*, his farewell note was famously titled "Méthode Is Frozen". The bandwidth-heavy CMS that was supposed to make email and word processing obsolete within teams in *HT* has managed to do neither of those things, reporters continue to file stories using email, and editors continue to edit in Microsoft Word, using Méthode only as the end of the filing and editing chain.

The second strand of Project Butterfly was to use space as an enabler. "Digital", it was felt, is all about effective, quick, efficient communication. To break the silos that once defined the print-only model, the new Digital First/better print model needed a new newsroom with more flows and less walls. This state-of-the-art newsroom that HT now inhabits is built on a "hub and spokes" model, with a central meeting table and seating all around it, in radials away from the centre. From any end of the newsroom, it does not take more than thirty seconds to reach any of the team heads and decision makers. And all the decision makers sit near each other.

The third strand was that of reskilling, and retiling the print operation. A print story might typically contain text, a graphic and a photo. In a digital story, the text could have to be updated several times in the day, in place of a photo there may be a photo gallery, in place of a graphic, there may have to be an interactive or a video. For the same story, there may have to be more effort for a digital story. This is a train of thought that is largely agreed upon that the digital project requires far more effort than the old print-only style of journalism. As Soumya Bhattacharya admitted, the workday has become longer, the effort put into each copy and each story package is more, and given the amount of noise in the online world, the amount of effort required to take your story to the end consumer has increased by many multiples.

The fourth strand was the change in workflows and people management. The digital cycle needed a change in the editorial cycles as well. And since online news is consumed throughout the day, a process was put into place to have a morning meeting to discuss online stories that would be published throughout the day; separate from the print meetings that happened at 2.00pm and 6.00pm. A twenty-four-hour news cycle needed online desk shifts, so that no part of the cycle was overwhelmed. People would have to be reorganised. Print resources had to be re-used in the digital effort. All resources were reorganised and reskilled into the digital process. New people who have been hired were integrated directly into the digital process. A morning news meeting at 9.00am was set up, which representatives from each team attended to plan publication strategies throughout the day and especially to capture what is seen as the morning peak for news stories.

What does "digital" do?

"Essentially", said R. Sukumar, Editor-in-Chief of *HT*, "digital has compressed the time we had in the news cycle. What could once be done over a week, must now be done in the space of a day". Taking the case of a story that breaks, say, at 9.00am on a particular day, he charts the way that news could have been done in an age before the Internet. While TV news could have blanket coverage of the event, the print cycle would have involved a reporter at the site, sending in a compiled incident report by evening for the morning paper, with a few images. The day after the event itself, there would have been more in-depth analysis, and even up to a week later, further analysis and well-researched opinion pieces.

In a digital cycle, if a piece of news breaks at 9.00am, by 9.30, there needs to be a preliminary story out. This means that the reporter is constantly in touch with the online desk, which can publish a basic story. Depending on whether the event is unfolding over a period of time, the website would have a live copy, regularly updated, while simultaneously establishing an online visibility by tweeting, posting and updating a Facebook post, and otherwise maintaining a social presence.

By 11.00am, when the event is likely over, the spot copy would give way to analysis and perhaps an interview or two with the principal actors. By 12.00, it would be time to have in place a quick expert comment and some research to give more depth to the reader in order to make sense of the event. Then by evening, a more detailed analysis, perhaps an opinion piece or two, would be in place. By the next day, a further plan to take forward the news cycle and give readers something more than just reported facts would have to be thought of.

"News is now consumed in binges", argues Sukumar. "People want to read all the news about a particular incident all at once". That could explain the sudden spurt of explainers, listicles and other "all you need to know about" style compressed news items. "In print", he says, "the work is done once the story is published. In digital, the work begins when the story is published". What this means is that once the story has a URL, it must then be made visible. Hence the presence of a team for social media amplification of each story.

That is one of the core things that digital "does". It allows the amplification and management of consumption of news. Only 25 to 30 per cent of stories can be expected to be "found" organically. The rest come from search results and social media. This increases the reliance that media houses have on companies such as Google and Facebook. Anup Gupta calls social media a "digital fireplace" – the space around which people would gather in order to talk about an article. "Each tweet that is read, each Facebook post is a digital fireplace", he maintains.

This also influences the bottom lines and revenue models in the digital world. Soumya Bhattacharya admits that no one has been able to figure out revenue models in the digital world. Almost everyone agrees that monetising the number of hits on a website with ads is really not the solution, since Facebook and Google will always have more hits than other websites. News organisations such as the *Financial Times* and *New York Times* are subscription-based, a model that has not yet worked very well in a market such as India.

What about print?

When a news cycle that could have spanned a week, happens within a day, where does it leave the printed word? What is the relevance of the newspaper in such a shortened news cycle? What would be the point of giving people news a whole day after it has occurred and been "consumed" on TV and on the web?

In 2013, there was an increasing realisation that newspapers can no longer provide what Mahapatra calls the "he said, she said spot news" a whole day after an event had taken place. It was said that TV news had no place for in-depth analysis and news, and that newspapers were the only way of getting details; but by 2013, online portals gave readers those details, a development that could have made newspaper copies redundant.

Newspapers were increasingly faced with the prospect of providing more than simply "what happened" news. There would have to be exclusive content, more investigative pieces, better analysis and more data to keep newspapers relevant. Digital news quickly became the go-to place for news – breaking or otherwise. Audiences had moved (and were continuing to move) to digital platforms. And if we were to keep our audience, we would have to move with them from print to online.

Other insights show that people consume news all day – on their commute, as they wait for friends to arrive, in offices, on desktops, tablets, computers, laptops and mobile phones. These insights created the need for *HT* to craft a workday around the digital cycle and the print cycle and to integrate one into the other seamlessly.

But the interesting thing is that the ninety-three-year-old paper is still going strong. The newspaper accounts for 97 per cent of *HT*'s revenue, says Bhattacharya. The digital presence brings in only 3 per cent. So, even if worldwide wisdom suggests that print is a dying medium, it will take a while before the medium finally breathes its last in India.

Conclusion

In conclusion, for a layman viewing Indian media from the outside, the digital transformation might look like a jumble – bits and pieces of western news practices agnostically put together and adopted to fit local news consumption requirements and practices. But our short investigation into how *HT* went through the process reveals that while certain parts of the transformation certainly involve flying blind, other sections are meticulously thought out and examined before adoption. The challenge, then, for *HT* as well as Indian media, is to continue to improve its overall news and editorial standards while also continuing to do well enough digitally to keep the integration process on track.

This is a strange conundrum – if editorial standards are poor and credibility of a news organisation is low, then building long-term brand recognition and sustainability is out of the question, and would then mean that the firm will be forever dependent on piecemeal, spot audience, and not any loyal, returning readers. Such processes are expensive, time-consuming, and most importantly, take focus and resources away from daily traffic building, which can have disastrous near-term consequences. This is further complicated by the fact that digital businesses will continue to be loss-making ventures, at least in the near term.

The trick, then, to going digital and sustaining the process, is finding that sweet spot, where journalism and "content" come together, as do readers and "consumers" of news. Where alongside paying for a physical newspaper, perhaps subscribers can pay to sustain a digital presence for a brand to which they are loyal.

Notes

1 Kohli-Khandekar, Vanita. "IRS: It Is Unclear Whether Four Measures of Readership Aid or Muddle Market" in Business Standard, 1 February 2018. <www.business-standard. com/article/economy-policy/irs-it-is-unclear-whether-four-measures-of-readership-aid-or-muddle-market-118020100040_1.html>, accessed 28 May 2018.
2 A content management system (CMS) is the back-end application that supports the creation and modification of digital content on a website.

References

Boczkowski, PJ, *Digitizing the News: Innovation in Online Newspapers*. Cambridge, MA: MIT Press, 2004.
Deuze, M, What Is Multimedia Journalism? *Journalism Studies*, 5(2), 139–152, 2004.
Domingo, D, and CA Paterson (Eds.), *Making Online News: Newsroom Ethnographies in the Second Decade of Internet Journalism*. New York: Peter Lang, 2011.
Parasie, S, and E Dagiral, Data-Driven Journalism and the Public Good: 'Computer-Assisted-Reporters' and 'Programmer-Journalists' in Chicago. *New Media and Society*, 15(6), 853–871, 2012.

15

DID DIGITAL KILL THE RADIO STAR?

The changing landscape of the audio industry with the advent of new digital media

Mae Mariyam Thomas

In April 2018, the BBC opened up its vast sound archive to the public. They made available more than 16,000 sound effects available for free from the BBC Library – from a South American parrot, or the interior of a Belgian post office, to the sound of rattling windows and furnace glass burners. The database is tagged, searchable and covers most of the BBC's lifespan, with effects from the 1920s onwards. This resource is a testament to one of the biggest and longest-standing radio broadcasters in the world embracing the digital age.

When I was young, I discovered music by listening to the radio. I would buy blank tapes, and using my trusty tape deck, I would record my favourite songs. There are drawers of cassettes that have half-eaten songs by Ace of Base, Michael Learns to Rock, TLC and Boyz II Men. This may be a sign of the times, but even back then, I could sit in a car or in my room, turn a dial, press a button or push a knob, and a disembodied friendly voice would speak to me, telling me about the day, the traffic and the song they were about to play.

Accessing radio seems easy, and yet behind those voices on the radio is a huge broadcast tower, studios, engineers, producers, radio presenters, office staff, big executives, music licensing, lawyers, a big bundle of overheads and more. A lot is happening to put sound on the radio. Currently in India, compared to any other media, radio is the slow tortoise in the race with no finish line. You can't talk about politics, religion or sex. Private radio stations cannot broadcast news. The two biggest cities in the country – Mumbai and Delhi – each has less than ten commercial FM radio stations. In the US state of New York, for instance, there are more than six hundred licensed radio stations. The population of New York is 85.4 lakh. The population of Mumbai is 1.84 crore.

Let's take it back to "once upon a time . . . there was a radio frequency, many radio frequencies to give away". A radio station begins with attaining a radio frequency (i.e. a radio license). Currently, radio frequencies are auctioned by the government to the highest bidder and this is the third batch of the private FM radio Phase-III, which will complete the coverage of private FM radio broadcasting across all States and six Union Territories. The Cabinet approved conducting the e-auction of 683 radio frequencies in 236 cities in subsequent batches, which will help expand the presence of FM radio in more cities.[1] These auctions were expected to generate a revenue of ₹1,100 crore for the government.[2] An example of how much it costs to buy a radio license, in the first batch of private channels sold, HT Media successfully bid for a frequency in Delhi for 169 crore for 107.2 FM.[3] This is a non-refundable one-time entry fee. This license will be for fifteen years. Then, you need to rent the tower you'll be broadcasting from. There are fifty-seven All India Radio towers which are shared with private FM broadcasters on a rental basis.[4] These are the first set of costs just to buy a radio frequency and put a signal out into the universe.

Radio is not cheap. Hence, content needs to cater to what will provide listenership numbers and money. Where's the money? Bollywood. If you look at the radio stations across India, 95 per cent play Bollywood music. Every big city – Mumbai, Delhi, Bangalore, Chennai – has one token English radio station. There is no genre-based radio in India. You can't listen to a rock station or a jazz station or a classical music station. Due to the high investment costs, there is a nervousness to take risks with what you say, do and play on a station.

The radio industry in India is controlled, has few players (with deep pockets), lacks variety, may seem relatively unprofitable and is restrained in terms of what you can broadcast on air. However, radio in India has the biggest reach and listenership in the world, it has the ability to create change, save lives during disasters and more. The power of the voice – someone in your ear, talking to you directly, brings comfort and a sense of belonging. Radio is such a powerful medium that even the Prime Minister of India has a monthly radio broadcast (compulsory to air by every radio station in the country), called *Mann Ki Baat*.

Now, technology is the big disruptor. All the limitations radio brings with it, vanishes with the arrival of digital players like streaming apps, online radio, podcasting and so on, similar to the advent of Netflix, Amazon Prime, Hotstar and others, where a big shift in viewership habits took place from broadcast to on-demand. People want to watch TV in their own time at their own pace, and within the purview of the subject areas they are interested in. A similar trend is happening in the audio space. Streaming-music apps, like Saavn, Gaana, Spotify or Apple Music, have bypassed radio and asked, "Why would you want the music you listen to be dictated by someone at a radio station, when you can listen to whatever song you want, at whatever time you want, as many times as you want?" But that's not the only thing that streaming apps provide. Apple Music has its own radio station called Beats 1, where Dr Dre, Drake, Elton John and Pharrell Williams have their own shows. Saavn dived into Saavn Originals, where they provide podcasts and talk shows on their app.

Compared to an FM station, the setup cost for a streaming service consists of the streaming cost (that is, the bandwidth usage), the music licensing cost (of playing a song which goes either to the author of the track or the publishing company that is a label) and hosting cost. Then there are the app development costs, and of course just like radio, you have costs for your programming team, tech support, hosts, office staff, big executives, music licensing, lawyers, a big bundle of overheads and more.

Currently, Saavn, for example, has 20 million unique listeners,[5] with 250 million streams per month.[6] Apple Music boasts 49.5 million users, while Spotify (which has just entered the Indian market) has 47.7 million unique users.[7] Here is an example of outgoings of one of the biggest streaming services:

Spotify

Streaming costs: £126,000 per month
Music streaming licence costs: £600,000 per month
Hosting costs: £100,000 per month
Bearing in mind, India has far lower costs for private server hosting for cloud services and streaming costs, a ballpark pricing would be anything between approximately 8–15 lakhs a month.[8]

For most streaming apps, the largest payout is for music licensing. A streaming app like Spotify, Saavn or Amazon Music will approach a label (like Sony, Universal, Warner or, in India, T-Series,[9] Tips, etc.) with different kinds of licensing deals where they do one of the following

a   Pay through equity
b   Pay at a per-stream rate
c   Pay for future streams in advance
d   Pay a percentage of the revenue[10]

Streaming apps make money from subscription, ad revenue and investment. For each app, subscription barely covers just the monthly overhead costs for the running of operations. For example, Apple Music in India charges Rs 120 per month, while an Amazon Prime membership is Rs 999 per year, Saavn is Rs 95 per month and Wynk is Rs 120 per month. And most of these streaming apps offer a freemium model – a combination of basic services provided free of charge while more advanced features must be paid for. Paid subscription could mean that your streaming is ad-free or that you get certain privileges like early song releases and so forth.

Based on their userbase, streaming apps, using programmatic audio advertising, can use ad-insertion technology to create "real-time buying, targeting, optimization, and reporting of audio ad inventory". However, currently, most streaming apps aren't profitable and require investment to grow their operations.[11] Spotify, in 2018, went public.[12] Jio Music and Saavn have come together with a transaction that's been valued at $1 billion, with Reliance investing $100 million for its growth.[13]

With digitalisation comes new paths forged. For instance, instead of going for the highest common denominator, creating niche content and cultivating communities is the direction of the drift. For example, there is a gentleman from the Indian heavy metal community called Sahil Makhija, a.k.a. Demonstealer, who has a band called Demonic Resurrection. He also likes to cook. So, he started his own YouTube channel called *Headbanger's Kitchen*. And he doesn't just have 100 followers or a 1,000 or even 10,000. He has 1.5 lakh subscribers on his YouTube channel. And not YouTube views. Subscribers!

Back to the audio industry: with the vastness the Internet brings, there is freedom and with that comes variety and nuance. There is a new need to make qualitative judgements on content and its impact – where you focus on a small number of people but their attention sticks better and for longer. There is a renewed value for content. For instance, Amazon is a place you go to buy books, perfume, headphones or toilet tissue; now they bring you Amazon Music and Amazon Prime. Bookmyshow has moved into providing audio content with Jukebox – you can listen to music, horror stories, comedy and more. All this new content to increase the stickiness of their app. These companies have a captive audience that comes to them for specific reasons. They want to increase the reasons for you to come to their brand and keep your attention on them for longer.

So, is there a shift from radio to online? We are living in a multimedia world. Our attention is being highly sought after, and there are more avenues for our distraction. People haven't stopped listening to the radio. People haven't stopped watching TV necessarily. There has been a diversification. With new media comes new platforms and new aggregators climbing on to the bandwagon.

I went through a shift. The transition from broadcast to podcast was liberating. On air with FM radio, one is restricted by sales commitments, company policy and time (where you're only allowed to talk for two minutes between songs and your interviews have to be short, sharp and meaningful). Podcasting, on the other hand, allows you take your time, drop a few F-bombs here and there and allow the person you're interviewing to tell their story at length; you can immortalise them in an episode forever on an RSS feed that's linked to every podcasting app you can think of.

Also, radio isn't just a presenter on air, talking between songs. It's stories, radio plays, comedy, soap operas, documentaries, soundscapes and works of art. Indian commercial FM radio stations don't have such diverse audio content. Podcasting does. So, instead of flipping through FM bands to find one playing something that you like, you can scroll through a streaming app finding what you prefer and getting it.

What you listen to on the radio is limited and controlled. Digital is liberating because everyone is a creator. It isn't a celebrity or media professional sitting behind a camera or a mic. User-generated content showcased alongside content by big media conglomerates, they are all on equal footing on the same platforms. This means there is an abundance to watch, read and listen to in the ever-expanding universe of the Internet – which is where aggregators create a platform of access where curation is king.

Radio is a medium free to access. All you need is a radio signal receiver. Digital media access requires more. Besides just a device, you need an Internet connection, which is becoming cheaper and more accessible in India. However, there are still teething issues where connections aren't constant, it varies in speed and bandwidth, and penetration hasn't reached all corners of the country. In 2015, only 26 per cent of the Indian population had access to the Internet. That is 460 million Internet users, the second-largest online market after China.[14] A majority of them used mobile Internet (mainly social networking sites) and were living in urban communities. The disparity is still so high in India when it comes to access of resources. The population of rural India is 938 million, and only 186 million are Internet users.[15] The gap between the privileged and the underprivileged is vast enough for it to constantly be a drawback to growth. And yet there is nothing to stop the inevitable – that is, change.

Digital is all about more access and more options. Digital not only gives you freedom to play, but to dig up archives and listen to them. Everything that gets broadcast on radiowaves will vanish into the atmosphere as soon as you hear it. You can't rewind or fast-forward radio. All you can do is play. With digital media, that is changing.

Notes

1 For more details, see "Cabinet Okays E-Auction of FM Radio Phase III", December 21, 2017, <www.thehindubusinessline.com/economy/policy/cabinet-okays-eauction-of-fm-radio-phase-iii/article9999499.ece>, accessed May 24, 2018.

2 Please see Press Trust of India, "Results of First Batch of Private FM Radio Phase III Declared", September 16, 2015, accessed May 24, 2018.

3 For more information, see Press Trust of India, "65% of Population Soon to Be Connected to FM Radio Network, Says Govt", <www.livemint.com/Politics/eUh208BfXawM8JmD1OgbEM/FM-radio-network-to-reach-65-population-soon-says-governme.html>, accessed May 24, 2018.

4 For more information, see Press Trust of India, "65% of Population Soon to Be Connected to FM Radio Network, Says Govt", <www.livemint.com/Politics/eUh208BfXawM8JmD1OgbEM/FM-radio-network-to-reach-65-population-soon-says-governme.html>, accessed May 24, 2018.

5 "Saavn Claims 10-Fold Increase in Daily Active Users in India", September 25, 2015, <https://gadgets.ndtv.com/apps/news/saavn-claims-10-fold-increase-in-daily-active-users-in-india-744428>, accessed May 27, 2018.

6 See Connie Hwang's article, "Verto Index: Streaming Music Services", March 22, 2018, <www.vertoanalytics.com/verto-index-streaming-music-services/>, accessed May 27, 2018.

7 For more on the numbers, please see Charles Arthur's article, "How Much Does Spotify Cost to Run? We Analyse the Numbers", <www.theguardian.com/technology/blog/2009/oct/08/spotify-internet>, accessed May 27, 2018.

8 Based on inquiries from tech experts and IT management specialists, as accessed on May 28, 2018.

9 To read more on this, please see "Amazon Prime Music Announces Deal with T-Series", February 21, 2018, <www.exchange4media.com/digital/amazon-prime-music-announces-deal-with-t-series_88563.html>, accessed May 27, 2018.

10 See more as written by Kamal Kishore, "How Much Does it Cost to Develop a Music Streaming Mobile App?", September 20, 2017, <www.octalsoftware.com/blog/how-much-does-it-cost-to-develop-a-music-streaming-mobile-app>, accessed May 27, 2018.

11 See more, as written by Stuart Dredge, "Saavn Says It Will Be Profitable by the End of 2018", July 5, 2017, <http://musically.com/2017/07/05/saavn-says-will-profitable-end-2018/>, accessed May 27, 2018.

12 Read Jill Disis and Seth Fiegerman's "Spotify Goes Public in an Unconventional IPO", <http://money.cnn.com/2018/04/02/technology/business/spotify-ipo/index.html>, accessed May 27, 2018.

13 To read more on this, see "Integration of Jio Music and Saavn in a Transaction Valued at over US $1 Billion", March 23, 2018, <www.saavn.com/corporate/blog/2018/03/23/integration-of-jio-music-and-saavn-in-a-transaction-valued-at-over-us-1-billion/>, accessed May 27, 2018.

14 See "Internet Usage in India: Statistics and Facts", <www.statista.com/topics/2157/internet-usage-in-india/>, accessed May 25, 2018.

15 For more, see Surabhi Agarwal's "Internet Users in India Expected to Reach 500 Million by June: IAMAI", February 20, 2018, <https://economictimes.indiatimes.com/tech/internet/internet-users-in-india-expected-to-reach-500-million-by-june-iamai/articleshow/63000198.cms>, accessed May 25, 2018.

INDEX

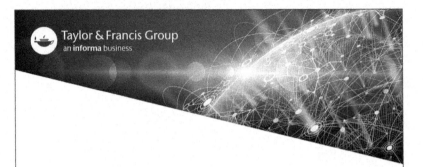

For Product Safety Concerns and Information please contact our EU
representative GPSR@taylorandfrancis.com
Taylor & Francis Verlag GmbH, Kaufingerstraße 24, 80331 München, Germany

www.ingramcontent.com/pod-product-compliance
Ingram Content Group UK Ltd.
Pitfield, Milton Keynes, MK11 3LW, UK
UKHW020956180425
457613UK00019B/717